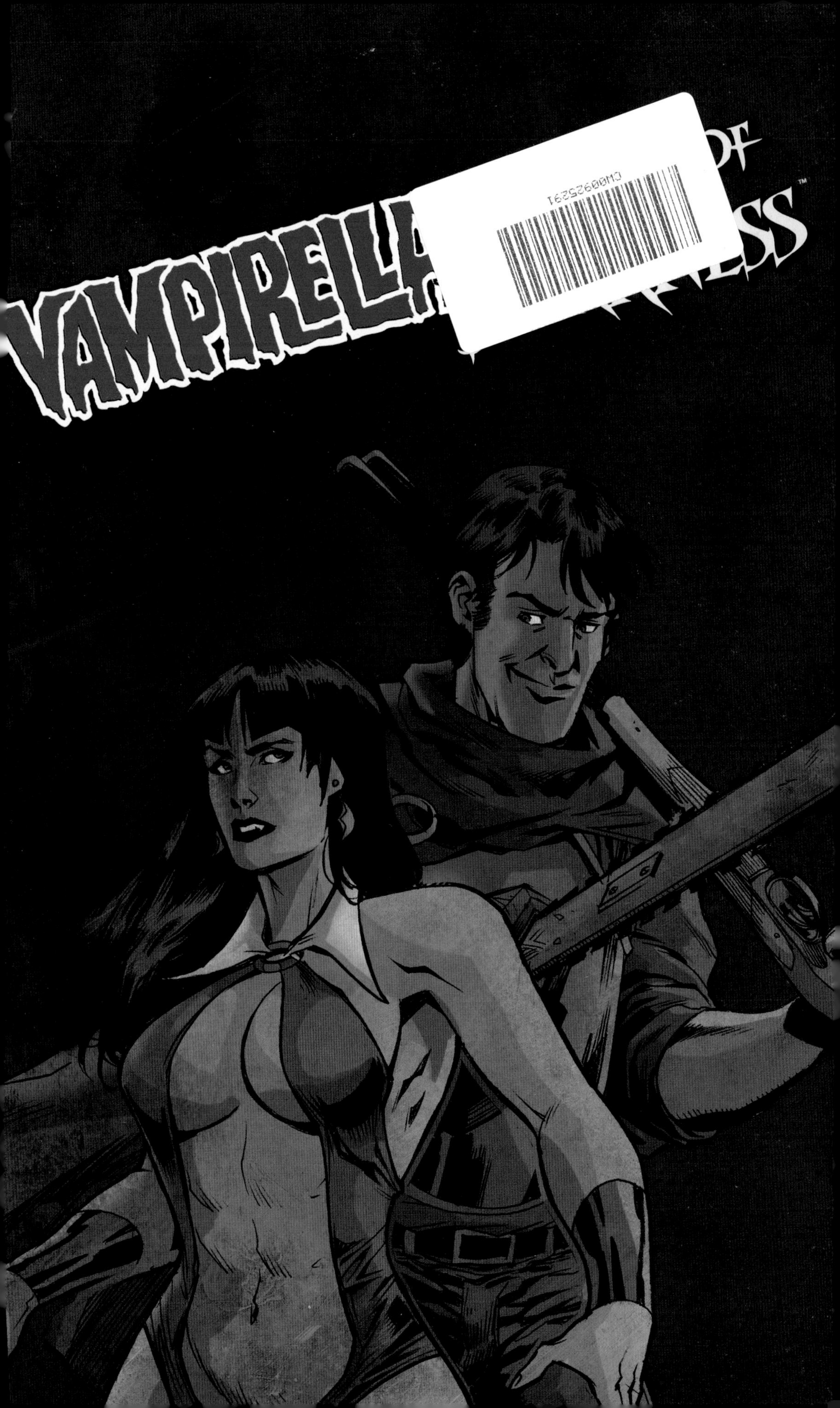
VAMPIRELLA
OF

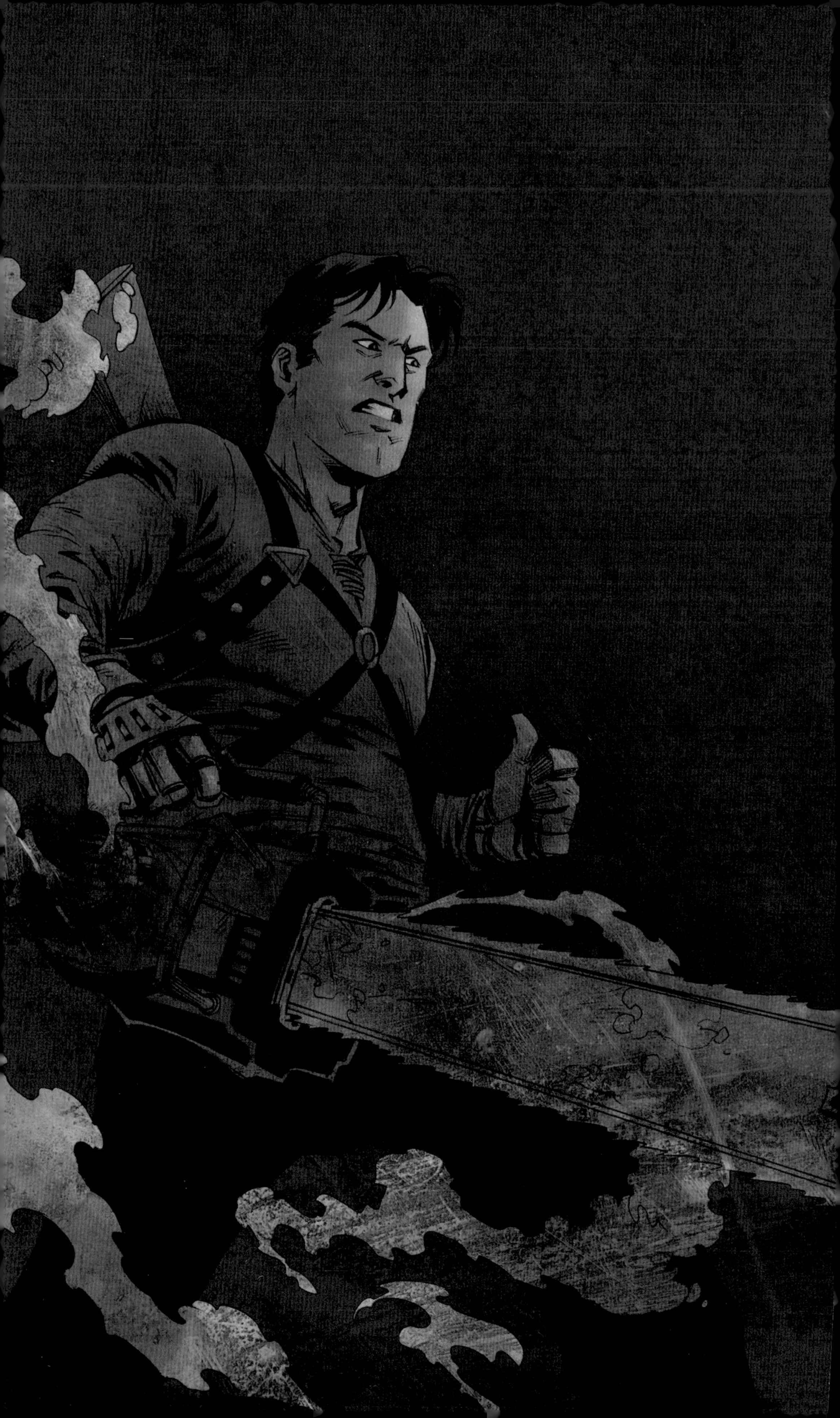

VAMPIRELLA ARMY of DARKNESS

WRITTEN BY
MARK RAHNER

ART BY
JETHRO MORALES

COLORS BY
MORGAN HICKMAN

LETTERS BY
MARSHALL DILLON

THIS VOLUME COLLECTS
ISSUES ONE THROUGH FOUR OF THE
DYNAMITE ENTERTAINMENT SERIES,
VAMPIRELLA / ARMY OF DARKNESS

COLLECTION DESIGN BY
JOSH JOHNSON

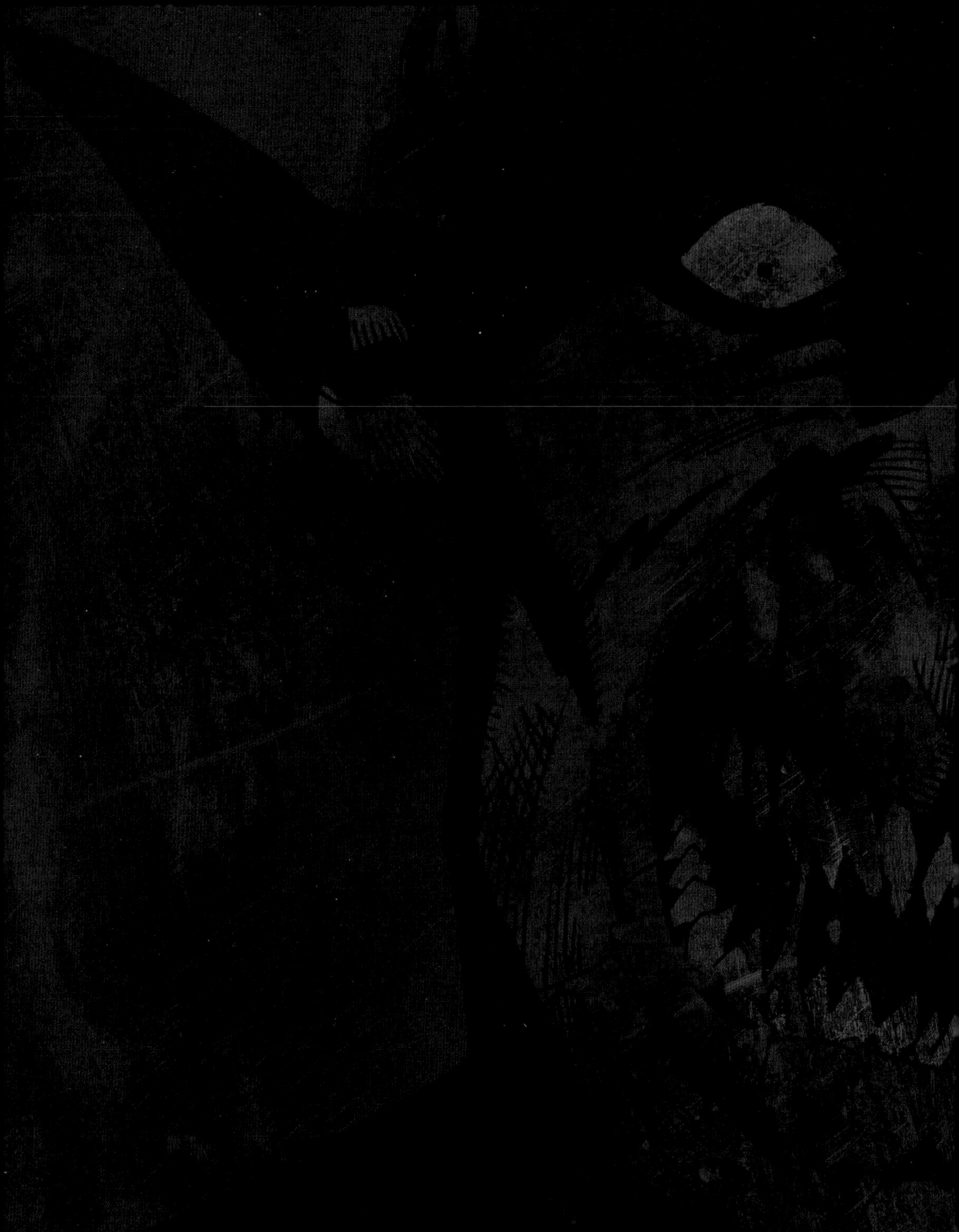

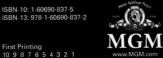

DYNAMITE®

Nick Barrucci, CEO / Publisher
Juan Collado, President / COO

Joe Rybandt, Senior Editor
Rachel Pinnelas, Associate Editor

Jason Ullmeyer, Design Director
Geoff Harkins, Graphic Designer
Chris Caniano, Digital Associate
Rachel Kilbury, Digital Assistant

Brandon Dante Primavera, Director of IT/Operations
Rich Young, Director of Business Development

Keith Davidsen, Marketing Manager
Kevin Pearl, Sales Associate

Online at **WWW.DYNAMITE.COM**
Twitter **@dynamitecomics**
Facebook **/Dynamitecomics**
Instagram **/Dynamitecomics**
YouTube **/Dynamitecomics**
Tumblr **dynamitecomics.tumblr.com**

VAMPIRELLA® / ARMY OF DARKNESS™ Volume 1. First printing. Contains materials originally published in Vampirella® / Army of Darkness™ #1-4. Published by Dynamite Entertainment. 113 Gaither Dr., STE 205, Mt. Laurel, NJ 08054.

Printed in China.

For media rights, foreign rights, promotions, licensing, and advertising: marketing@dynamite.com

ISBN-10: 1-60690-837-5
ISBN-13: 978-1-60690-837-2

MGM
www.MGM.com

First Printing
10 9 8 7 6 5 4 3 2 1

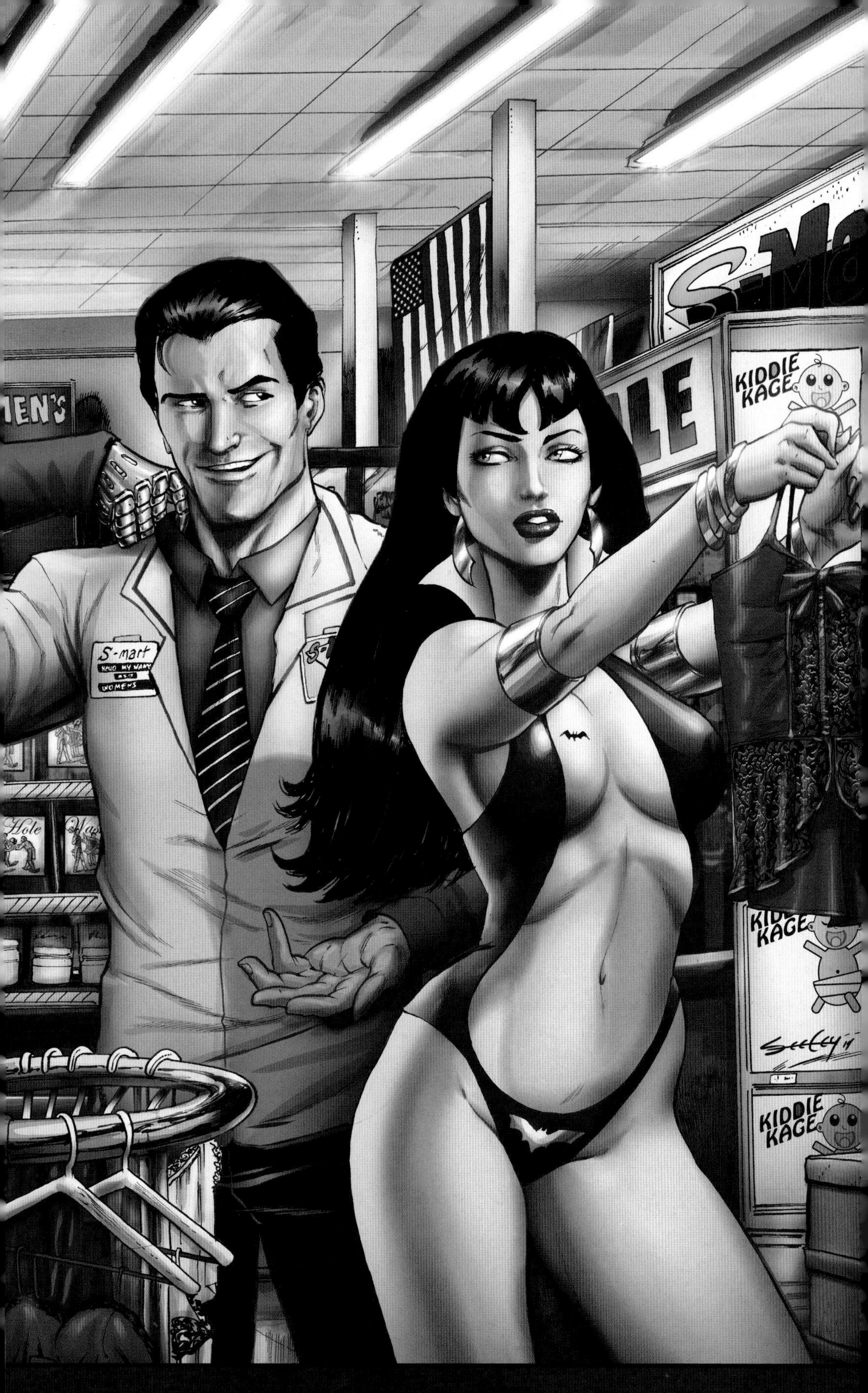
KIDDIE KAGE
S-mart
KIDDIE KAGE
KIDDIE KAGE

ISSUE #1 COVER ART BY TIM SEELEY COLORS BY VINICIUS ANDRADE

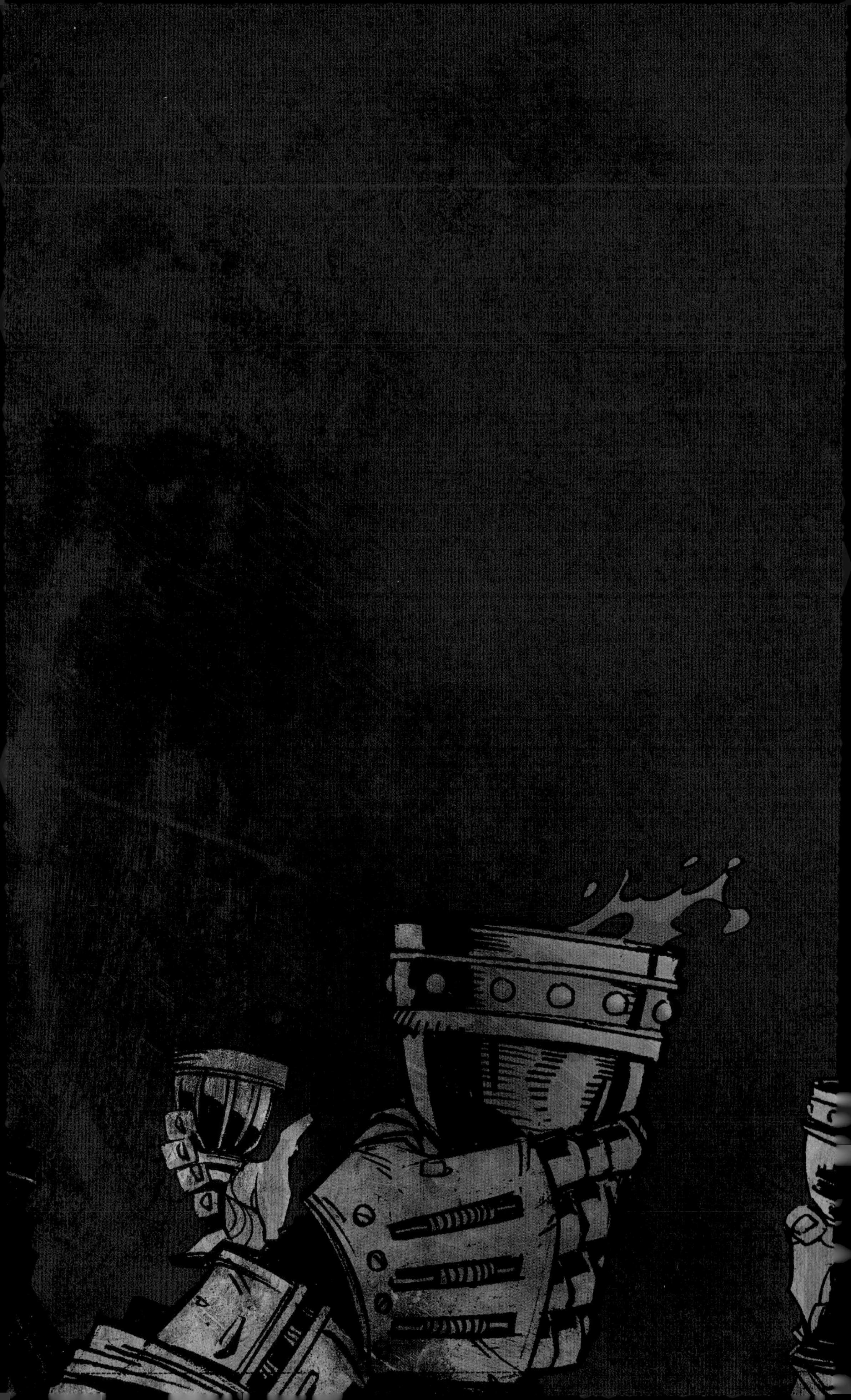

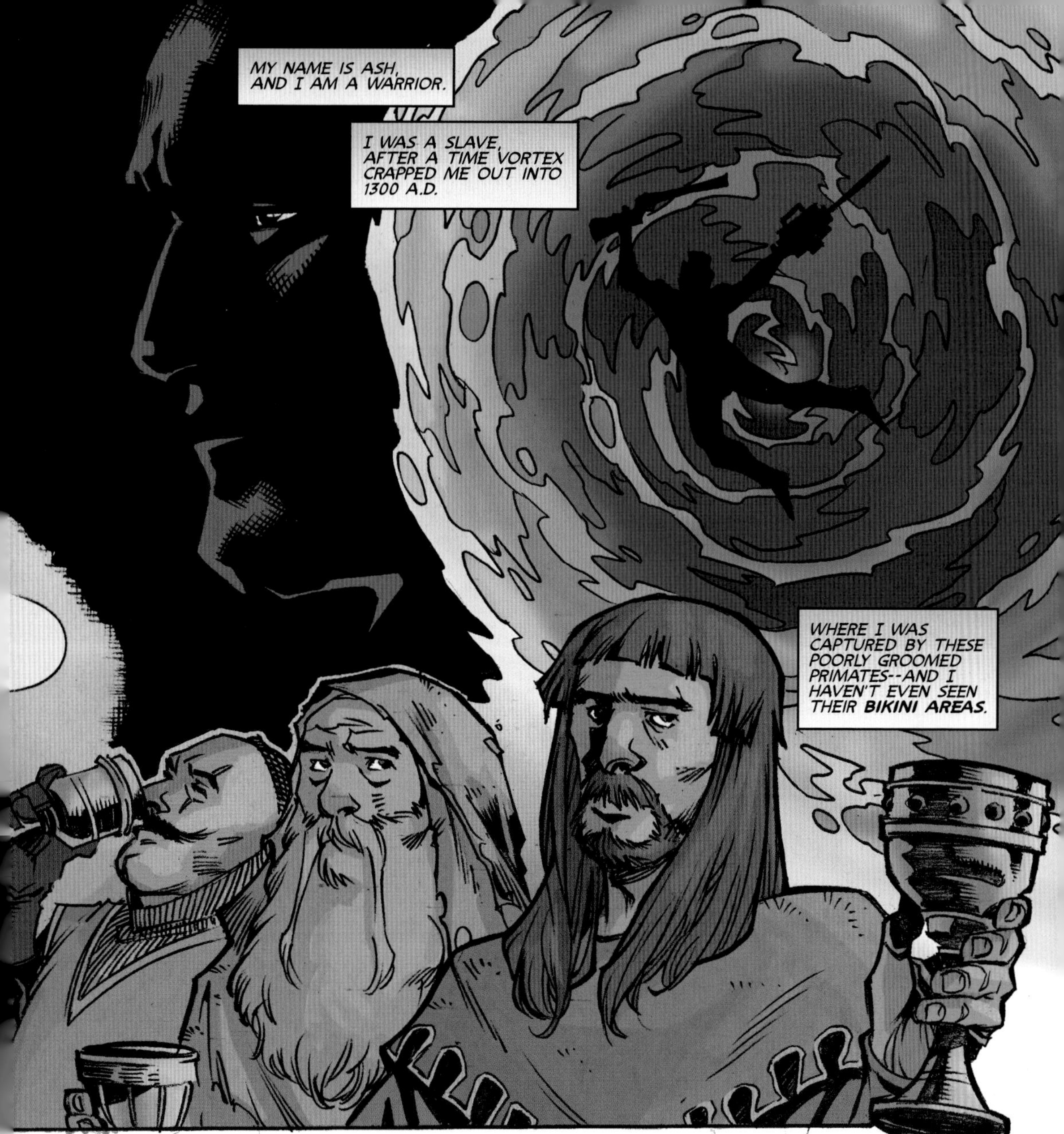
MY NAME IS ASH, AND I AM A WARRIOR.
I WAS A SLAVE, AFTER A TIME VORTEX CRAPPED ME OUT INTO 1300 A.D.
WHERE I WAS CAPTURED BY THESE POORLY GROOMED PRIMATES--AND I HAVEN'T EVEN SEEN THEIR **BIKINI AREAS**.

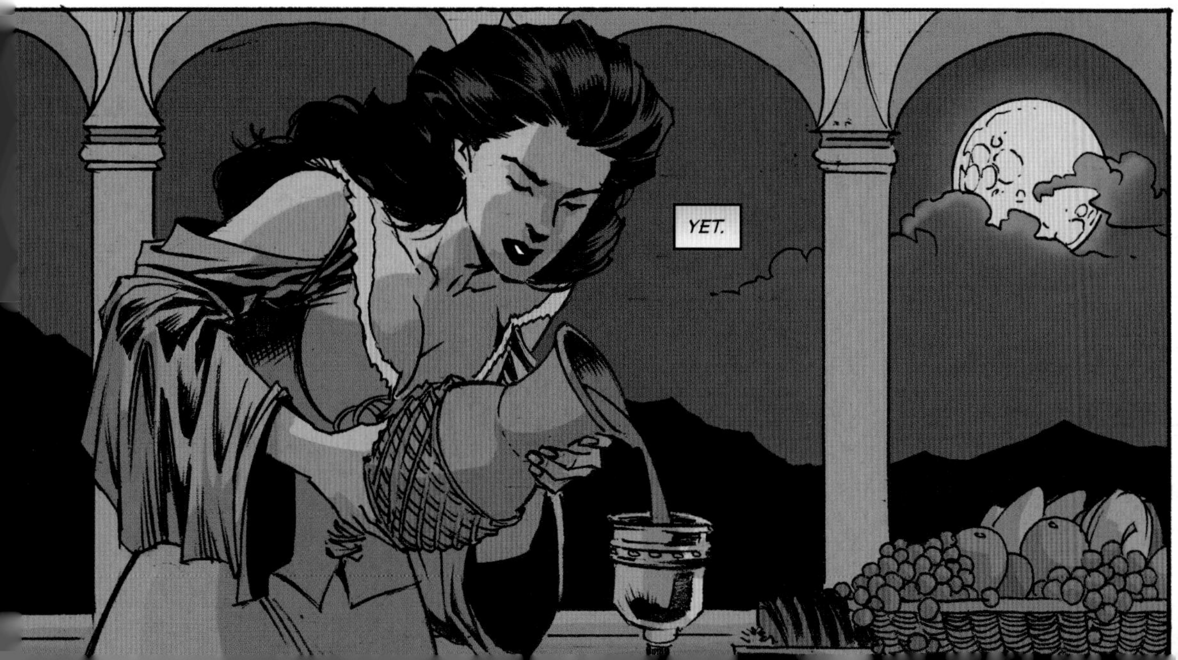
YET.

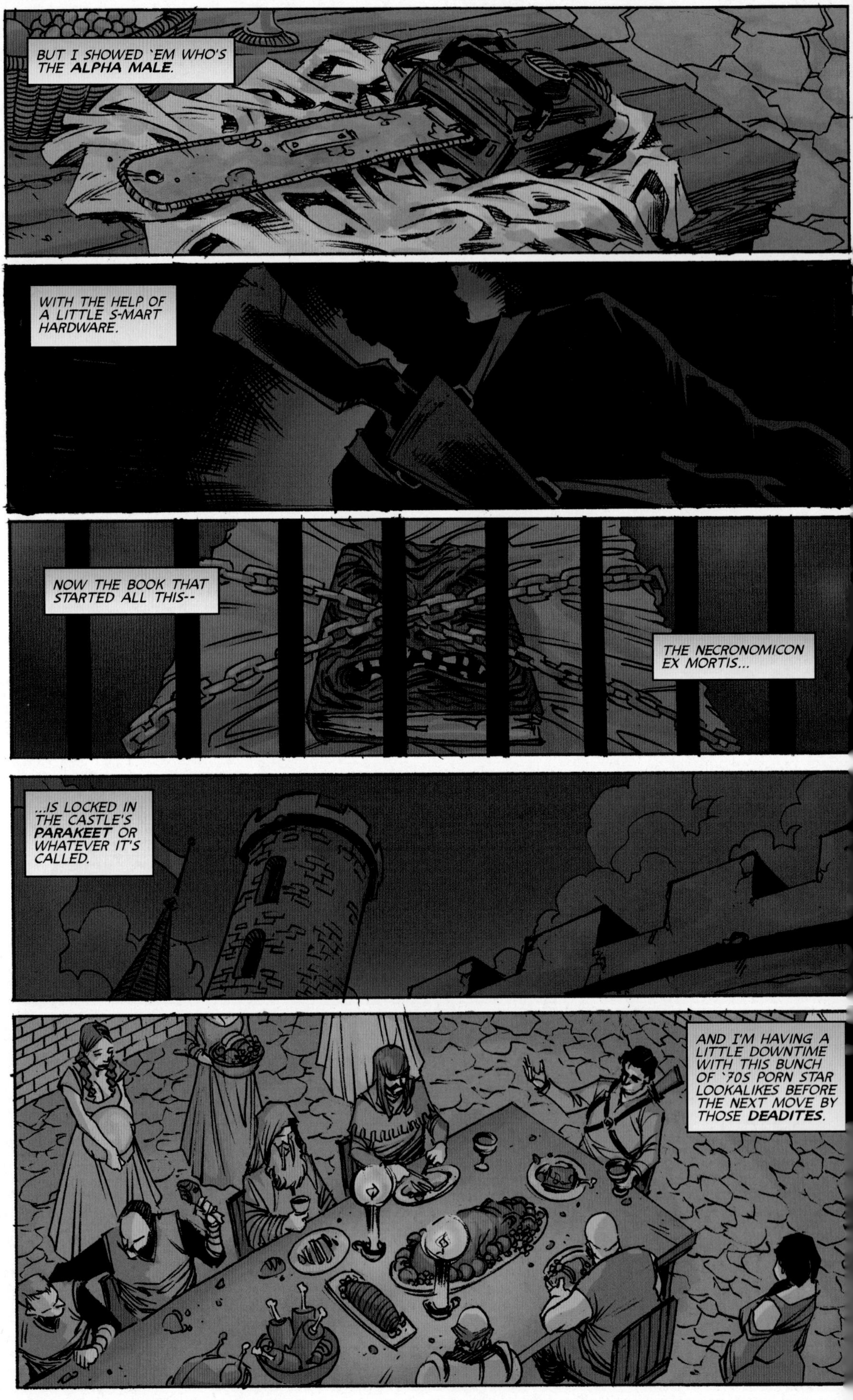
BUT I SHOWED 'EM WHO'S THE ALPHA MALE.
WITH THE HELP OF A LITTLE S-MART HARDWARE.
NOW THE BOOK THAT STARTED ALL THIS--
THE NECRONOMICON EX MORTIS...
...IS LOCKED IN THE CASTLE'S PARAKEET OR WHATEVER IT'S CALLED.
AND I'M HAVING A LITTLE DOWNTIME WITH THIS BUNCH OF '70S PORN STAR LOOKALIKES BEFORE THE NEXT MOVE BY THOSE DEADITES.

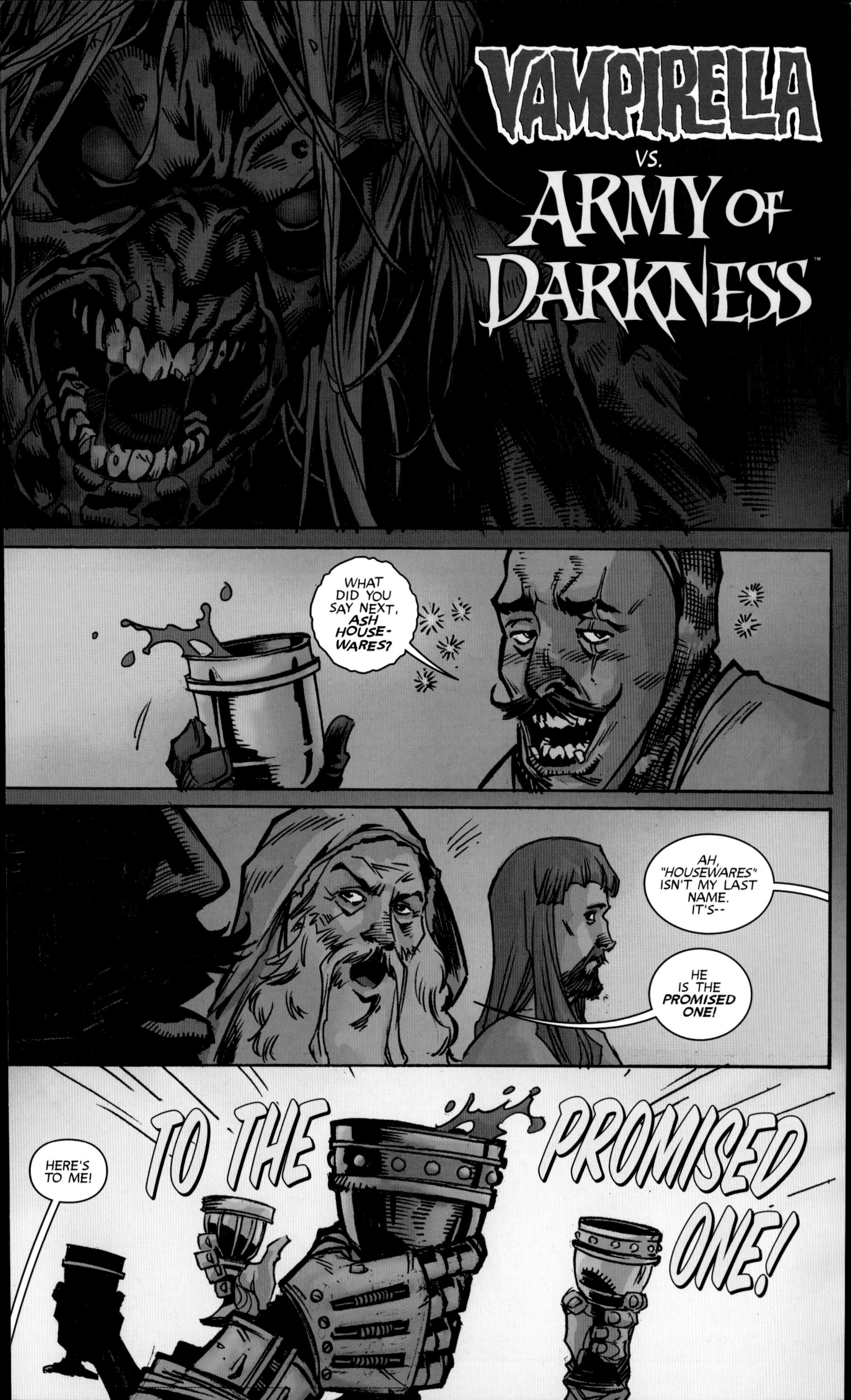
VAMPIRELLA VS. ARMY OF DARKNESS
WHAT DID YOU SAY NEXT, ASH HOUSE-WARES?
AH, "HOUSEWARES" ISN'T MY LAST NAME. IT'S--
HE IS THE PROMISED ONE!
HERE'S TO ME!
TO THE PROMISED ONE!

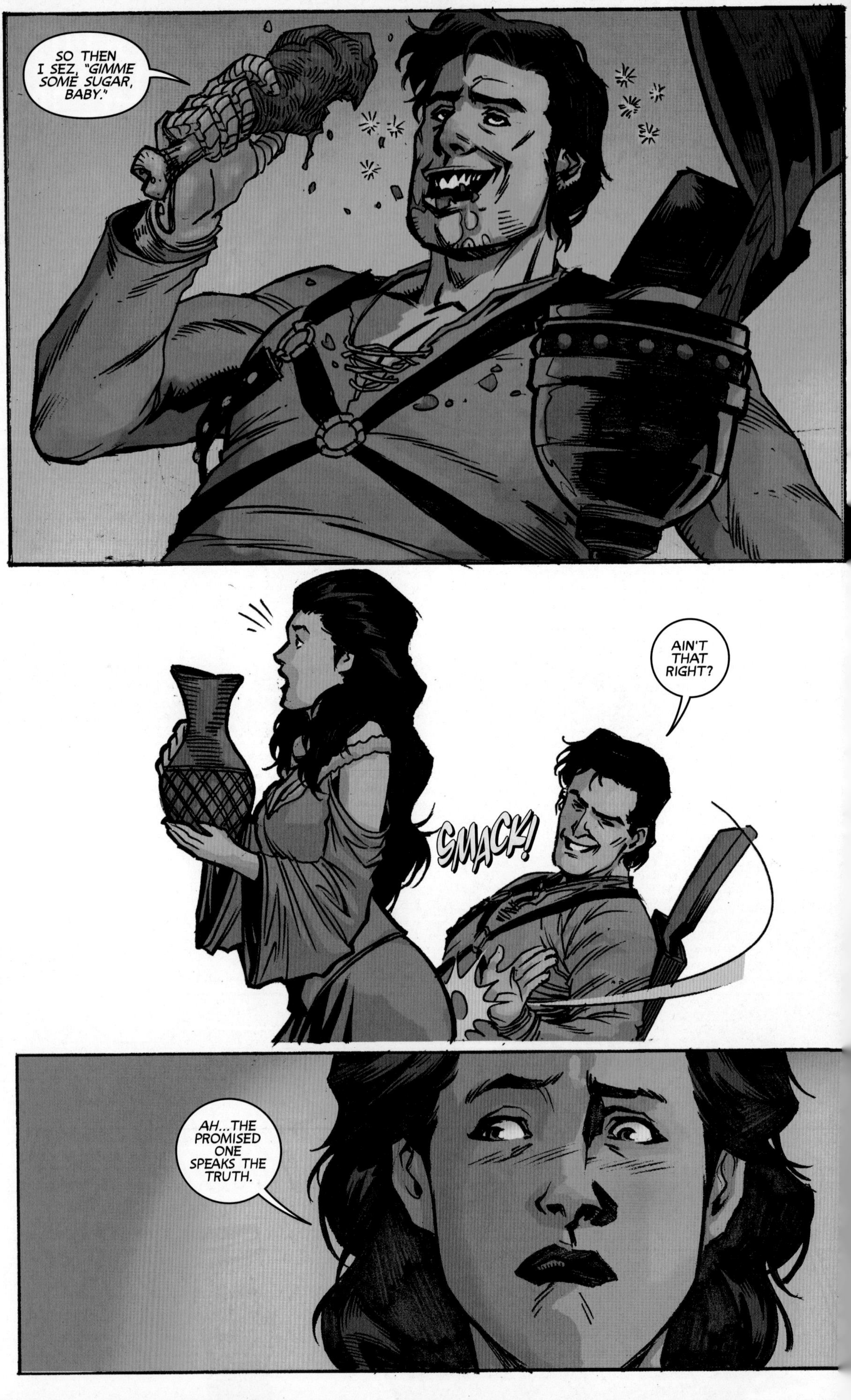
SO THEN I SEZ, "GIMME SOME SUGAR, BABY."
AIN'T THAT RIGHT?
SMACK!
AH...THE PROMISED ONE SPEAKS THE TRUTH.

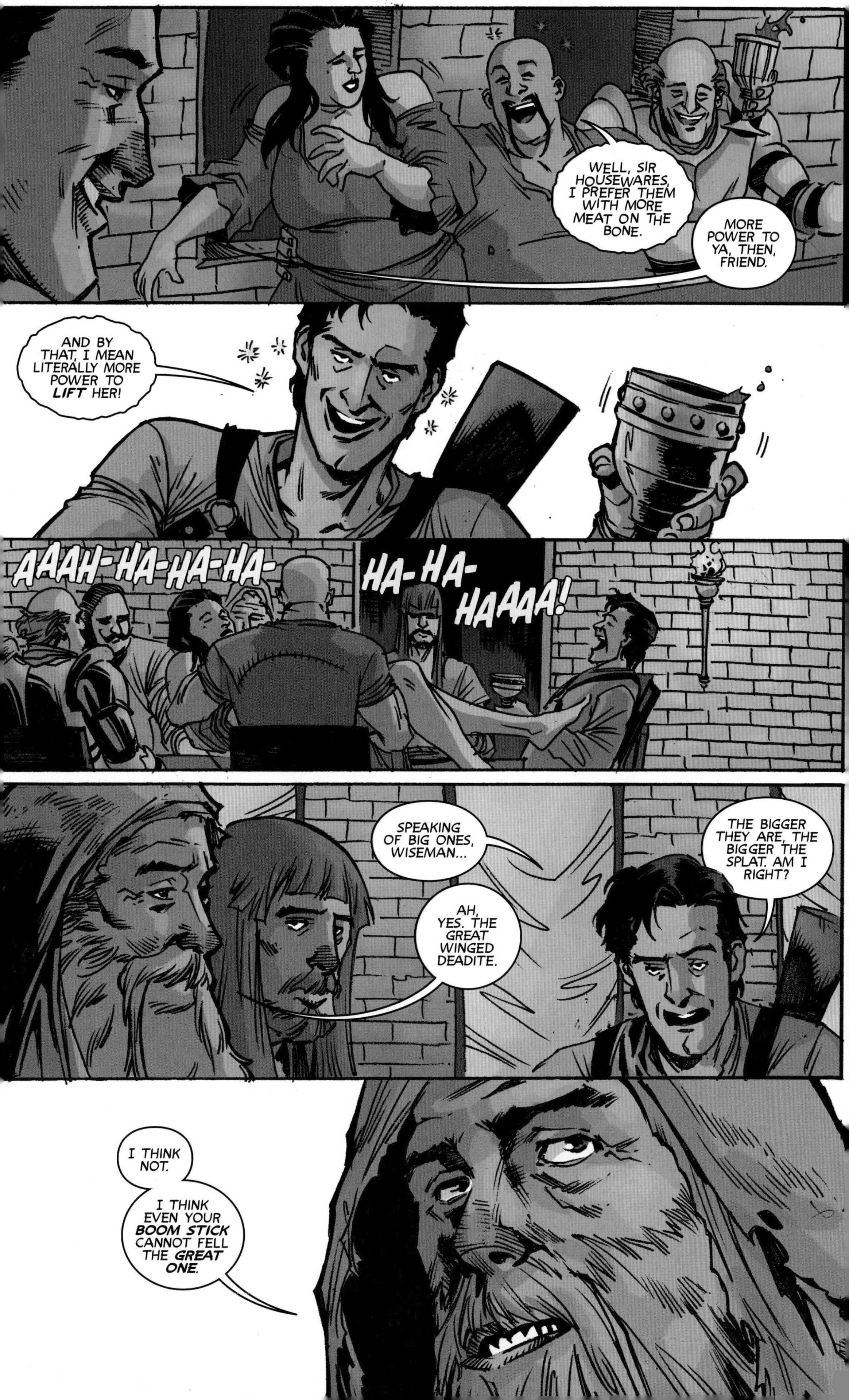
WELL, SIR HOUSEWARES, I PREFER THEM WITH MORE MEAT ON THE BONE.
MORE POWER TO YA, THEN, FRIEND.
AND BY THAT, I MEAN LITERALLY MORE POWER TO LIFT HER!
AAAH-HA-HA-HA-HA-HA-HAAAA!
SPEAKING OF BIG ONES, WISEMAN...
THE BIGGER THEY ARE, THE BIGGER THE SPLAT. AM I RIGHT?
AH, YES. THE GREAT WINGED DEADITE.
I THINK NOT.
I THINK EVEN YOUR BOOM STICK CANNOT FELL THE GREAT ONE.

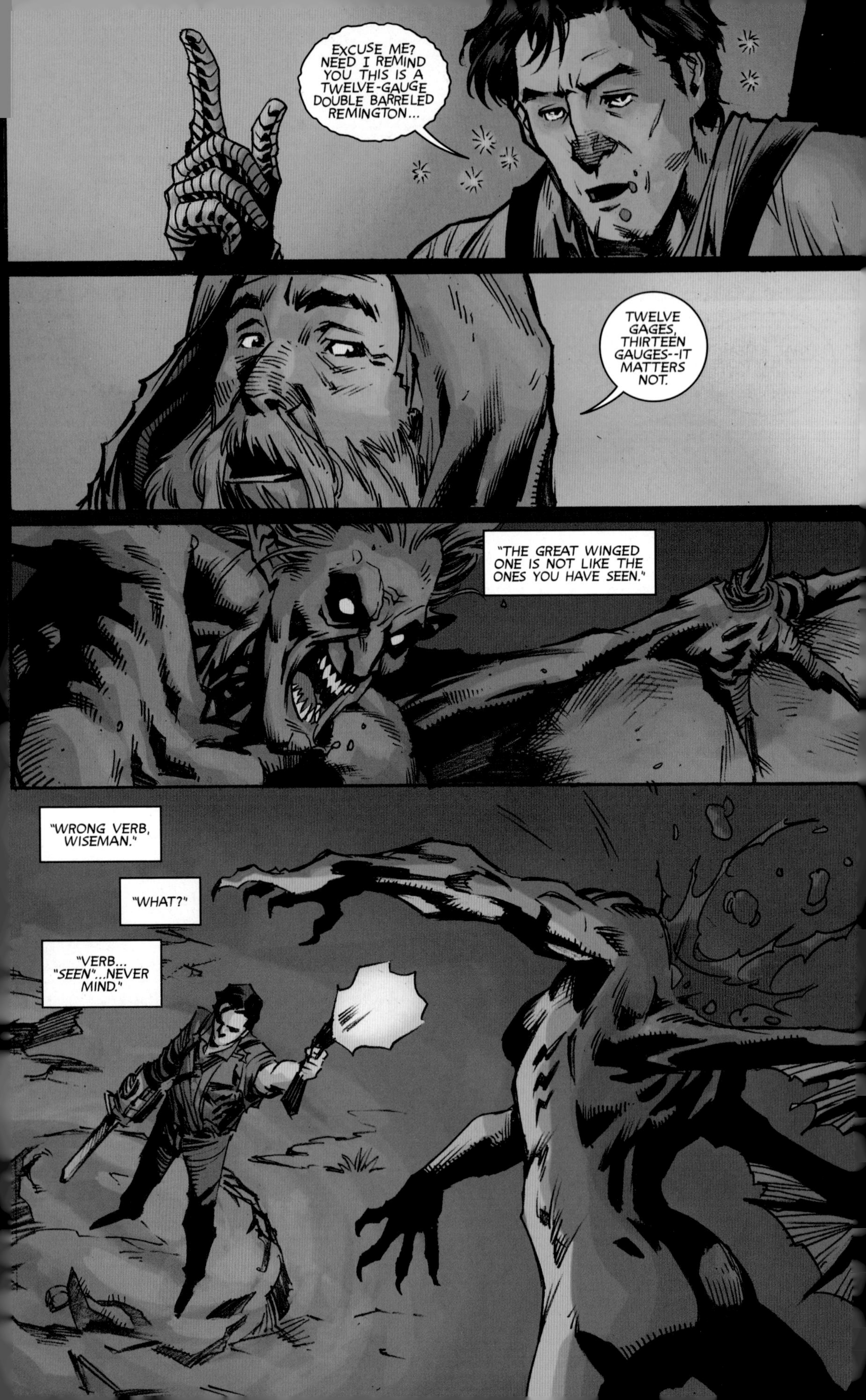
EXCUSE ME? NEED I REMIND YOU THIS IS A TWELVE-GAUGE DOUBLE BARRELED REMINGTON...
TWELVE GAGES, THIRTEEN GAUGES--IT MATTERS NOT.
"THE GREAT WINGED ONE IS NOT LIKE THE ONES YOU HAVE SEEN."
"WRONG VERB, WISEMAN."
"WHAT?"
"VERB... *"SEEN"*...NEVER MIND."

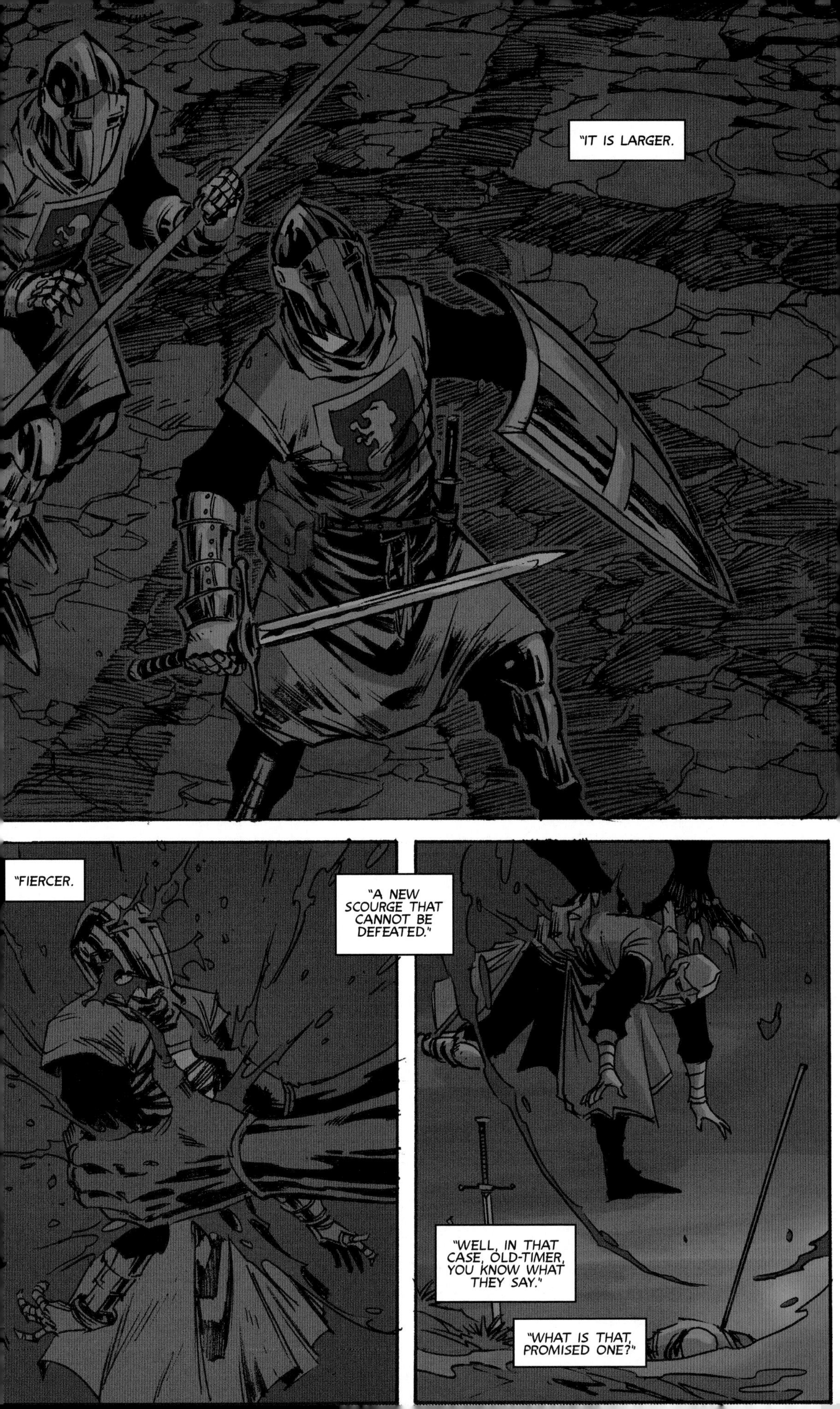
"IT IS LARGER.
"FIERCER.
"A NEW SCOURGE THAT CANNOT BE DEFEATED."
"WELL, IN THAT CASE, OLD-TIMER, YOU KNOW WHAT THEY SAY."
"WHAT IS THAT, PROMISED ONE?"

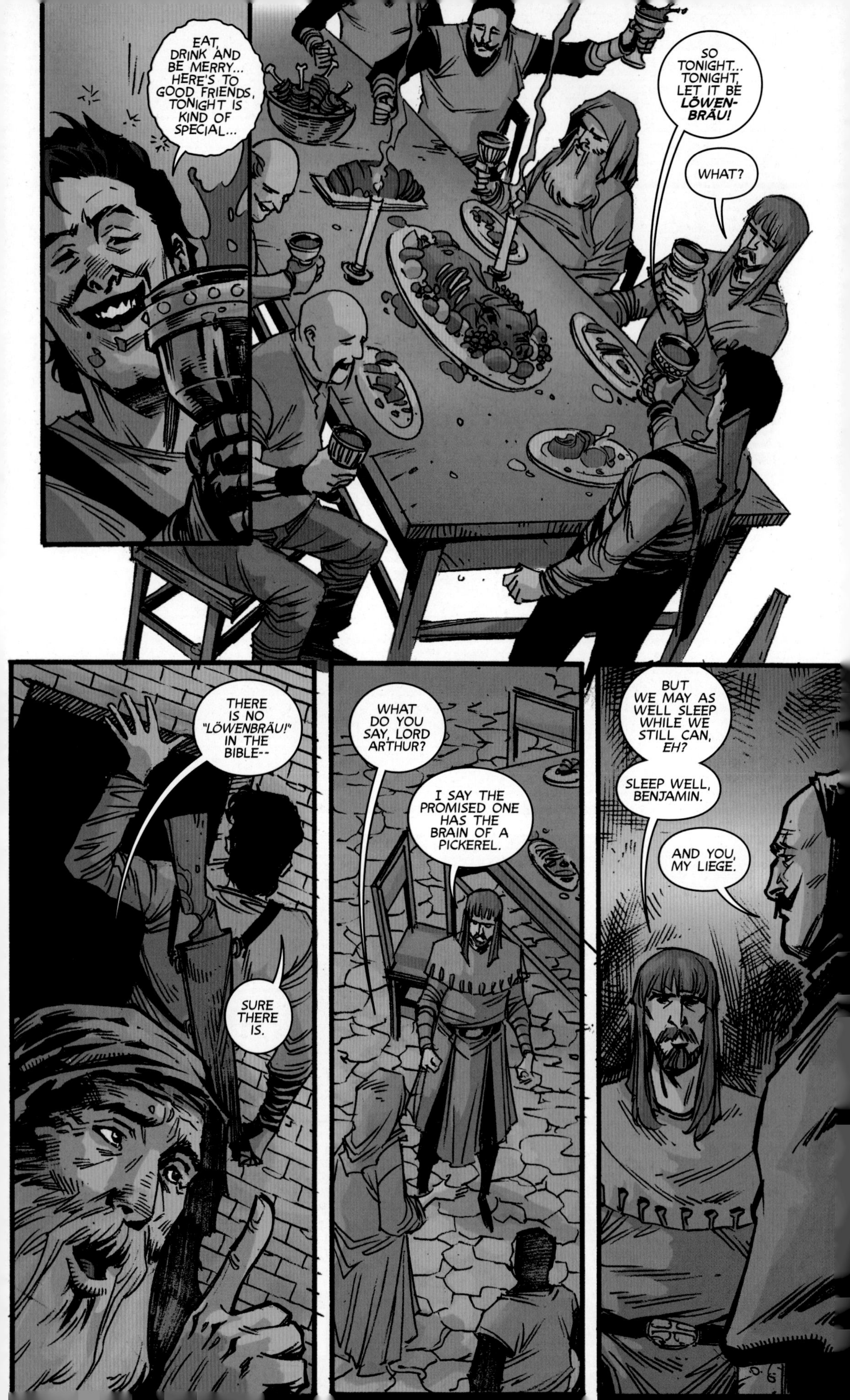
EAT, DRINK AND BE MERRY... HERE'S TO GOOD FRIENDS, TONIGHT IS KIND OF SPECIAL...
SO TONIGHT... TONIGHT, LET IT BE ***LÖWENBRÄU!***
WHAT?
THERE IS NO "LÖWENBRÄU!" IN THE BIBLE--
SURE THERE IS.
WHAT DO YOU SAY, LORD ARTHUR?
I SAY THE PROMISED ONE HAS THE BRAIN OF A PICKEREL.
BUT WE MAY AS WELL SLEEP WHILE WE STILL CAN, *EH?*
SLEEP WELL, BENJAMIN.
AND YOU, MY LIEGE.

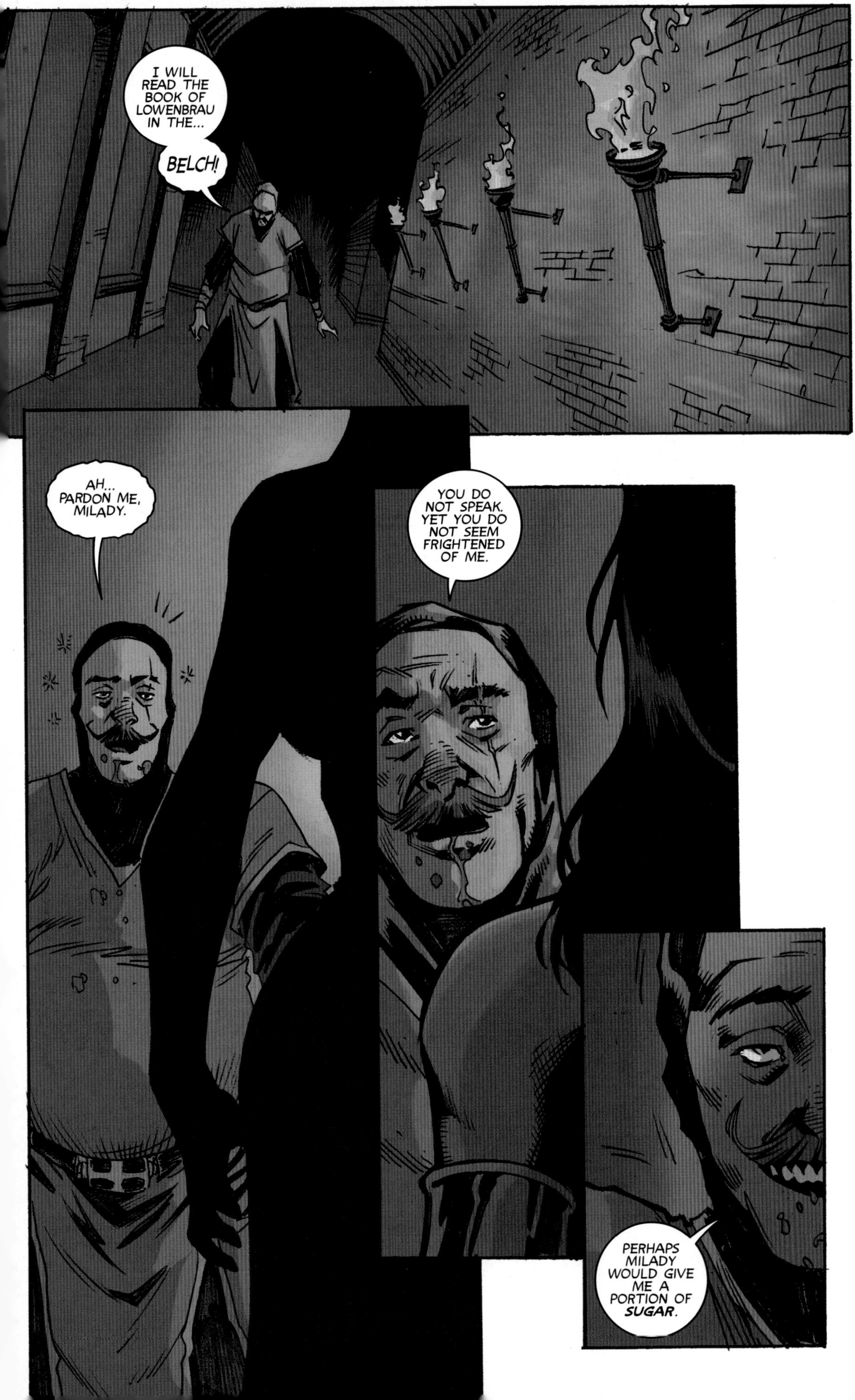

I WILL READ THE BOOK OF LOWENBRAU IN THE...
BELCH!
AH... PARDON ME, MILADY.
YOU DO NOT SPEAK. YET YOU DO NOT SEEM FRIGHTENED OF ME.
PERHAPS MILADY WOULD GIVE ME A PORTION OF **SUGAR**.

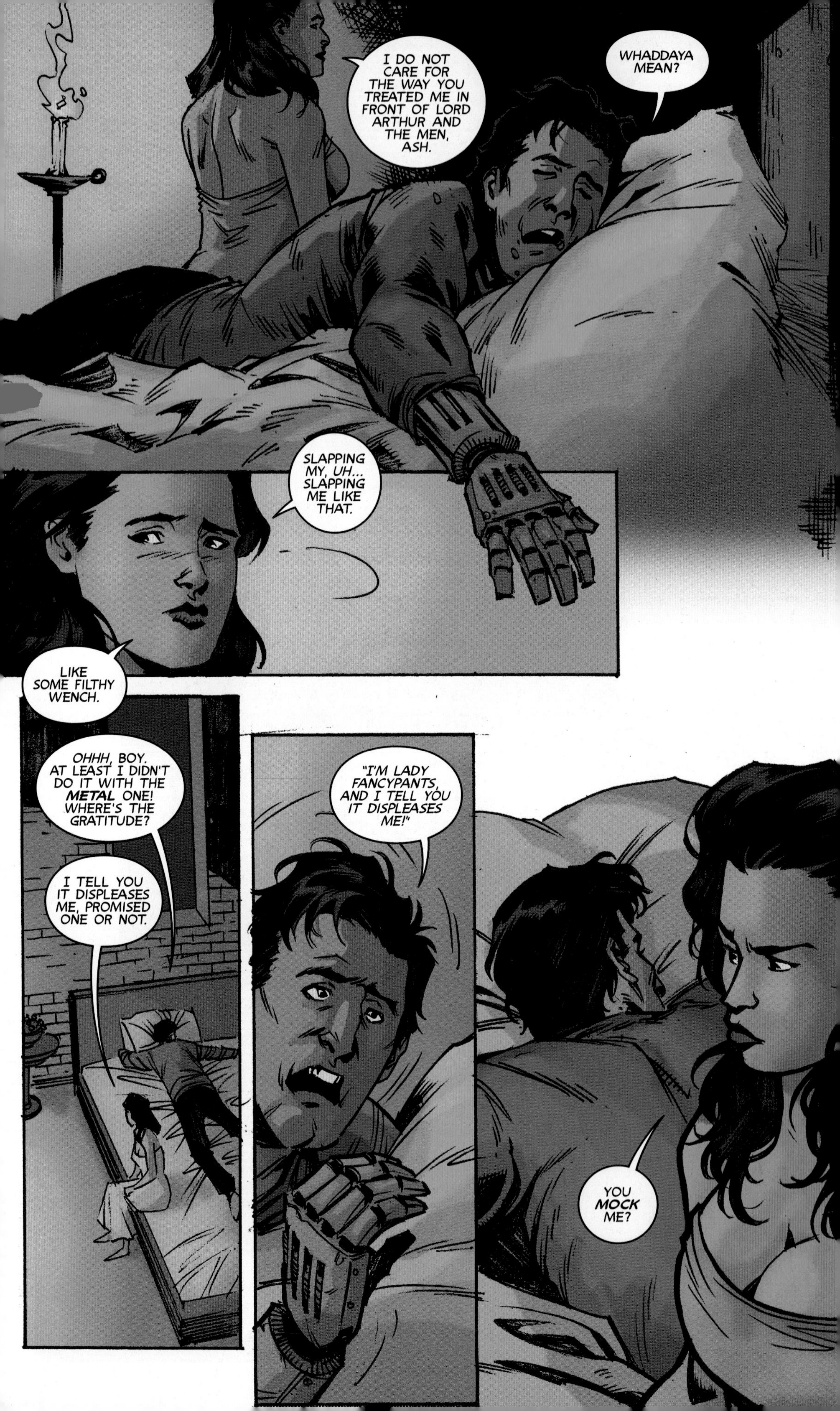

I DO NOT CARE FOR THE WAY YOU TREATED ME IN FRONT OF LORD ARTHUR AND THE MEN, ASH.
WHADDAYA MEAN?
SLAPPING MY, *UH*... SLAPPING ME LIKE THAT.
LIKE SOME FILTHY WENCH.
OHHH, BOY. AT LEAST I DIDN'T DO IT WITH THE ***METAL*** ONE! WHERE'S THE GRATITUDE?
I TELL YOU IT DISPLEASES ME, PROMISED ONE OR NOT.
"I'M LADY FANCYPANTS, AND I TELL YOU IT DISPLEASES ME!"
YOU ***MOCK*** ME?

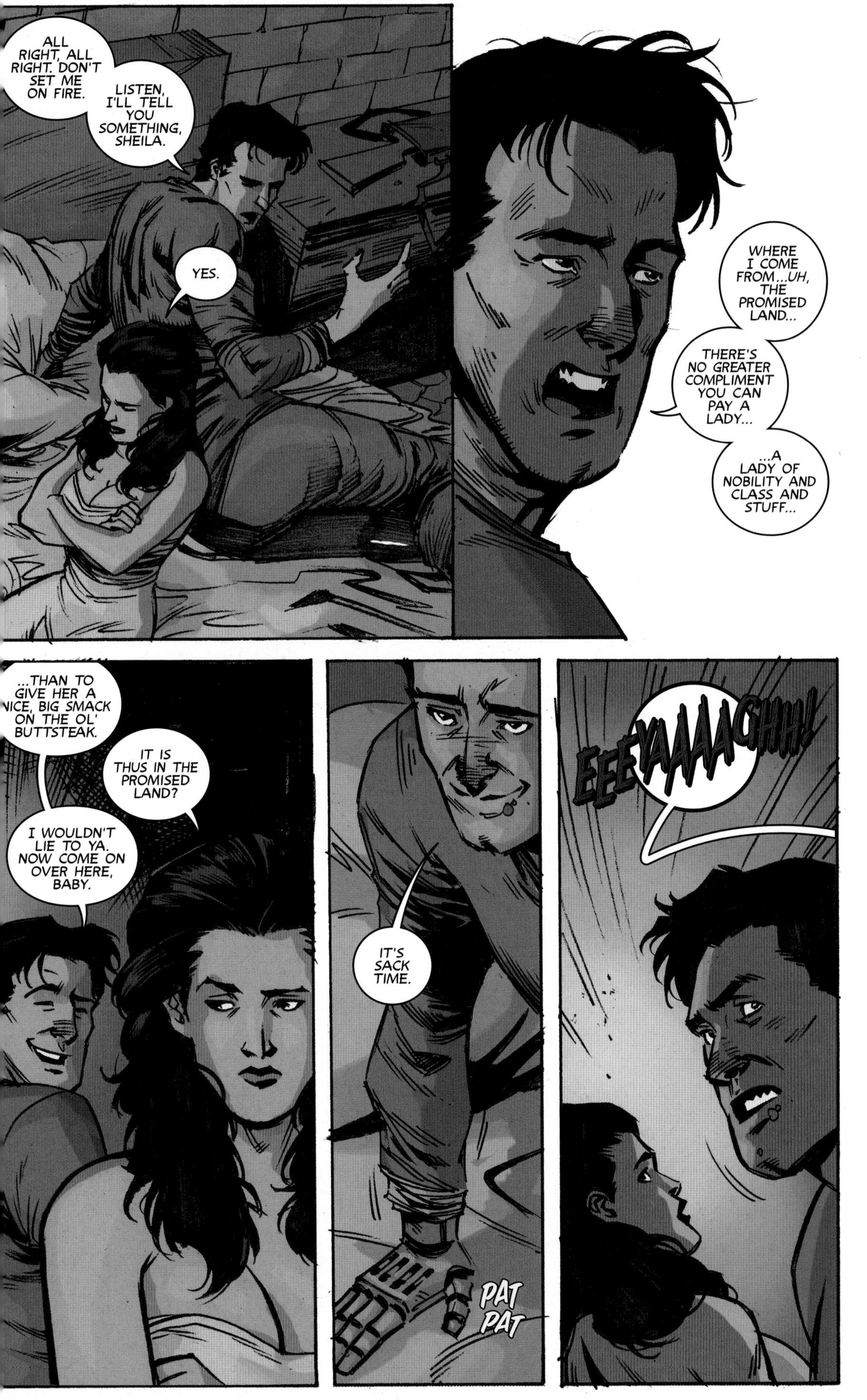

ALL RIGHT, ALL RIGHT. DON'T SET ME ON FIRE.
LISTEN, I'LL TELL YOU SOMETHING, SHEILA.
YES.
WHERE I COME FROM...UH, THE PROMISED LAND...
THERE'S NO GREATER COMPLIMENT YOU CAN PAY A LADY...
...A LADY OF NOBILITY AND CLASS AND STUFF...
...THAN TO GIVE HER A NICE, BIG SMACK ON THE OL' BUTTSTEAK.
IT IS THUS IN THE PROMISED LAND?
I WOULDN'T LIE TO YA. NOW COME ON OVER HERE, BABY.
IT'S SACK TIME.
PAT PAT
EEEYAAAAGHH!

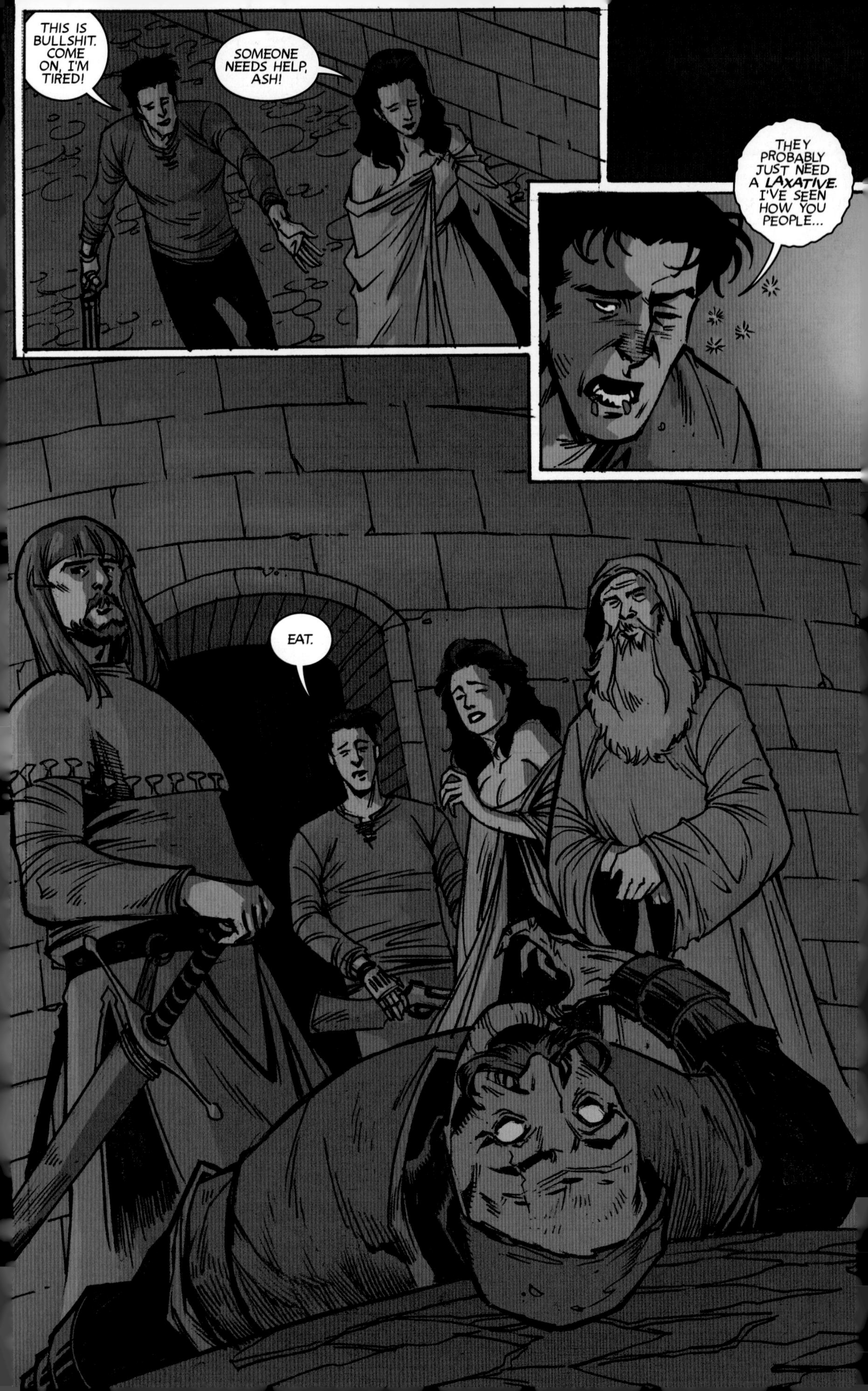
THIS IS BULLSHIT. COME ON, I'M TIRED!
SOMEONE NEEDS HELP, ASH!
THEY PROBABLY JUST NEED A LAXATIVE. I'VE SEEN HOW YOU PEOPLE...
EAT.

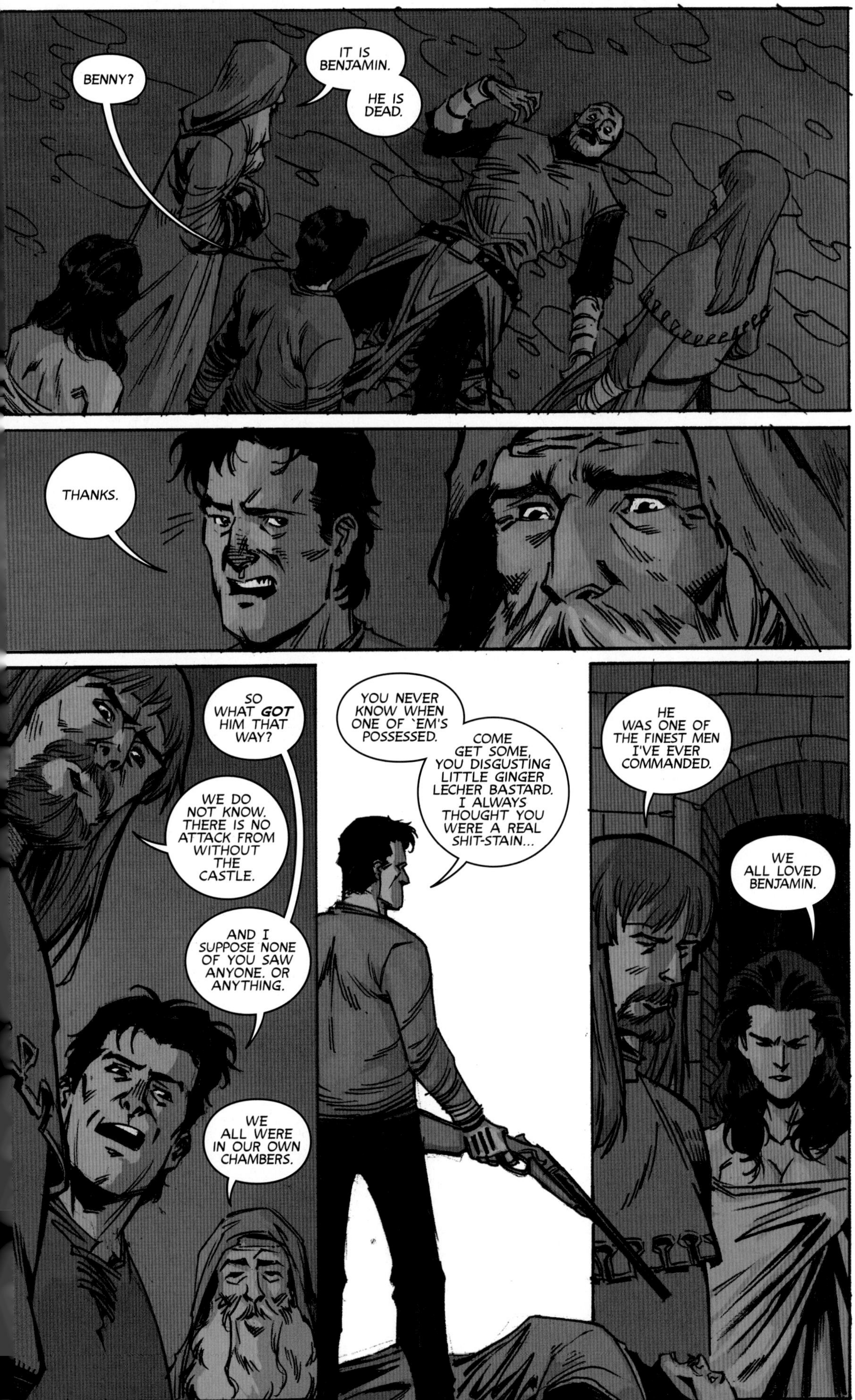
BENNY?
IT IS BENJAMIN.
HE IS DEAD.
THANKS.
SO WHAT **GOT** HIM THAT WAY?
WE DO NOT KNOW. THERE IS NO ATTACK FROM WITHOUT THE CASTLE.
AND I SUPPOSE NONE OF YOU SAW ANYONE. OR ANYTHING.
WE ALL WERE IN OUR OWN CHAMBERS.
YOU NEVER KNOW WHEN ONE OF `EM'S POSSESSED.
COME GET SOME, YOU DISGUSTING LITTLE GINGER LECHER BASTARD. I ALWAYS THOUGHT YOU WERE A REAL SHIT-STAIN...
HE WAS ONE OF THE FINEST MEN I'VE EVER COMMANDED.
WE ALL LOVED BENJAMIN.

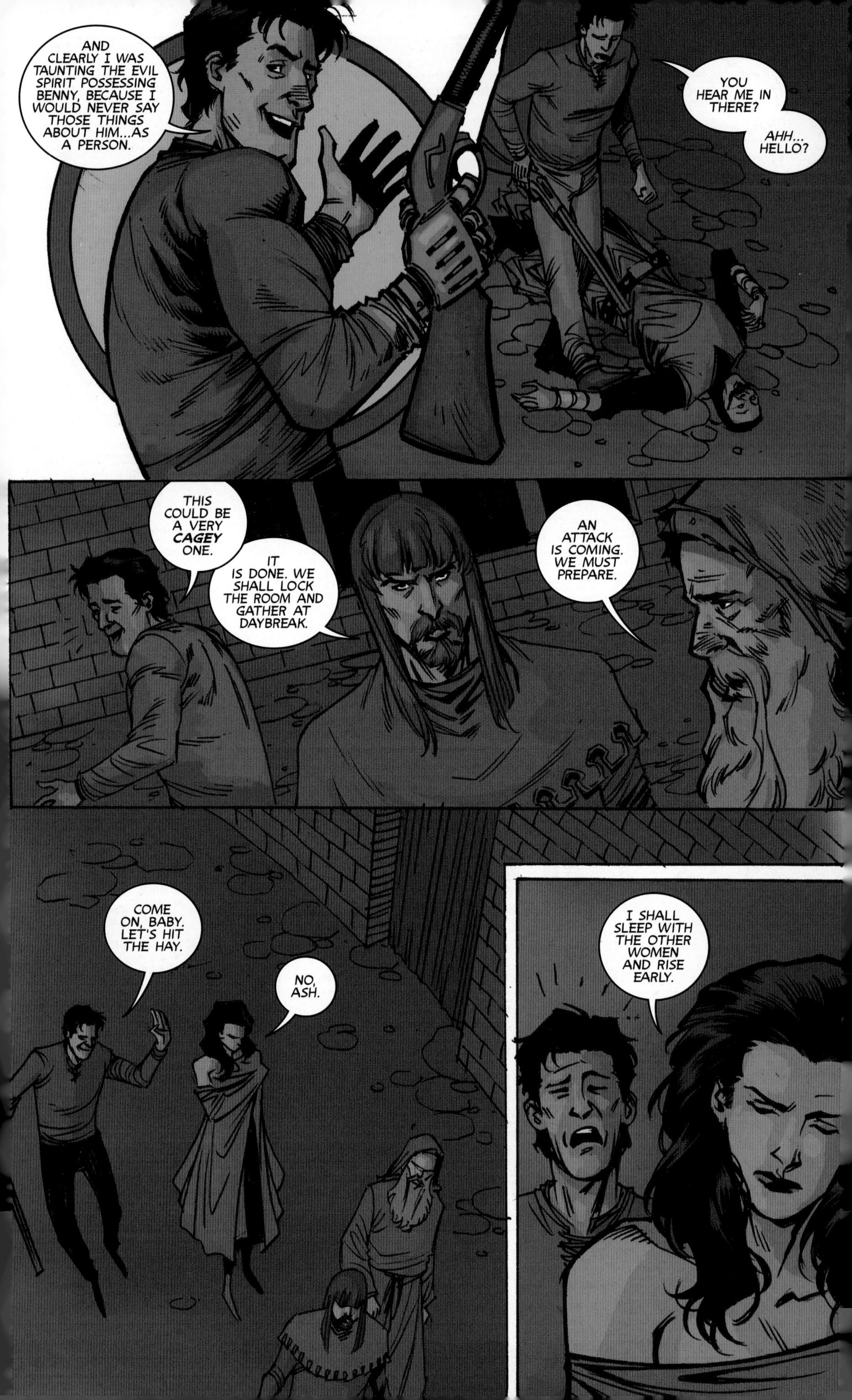
AND CLEARLY I WAS TAUNTING THE EVIL SPIRIT POSSESSING BENNY, BECAUSE I WOULD NEVER SAY THOSE THINGS ABOUT HIM...AS A PERSON.
YOU HEAR ME IN THERE?
AHH... HELLO?
THIS COULD BE A VERY CAGEY ONE.
IT IS DONE. WE SHALL LOCK THE ROOM AND GATHER AT DAYBREAK.
AN ATTACK IS COMING. WE MUST PREPARE.
COME ON, BABY. LET'S HIT THE HAY.
NO, ASH.
I SHALL SLEEP WITH THE OTHER WOMEN AND RISE EARLY.

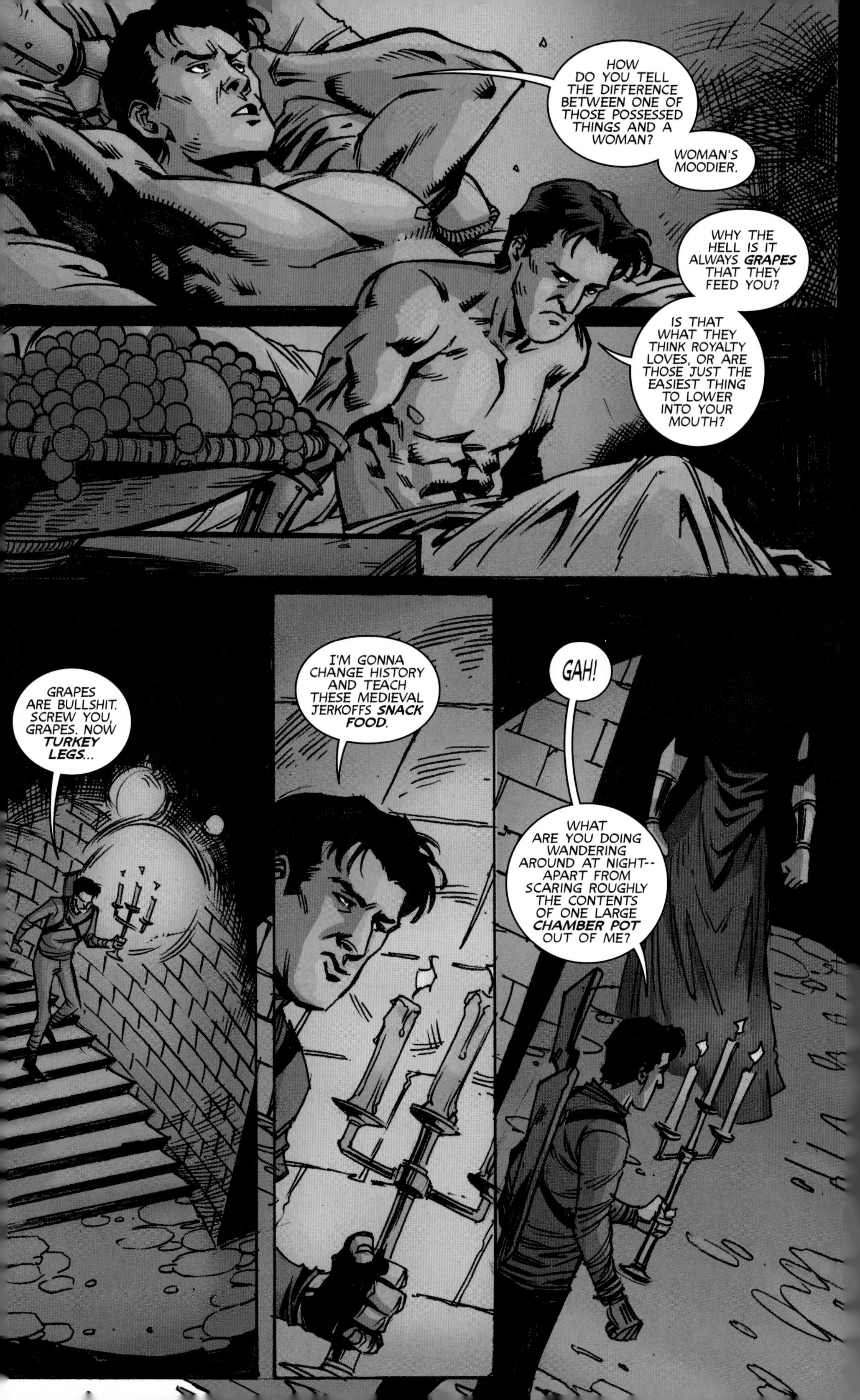

HOW DO YOU TELL THE DIFFERENCE BETWEEN ONE OF THOSE POSSESSED THINGS AND A WOMAN?
WOMAN'S MOODIER.
WHY THE HELL IS IT ALWAYS **GRAPES** THAT THEY FEED YOU?
IS THAT WHAT THEY THINK ROYALTY LOVES, OR ARE THOSE JUST THE EASIEST THING TO LOWER INTO YOUR MOUTH?
GRAPES ARE BULLSHIT. SCREW YOU, GRAPES. NOW **TURKEY LEGS**...
I'M GONNA CHANGE HISTORY AND TEACH THESE MEDIEVAL JERKOFFS **SNACK FOOD**.
GAH!
WHAT ARE YOU DOING WANDERING AROUND AT NIGHT-- APART FROM SCARING ROUGHLY THE CONTENTS OF ONE LARGE **CHAMBER POT** OUT OF ME?

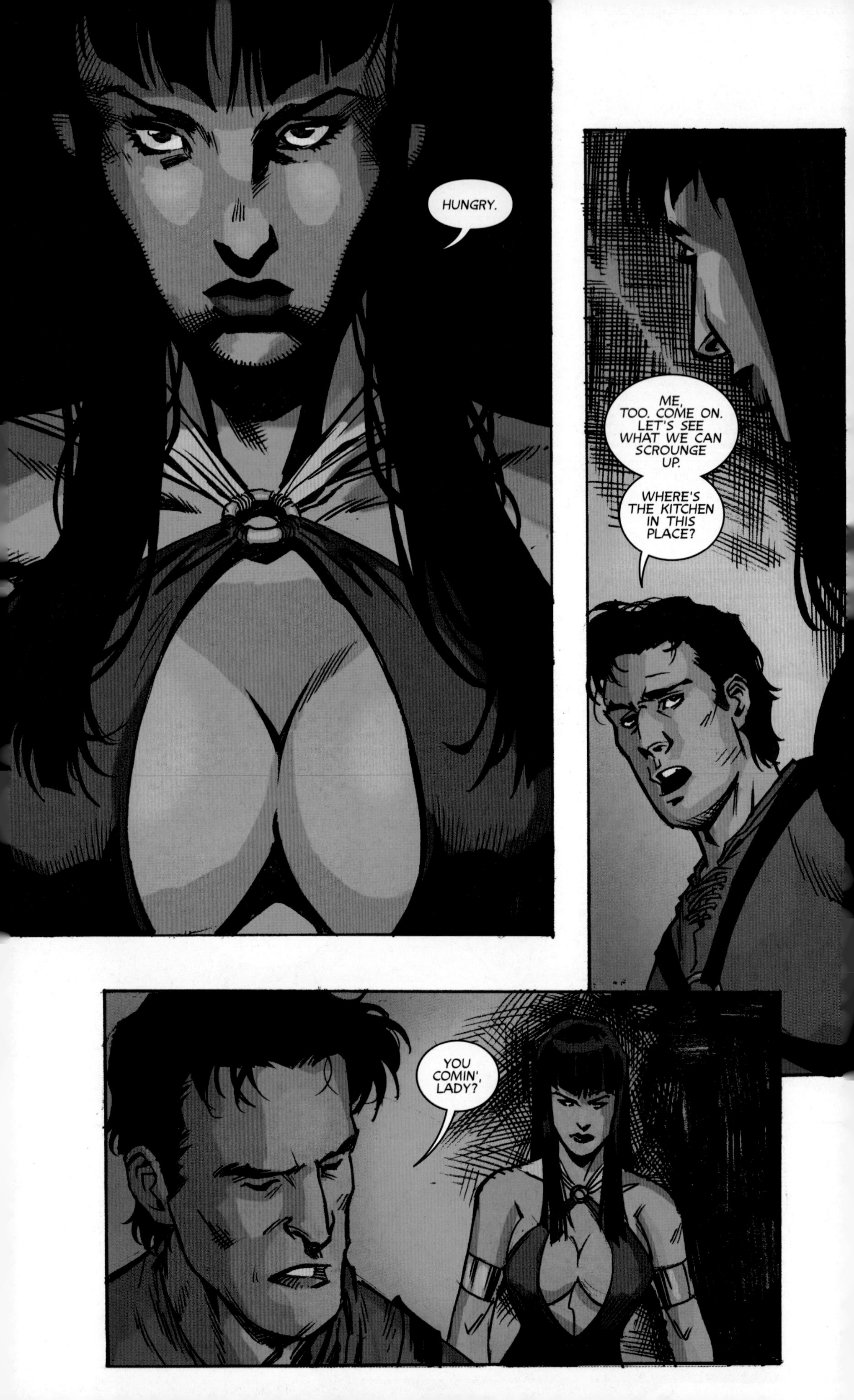
HUNGRY.
ME, TOO. COME ON. LET'S SEE WHAT WE CAN SCROUNGE UP.
WHERE'S THE KITCHEN IN THIS PLACE?
YOU COMIN', LADY?

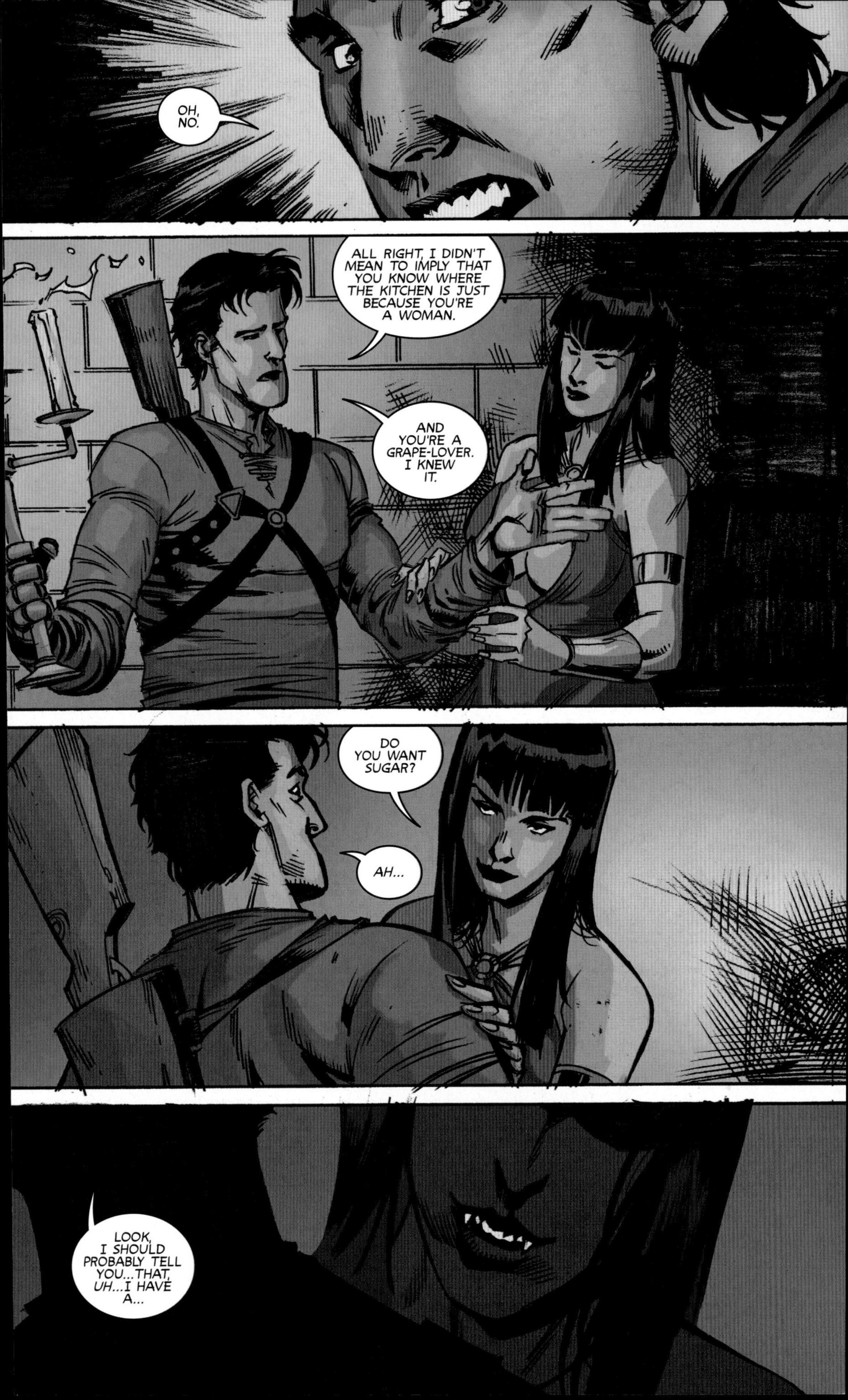
OH, NO.
ALL RIGHT, I DIDN'T MEAN TO IMPLY THAT YOU KNOW WHERE THE KITCHEN IS JUST BECAUSE YOU'RE A WOMAN.
AND YOU'RE A GRAPE-LOVER. I KNEW IT.
DO YOU WANT SUGAR?
AH...
LOOK, I SHOULD PROBABLY TELL YOU...THAT, UH...I HAVE A...

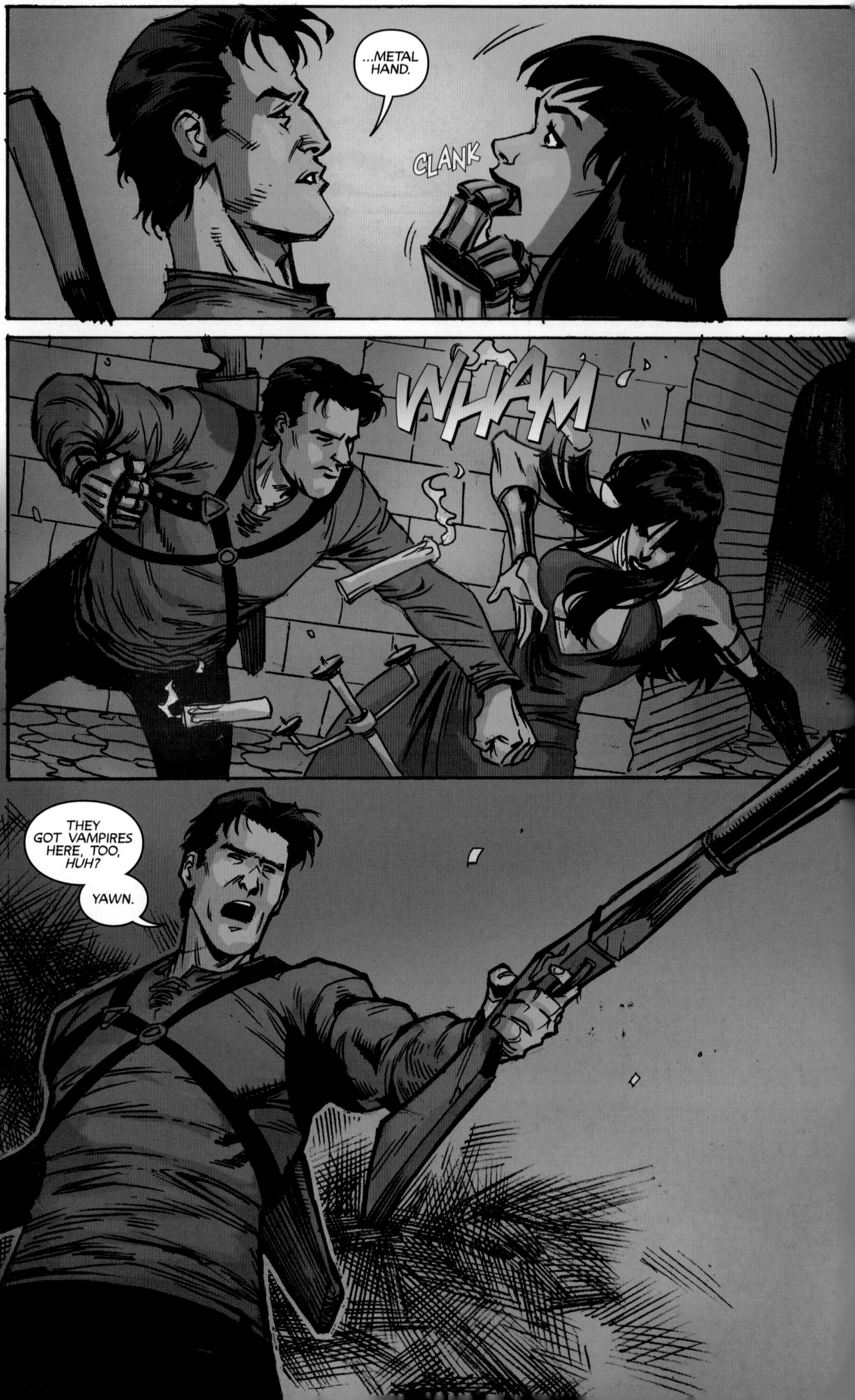
...METAL HAND.
CLANK
WHAM
THEY GOT VAMPIRES HERE, TOO, HUH?
YAWN.

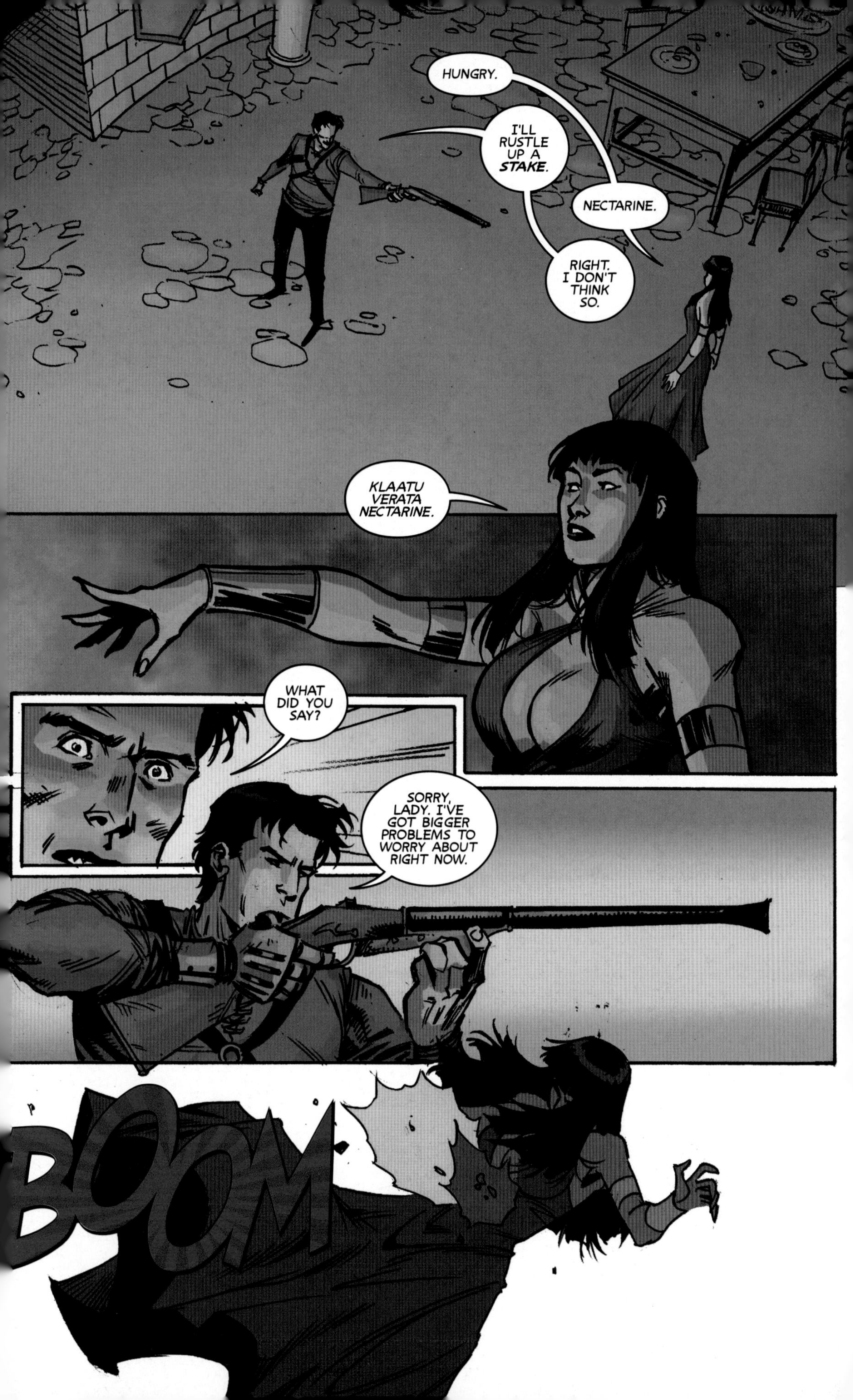
HUNGRY.
I'LL RUSTLE UP A *STAKE*.
NECTARINE.
RIGHT. I DON'T THINK SO.
KLAATU VERATA NECTARINE.
WHAT DID YOU SAY?
SORRY, LADY. I'VE GOT BIGGER PROBLEMS TO WORRY ABOUT RIGHT NOW.
BOOM

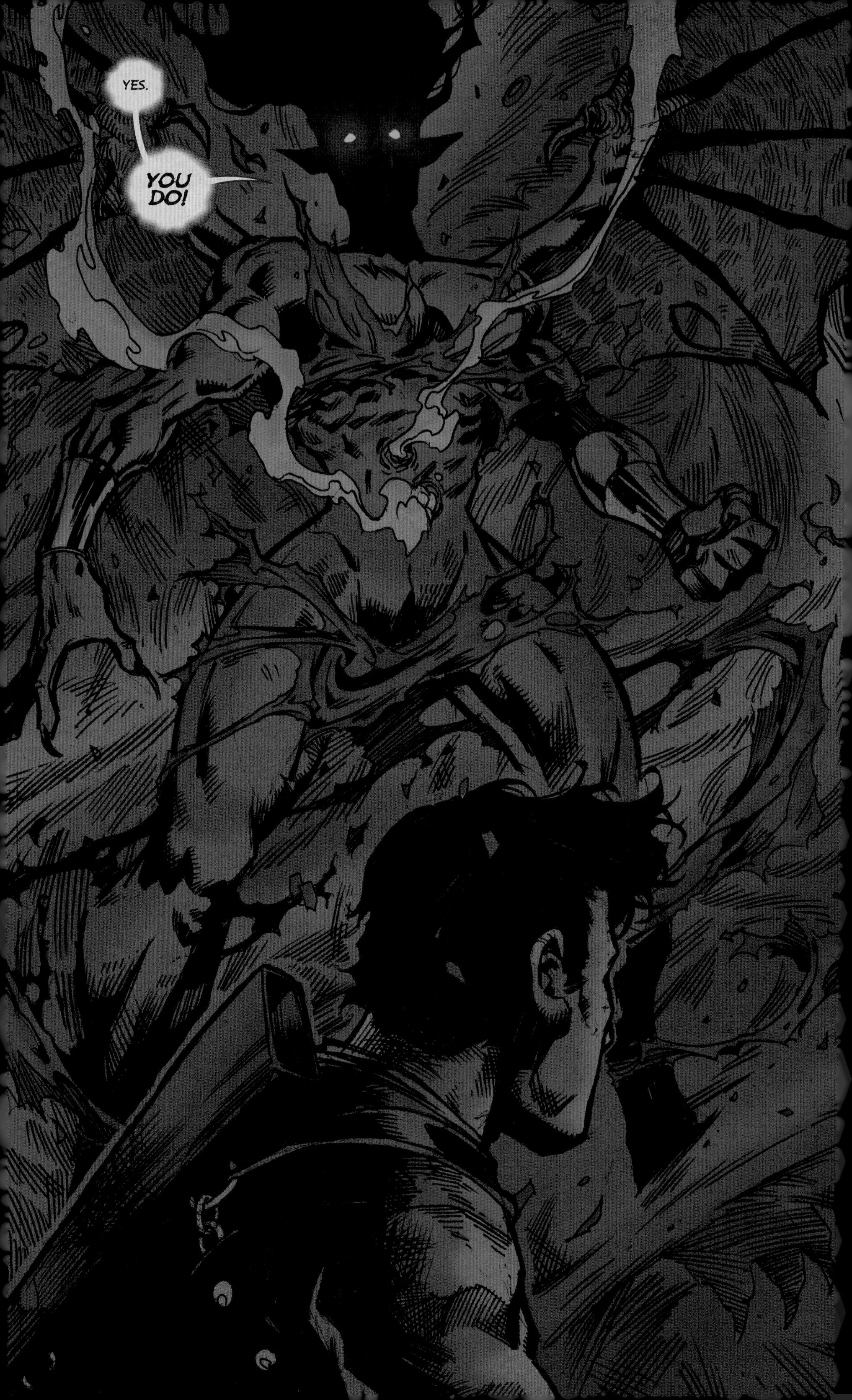
YES.
YOU DO!

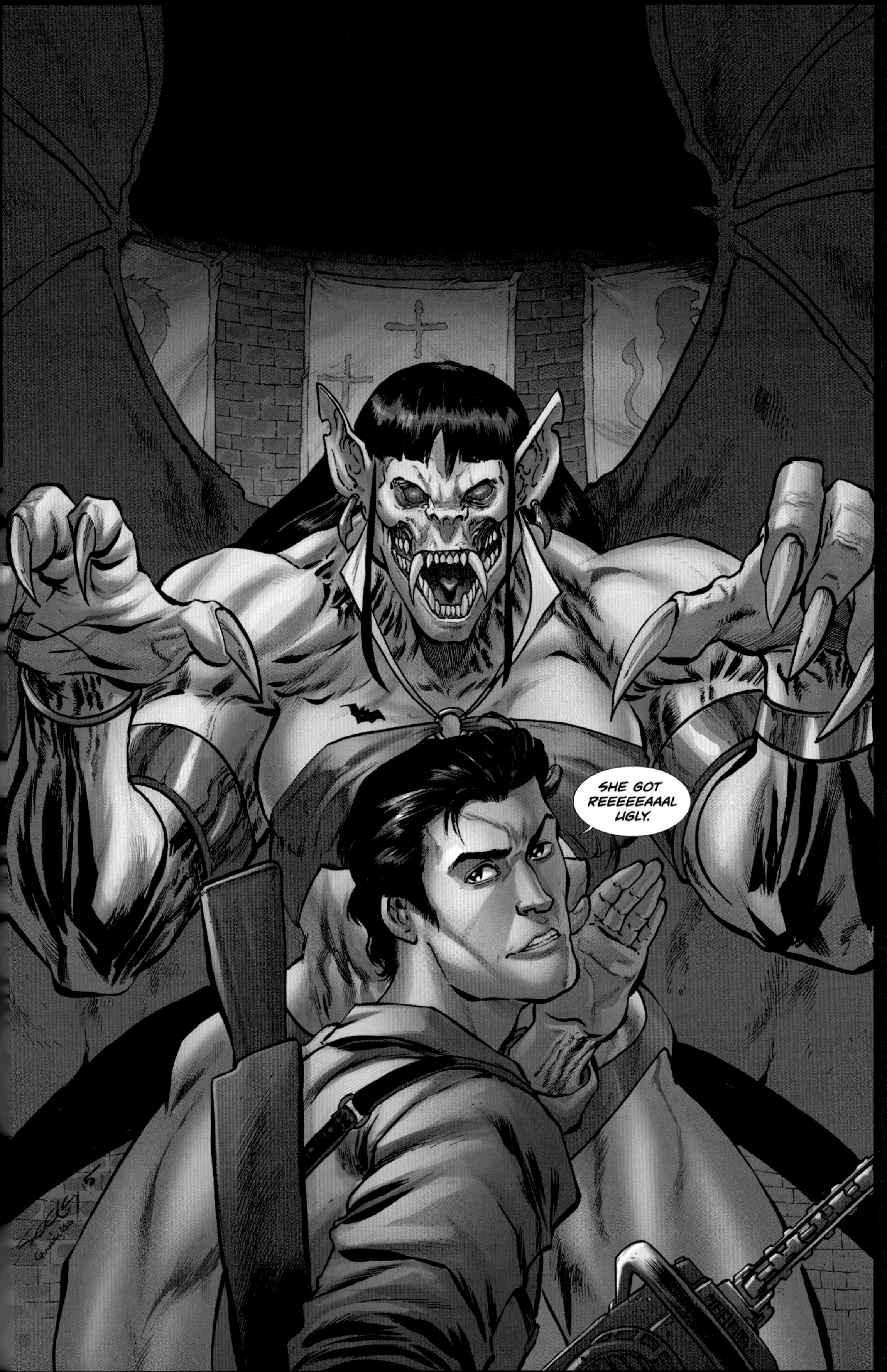
SHE GOT REEEEEAAAL UGLY.

ISSUE #2 COVER ART BY TIM SEELEY COLORS BY ALEX GUIMARAES

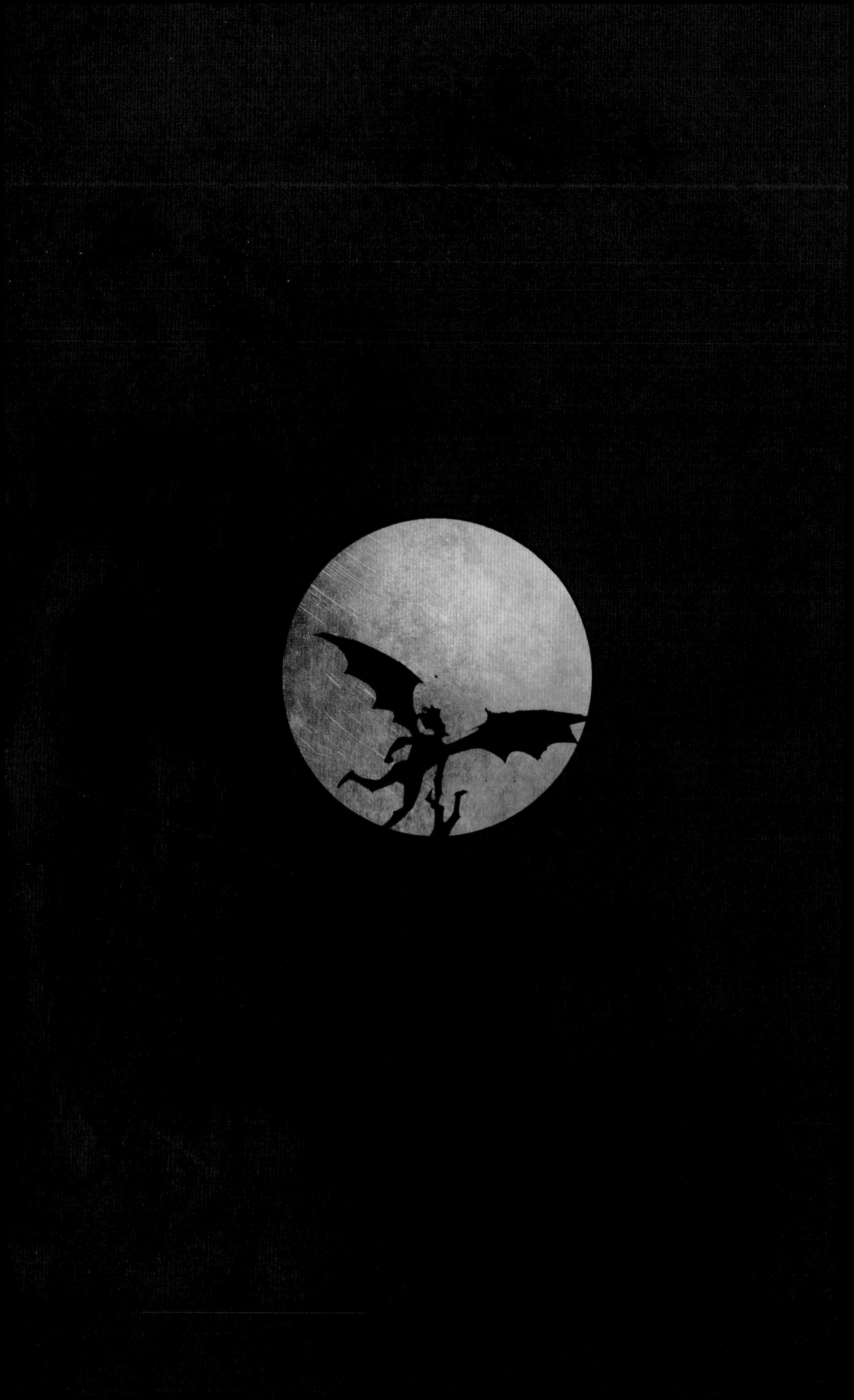

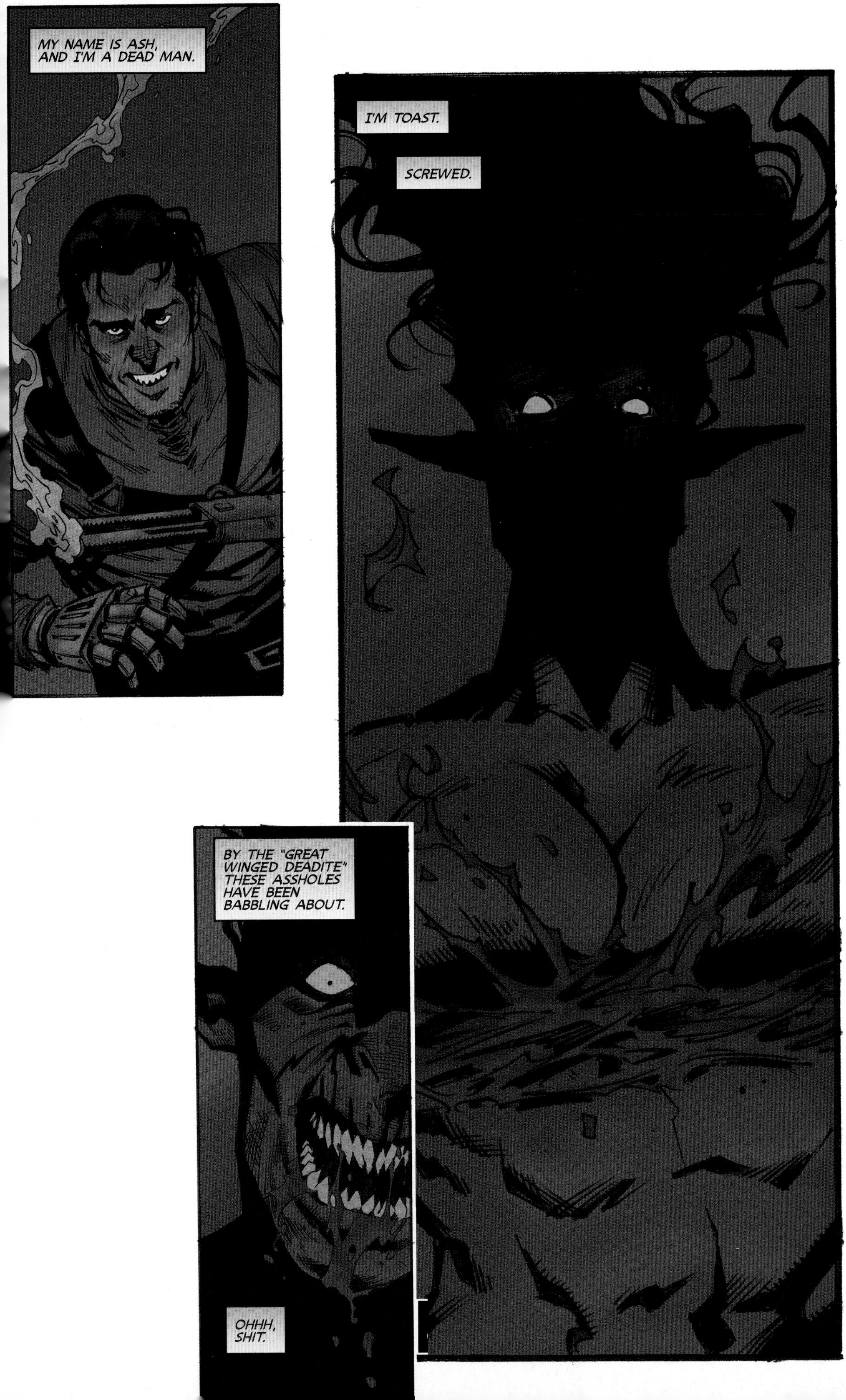
MY NAME IS ASH, AND I'M A DEAD MAN.
I'M TOAST.
SCREWED.
BY THE "GREAT WINGED DEADITE" THESE ASSHOLES HAVE BEEN BABBLING ABOUT.
OHHH, SHIT.

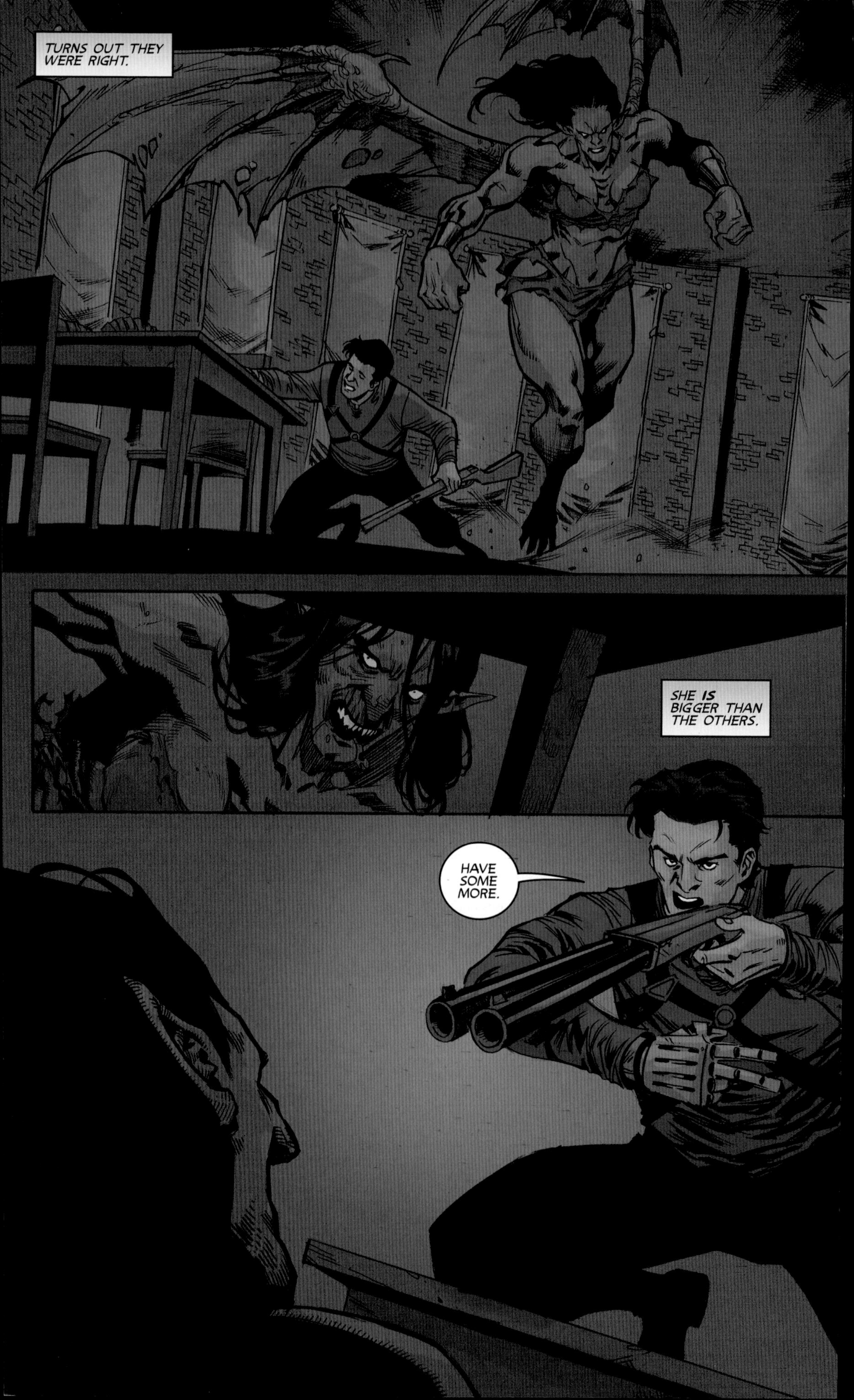
TURNS OUT THEY WERE RIGHT.
SHE IS BIGGER THAN THE OTHERS.
HAVE SOME MORE.

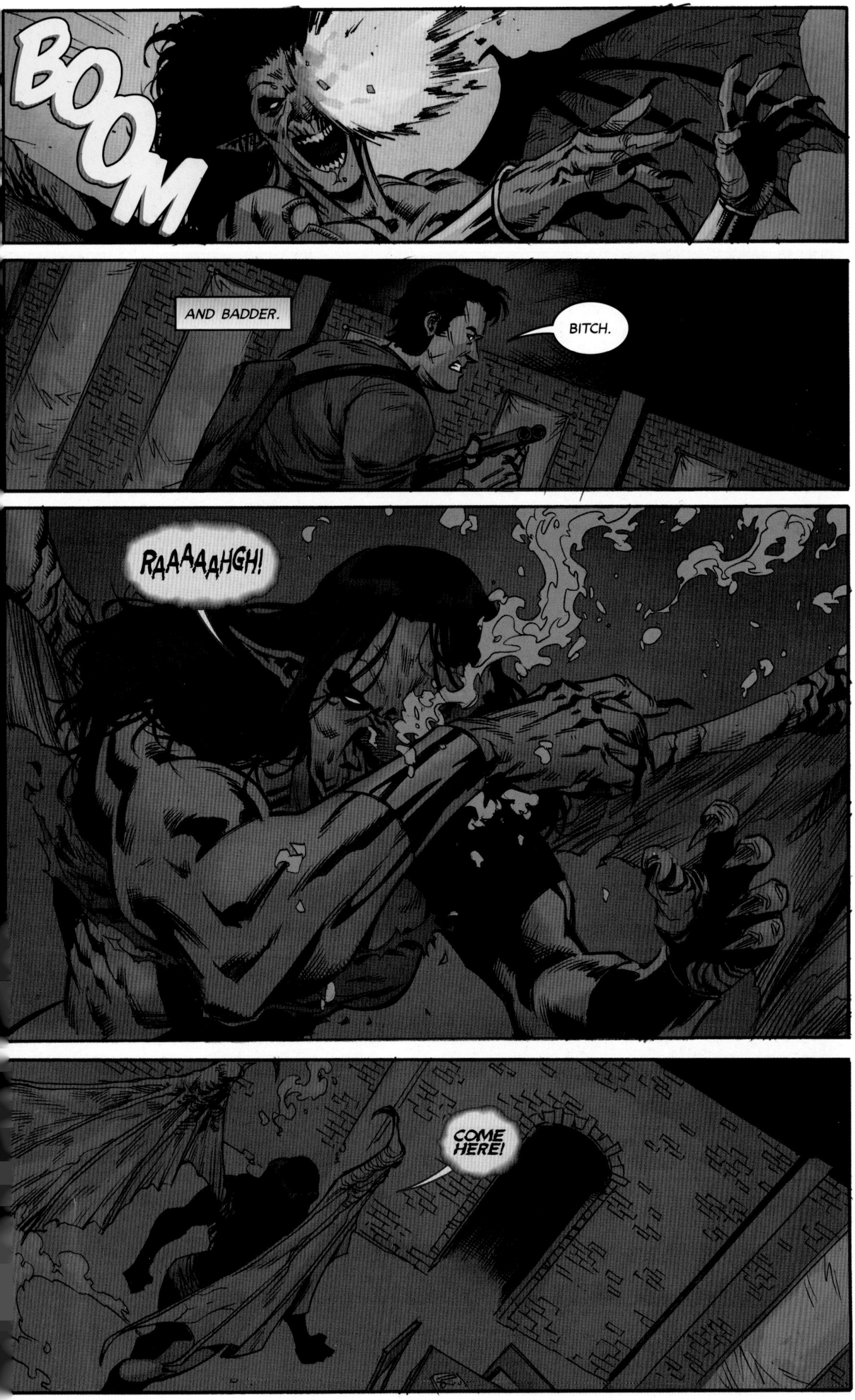
BOOM
AND BADDER.
BITCH.
RAAAAAHGH!
COME HERE!

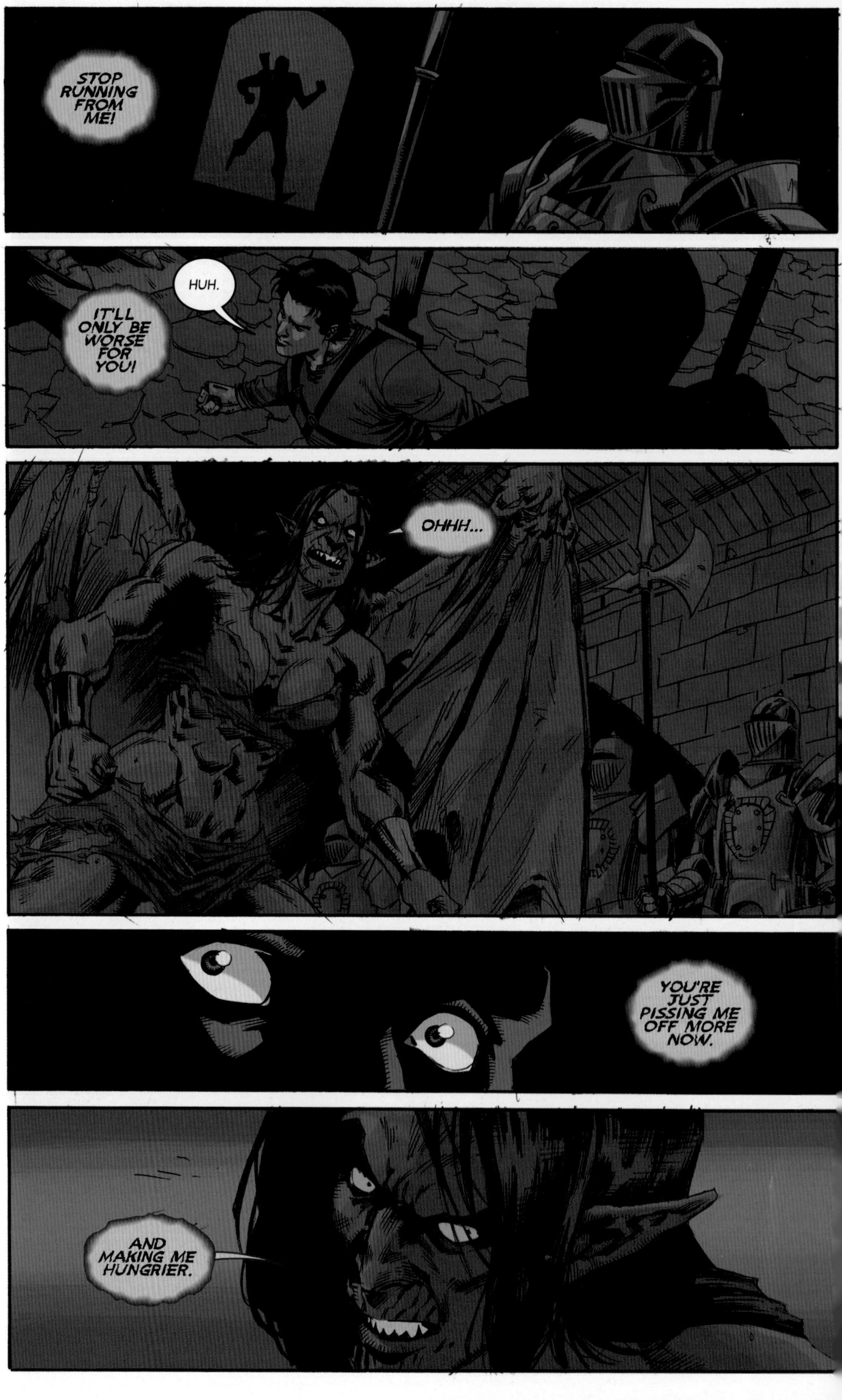
STOP RUNNING FROM ME!
HUH.
IT'LL ONLY BE WORSE FOR YOU!
OHHH...
YOU'RE JUST PISSING ME OFF MORE NOW.
AND MAKING ME HUNGRIER.

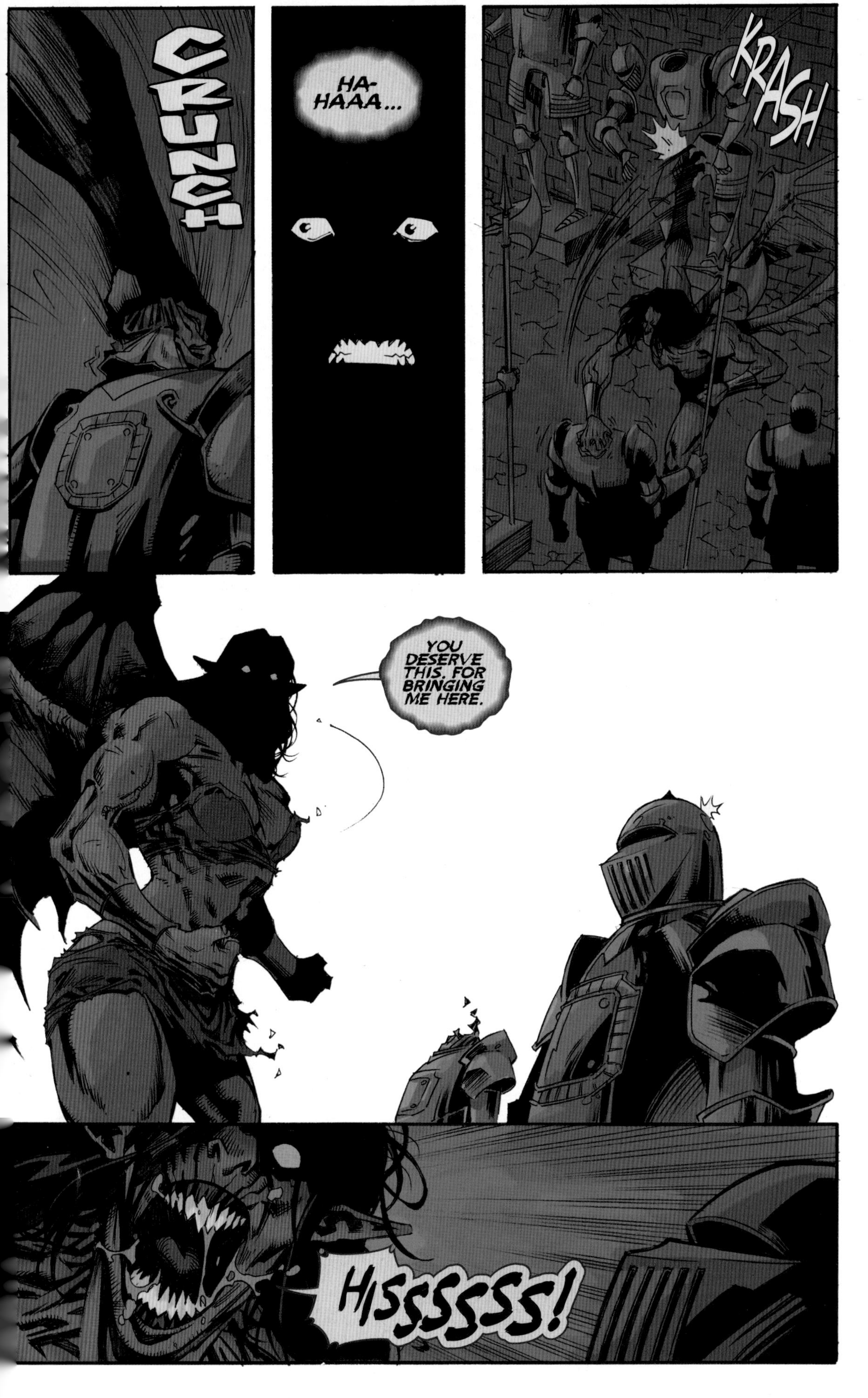
CRUNCH!
HA-HAAA...
KRASH
YOU DESERVE THIS. FOR BRINGING ME HERE.
HISSSSSS!

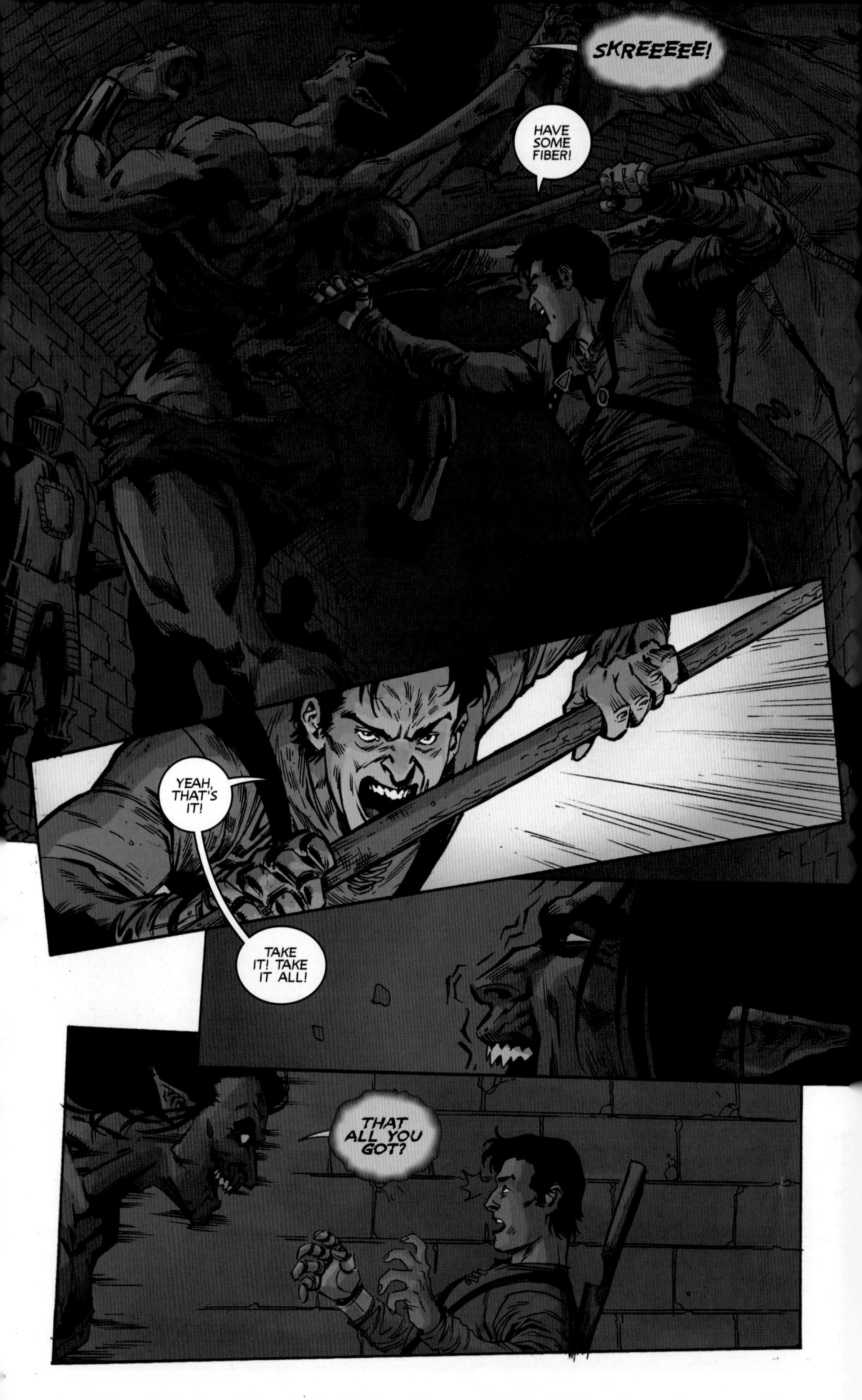
SKREEEEE!
HAVE SOME FIBER!
YEAH, THAT'S IT!
TAKE IT! TAKE IT ALL!
THAT ALL YOU GOT?

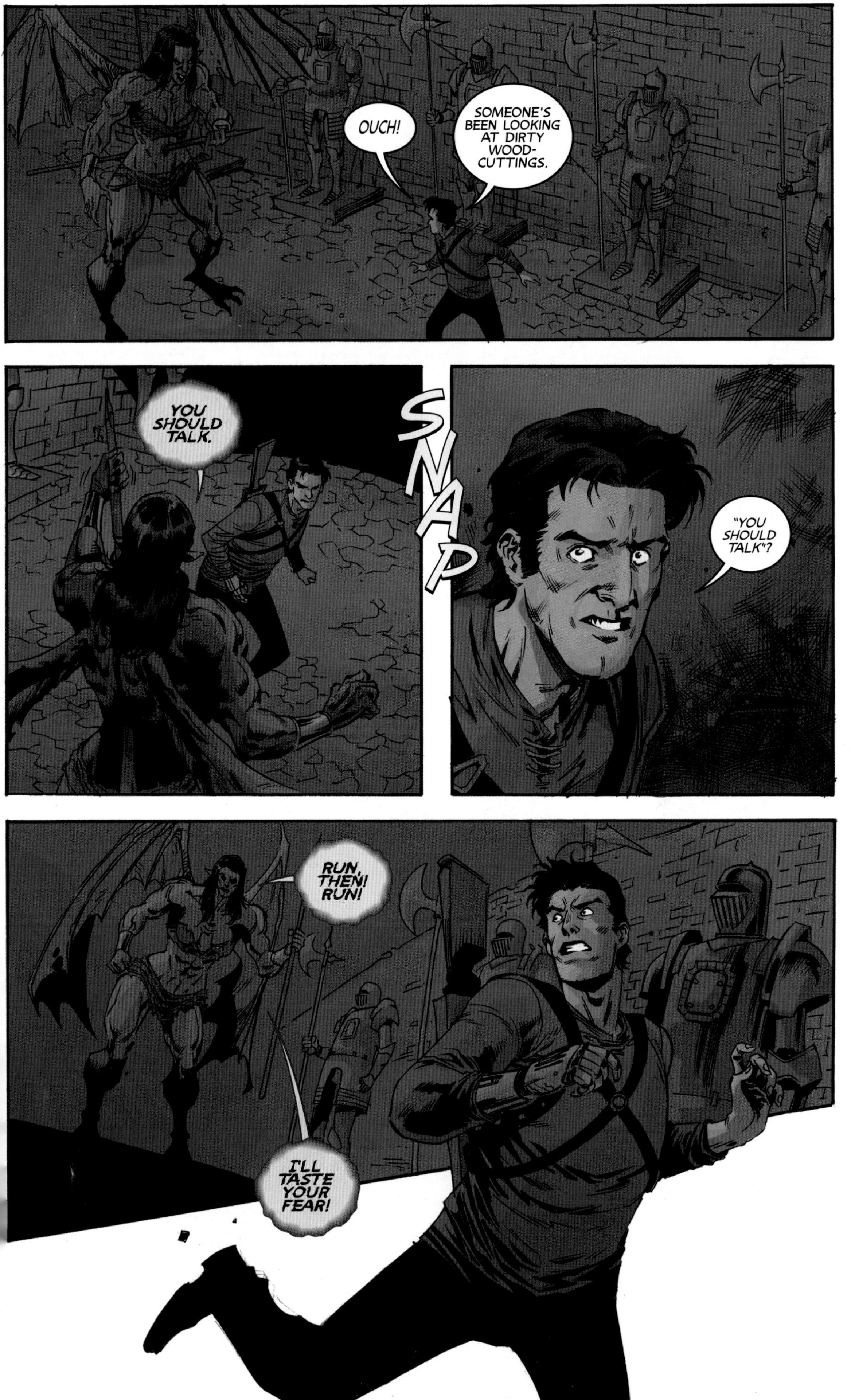
OUCH!
SOMEONE'S BEEN LOOKING AT DIRTY WOOD-CUTTINGS.
YOU SHOULD TALK.
SNAP
"YOU SHOULD TALK"?
RUN, THEN! RUN!
I'LL TASTE YOUR FEAR!

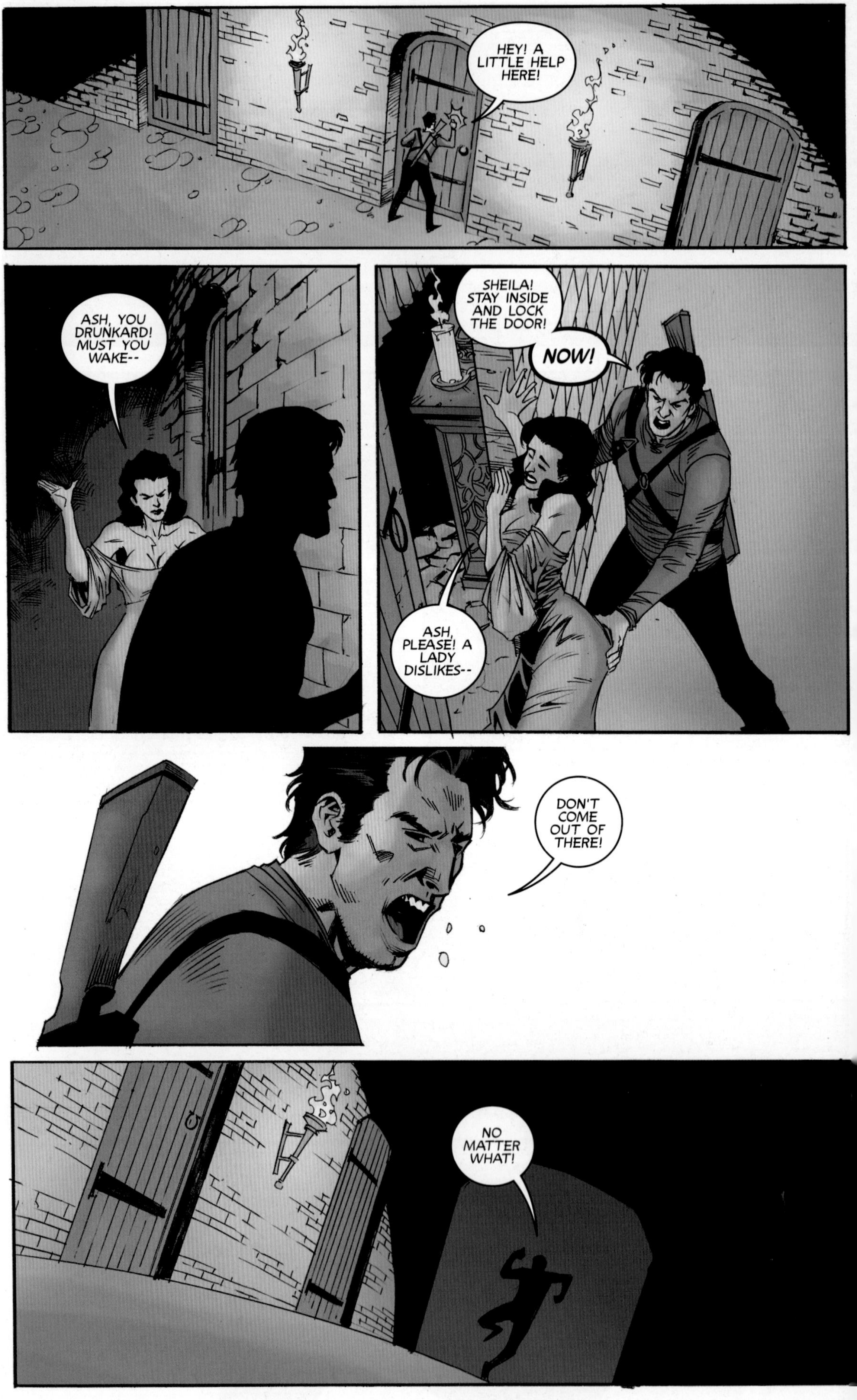
HEY! A LITTLE HELP HERE!
ASH, YOU DRUNKARD! MUST YOU WAKE--
SHEILA! STAY INSIDE AND LOCK THE DOOR!
NOW!
ASH, PLEASE! A LADY DISLIKES--
DON'T COME OUT OF THERE!
NO MATTER WHAT!

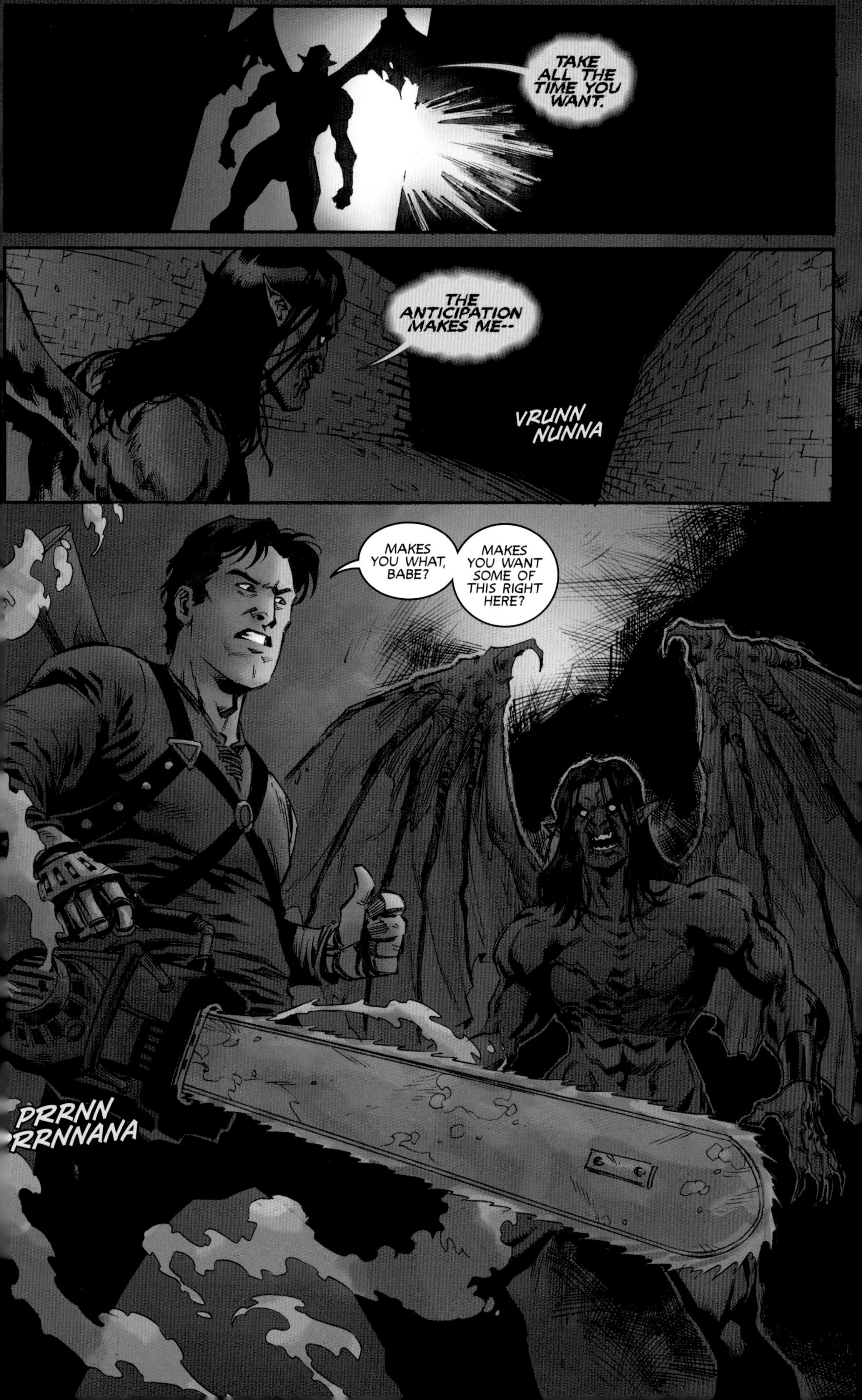
TAKE ALL THE TIME YOU WANT.
THE ANTICIPATION MAKES ME--
VRUNN NUNNA
MAKES YOU WHAT, BABE?
MAKES YOU WANT SOME OF THIS RIGHT HERE?
PRRNN RRNNANA

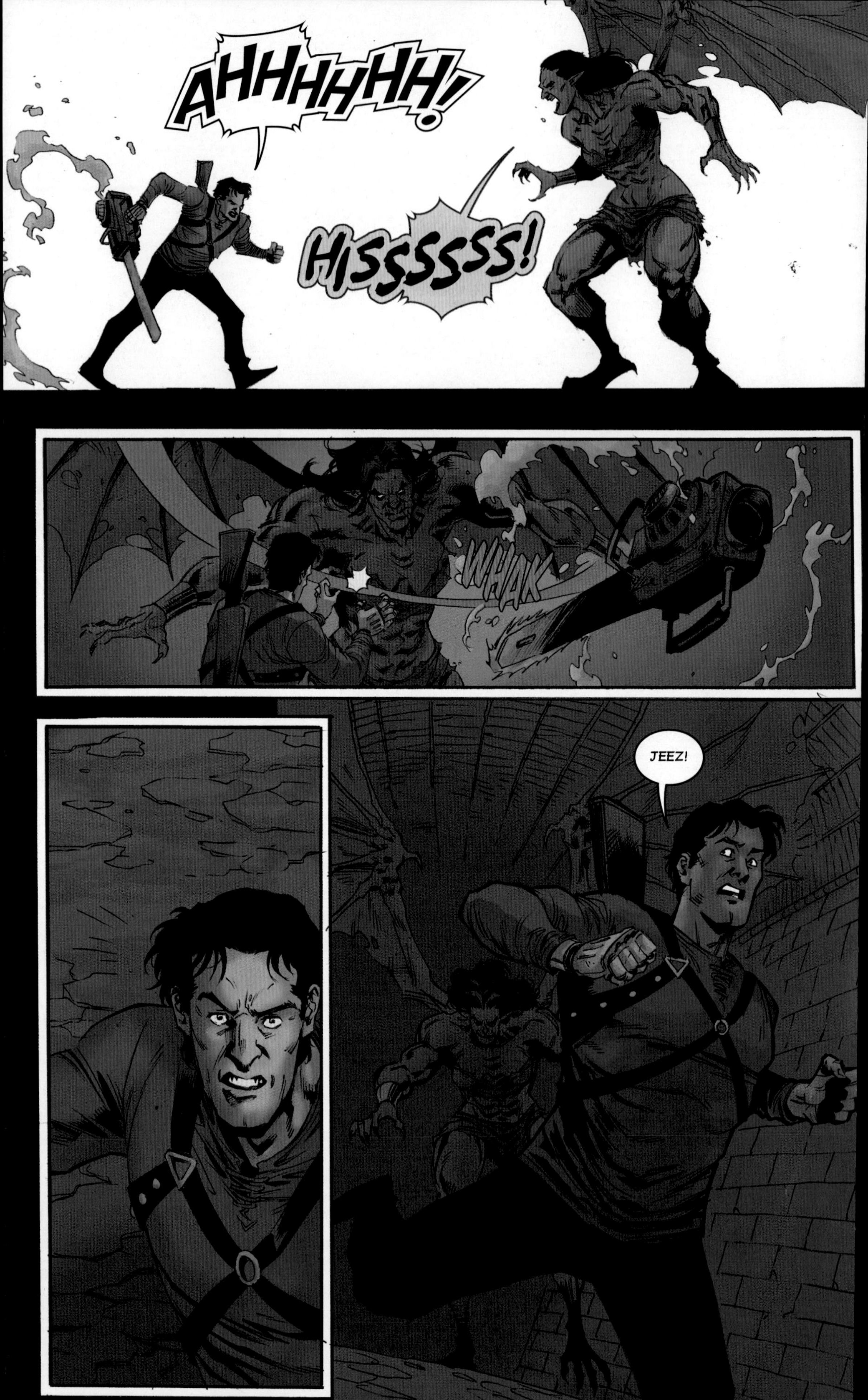
AHHHHHH!
HISSSSSS!
WHAK
JEEZ!

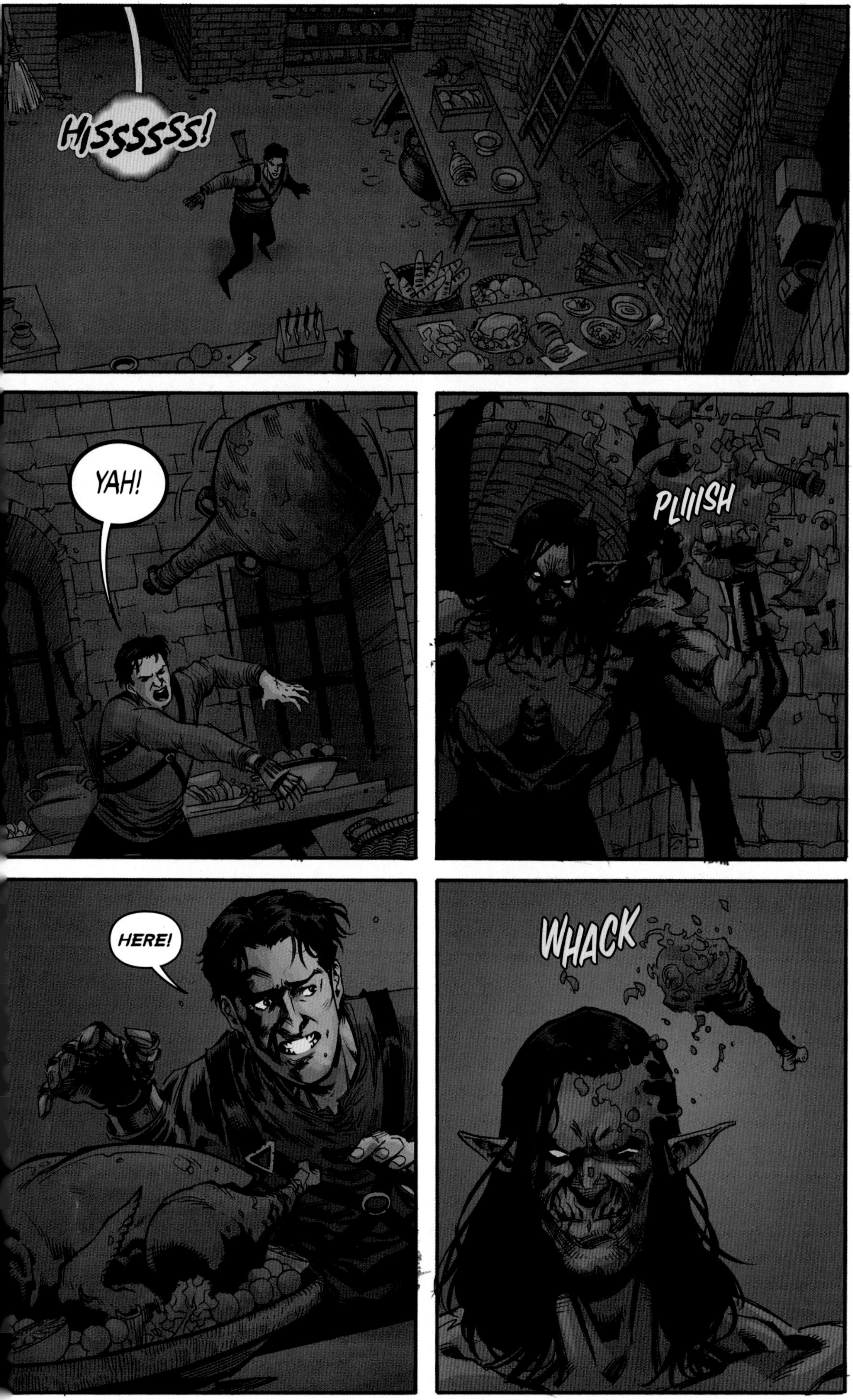
HISSSSSS!
YAH!
PLIIISH
HERE!
WHACK

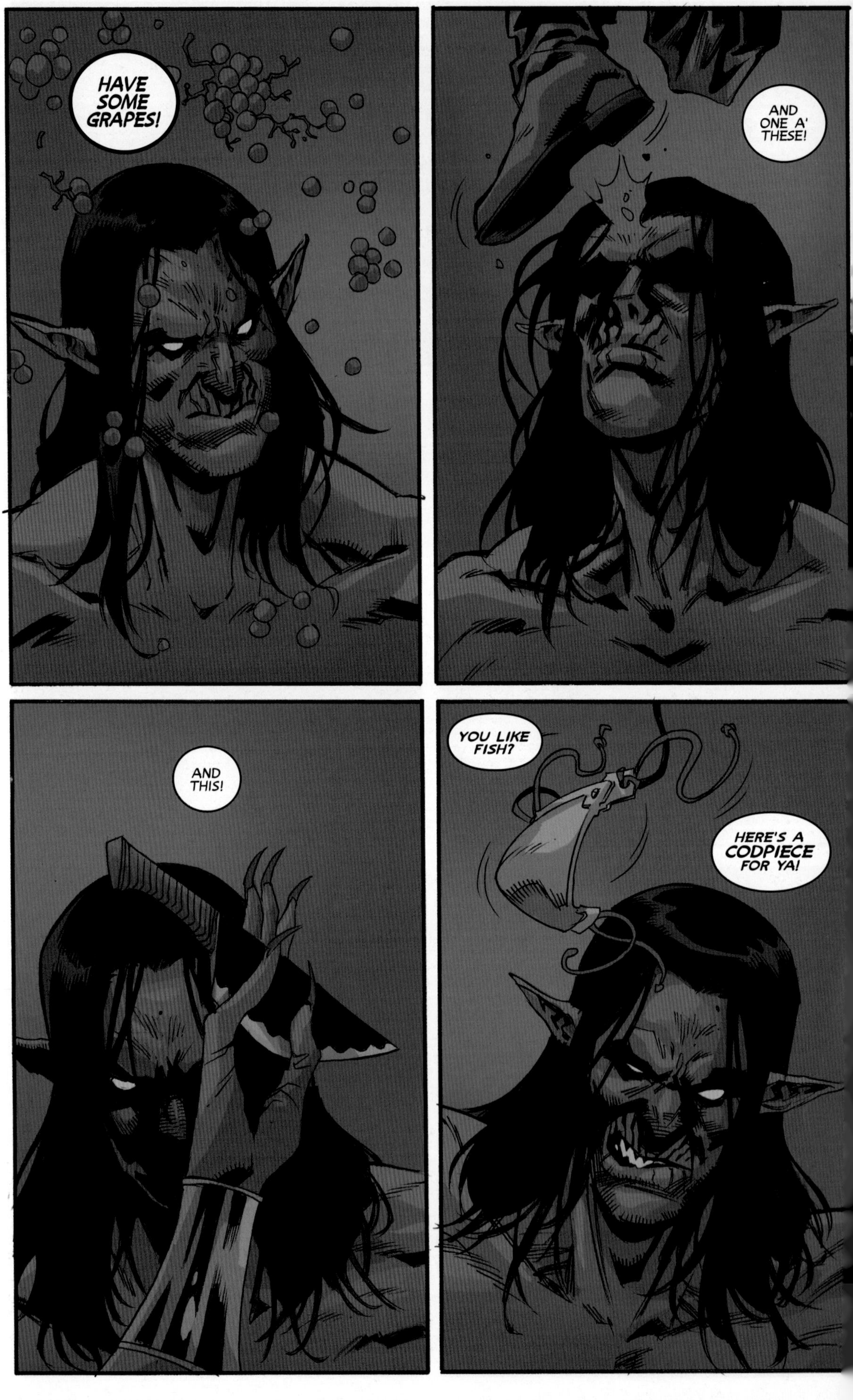
HAVE SOME GRAPES!
AND ONE A' THESE!
AND THIS!
YOU LIKE FISH?
HERE'S A CODPIECE FOR YA!

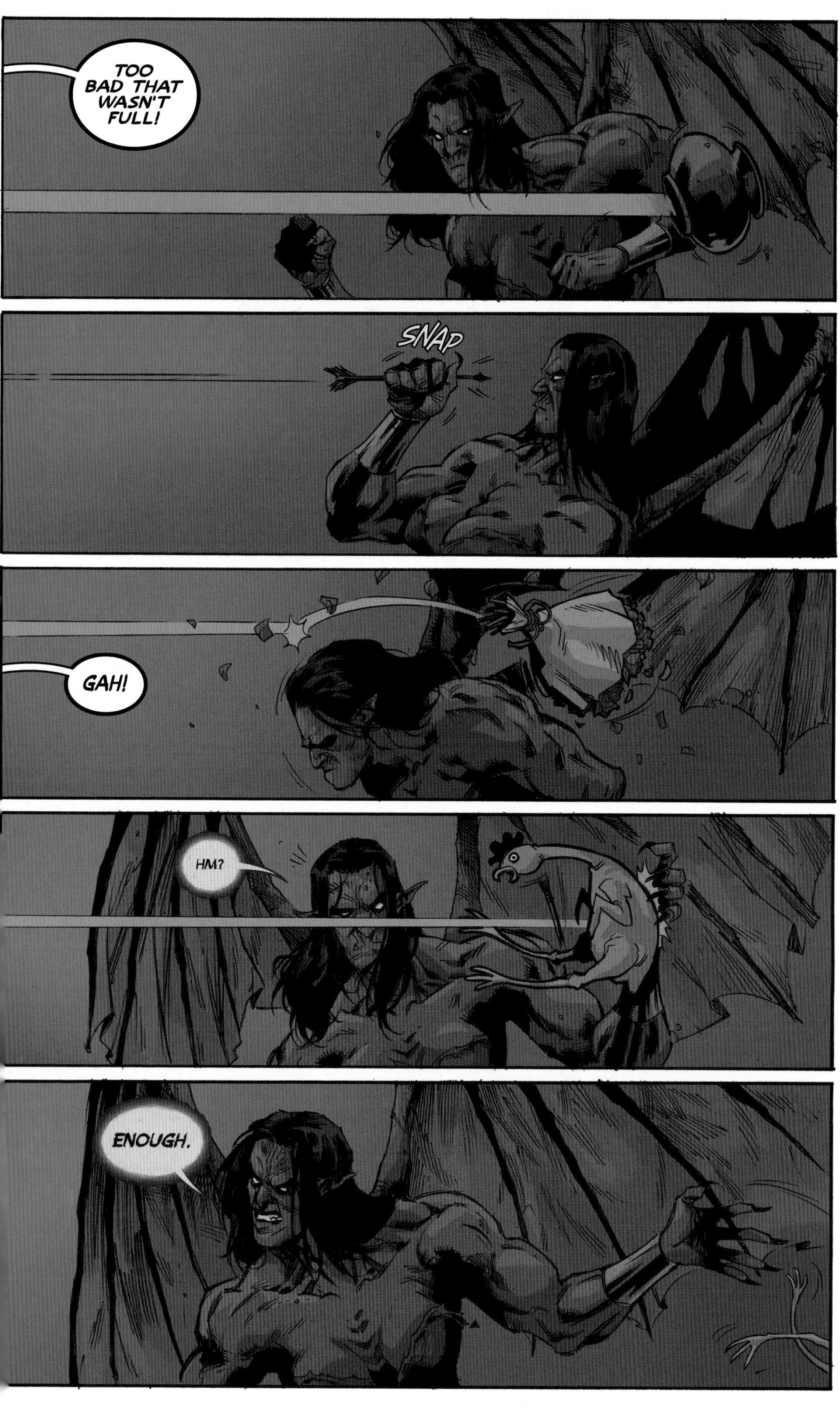

TOO BAD THAT WASN'T FULL!
SNAP
GAH!
HM?
ENOUGH.

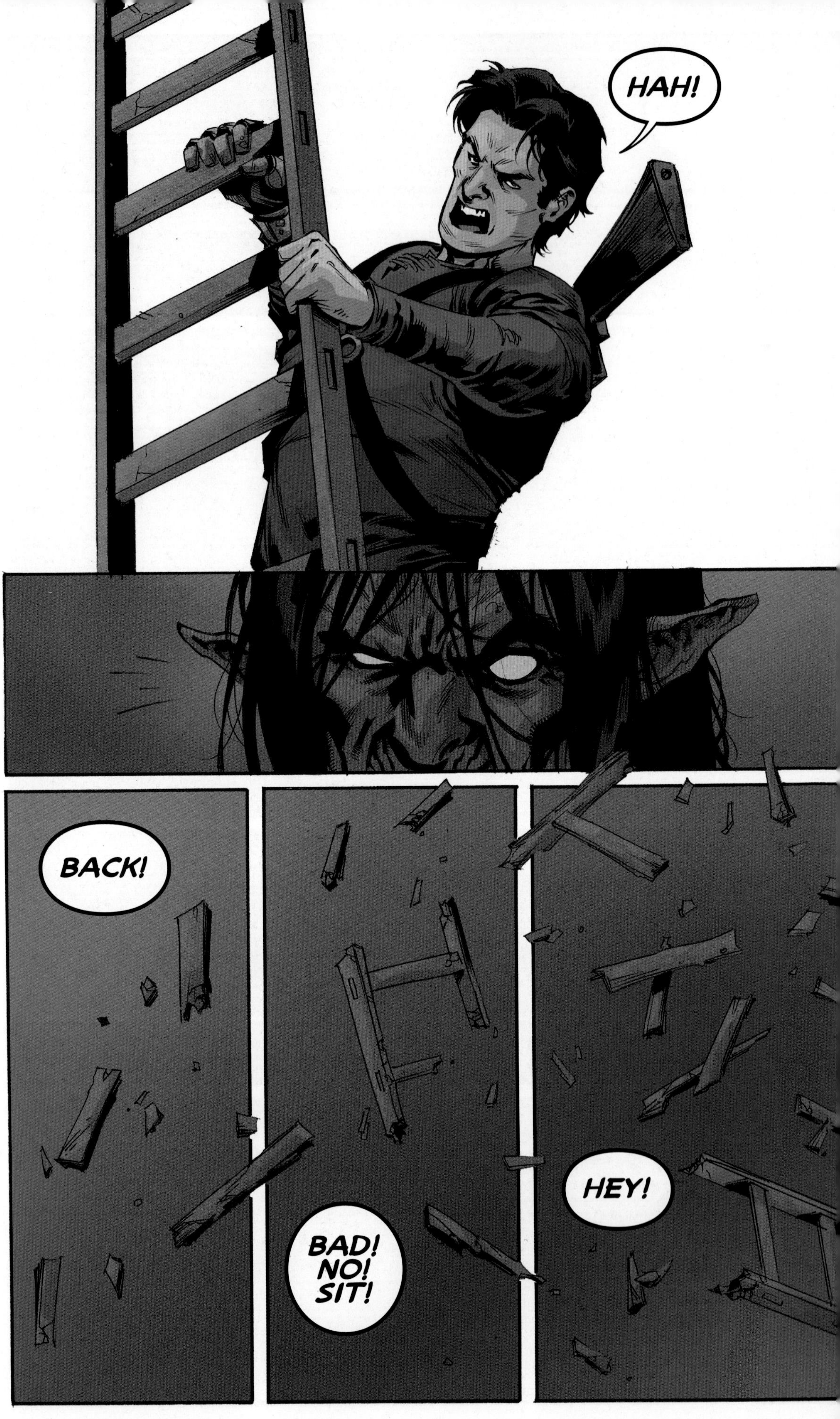
HAH!
BACK!
BAD! NO! SIT!
HEY!

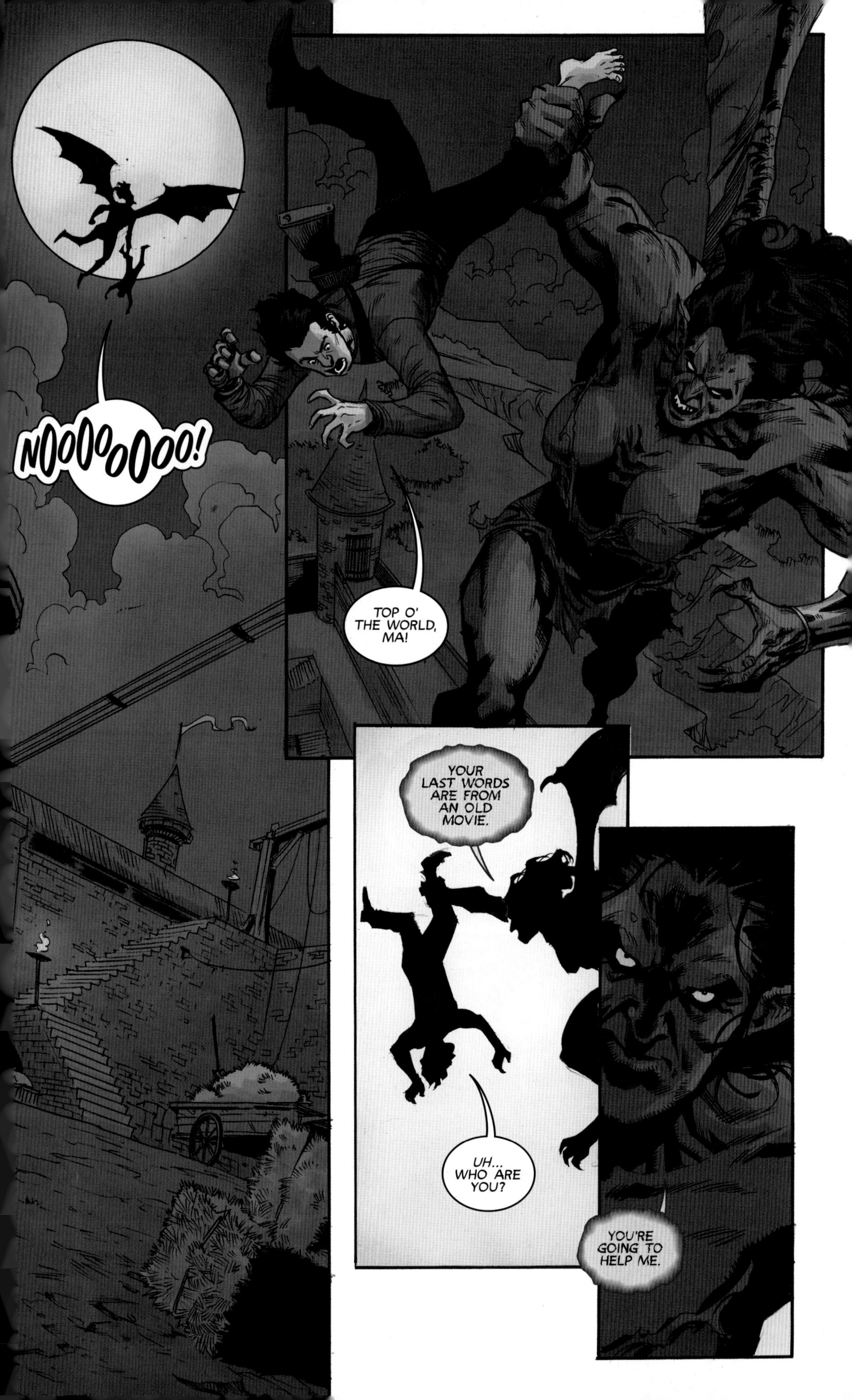
NOOOOOOOO!
TOP O' THE WORLD, MA!
YOUR LAST WORDS ARE FROM AN OLD MOVIE.
UH... WHO ARE YOU?
YOU'RE GOING TO HELP ME.

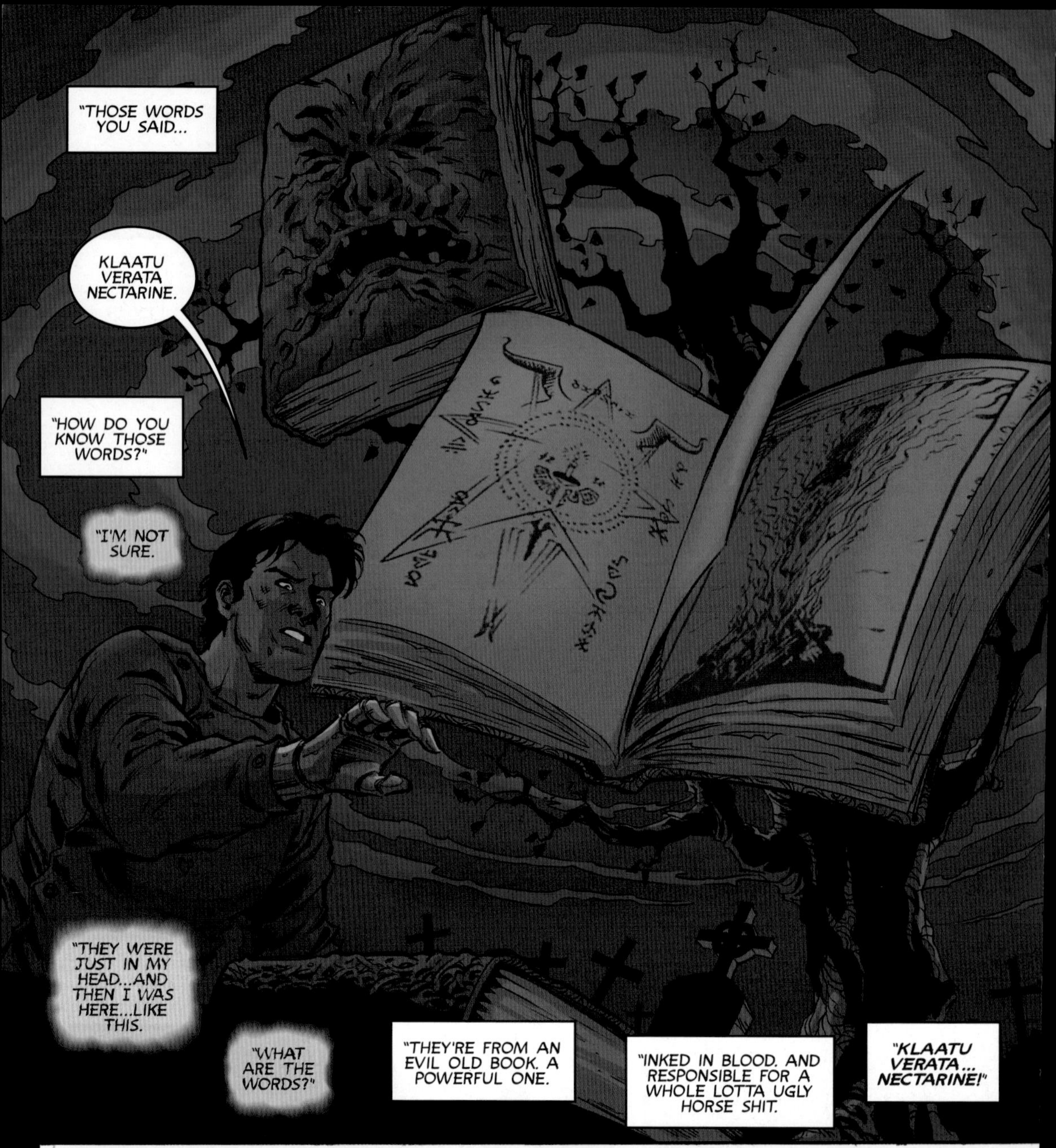
"THOSE WORDS YOU SAID...
KLAATU VERATA NECTARINE.
"HOW DO YOU KNOW THOSE WORDS?"
"I'M NOT SURE.
"THEY WERE JUST IN MY HEAD...AND THEN I WAS HERE...LIKE THIS.
"WHAT ARE THE WORDS?"
"THEY'RE FROM AN EVIL OLD BOOK. A POWERFUL ONE.
"INKED IN BLOOD. AND RESPONSIBLE FOR A WHOLE LOTTA UGLY HORSE SHIT.
"KLAATU VERATA... NECTARINE!"
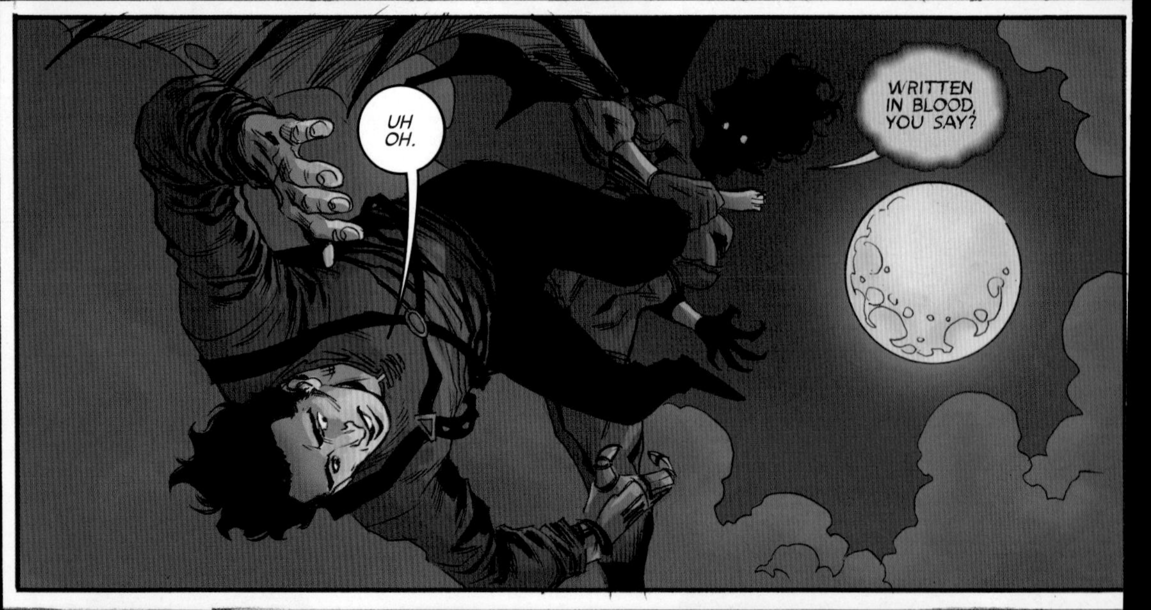
UH OH.
WRITTEN IN BLOOD, YOU SAY?

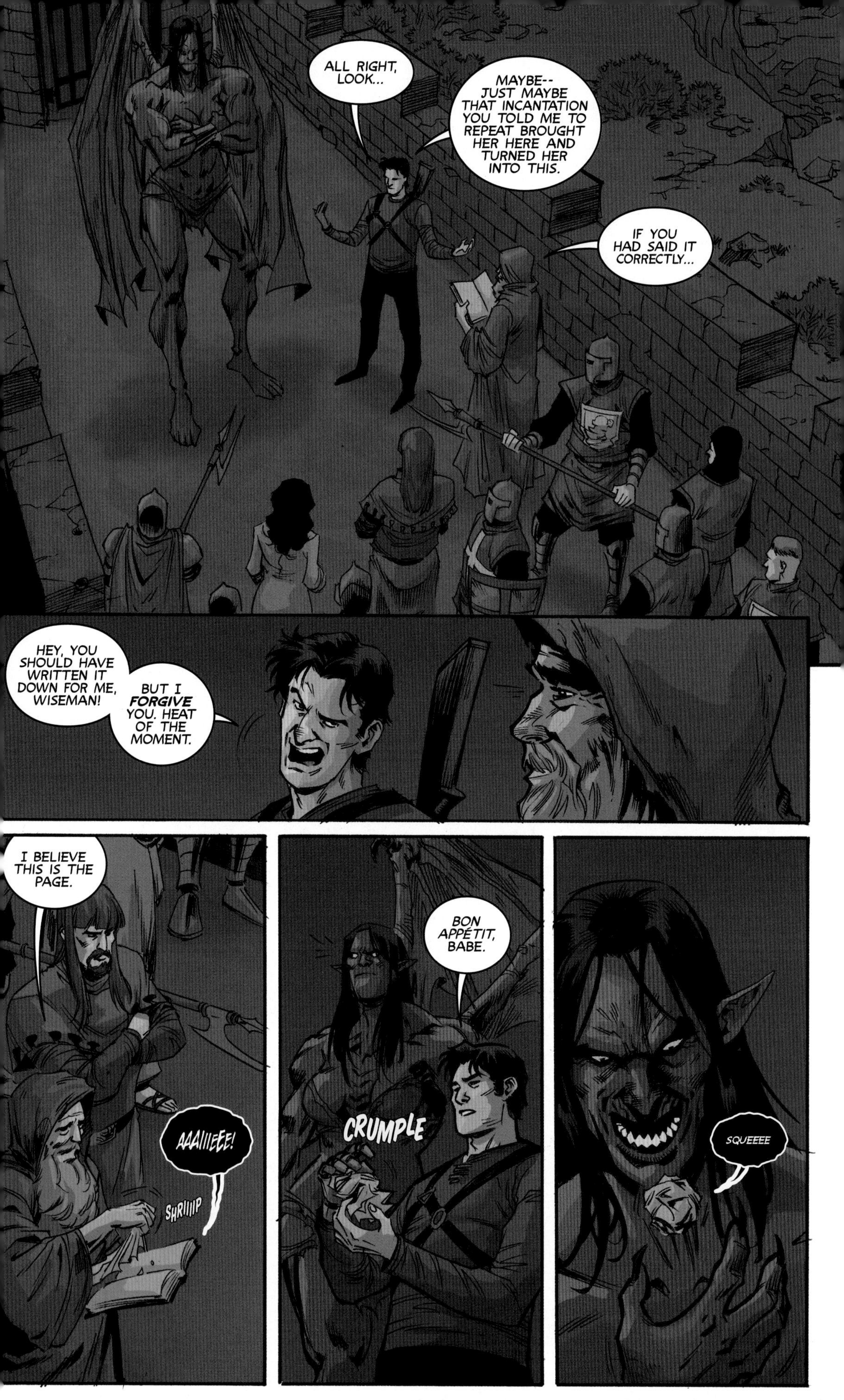
ALL RIGHT, LOOK...
MAYBE-- JUST MAYBE THAT INCANTATION YOU TOLD ME TO REPEAT BROUGHT HER HERE AND TURNED HER INTO THIS.
IF YOU HAD SAID IT CORRECTLY...
HEY, YOU SHOULD HAVE WRITTEN IT DOWN FOR ME, WISEMAN!
BUT I *FORGIVE* YOU. HEAT OF THE MOMENT.
I BELIEVE THIS IS THE PAGE.
AAAIIIEEE!
SHRIIIP
BON APPÉTIT, BABE.
CRUMPLE
SQUEEEE

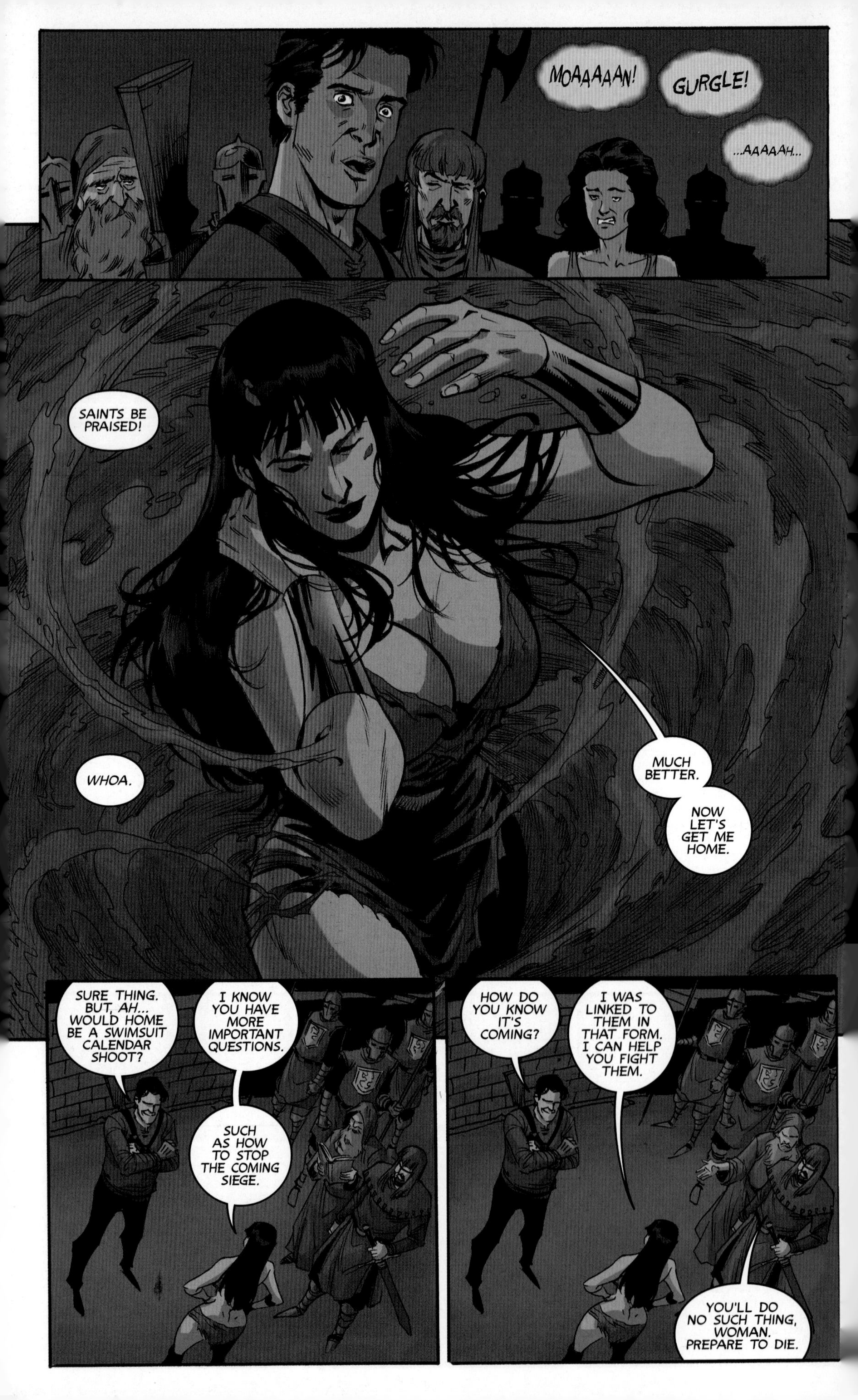
MOAAAAAN!
GURGLE!
...AAAAAH...
SAINTS BE PRAISED!
WHOA.
MUCH BETTER.
NOW LET'S GET ME HOME.
SURE THING. BUT, AH... WOULD HOME BE A SWIMSUIT CALENDAR SHOOT?
I KNOW YOU HAVE MORE IMPORTANT QUESTIONS.
SUCH AS HOW TO STOP THE COMING SIEGE.
HOW DO YOU KNOW IT'S COMING?
I WAS LINKED TO THEM IN THAT FORM. I CAN HELP YOU FIGHT THEM.
YOU'LL DO NO SUCH THING, WOMAN. PREPARE TO DIE.

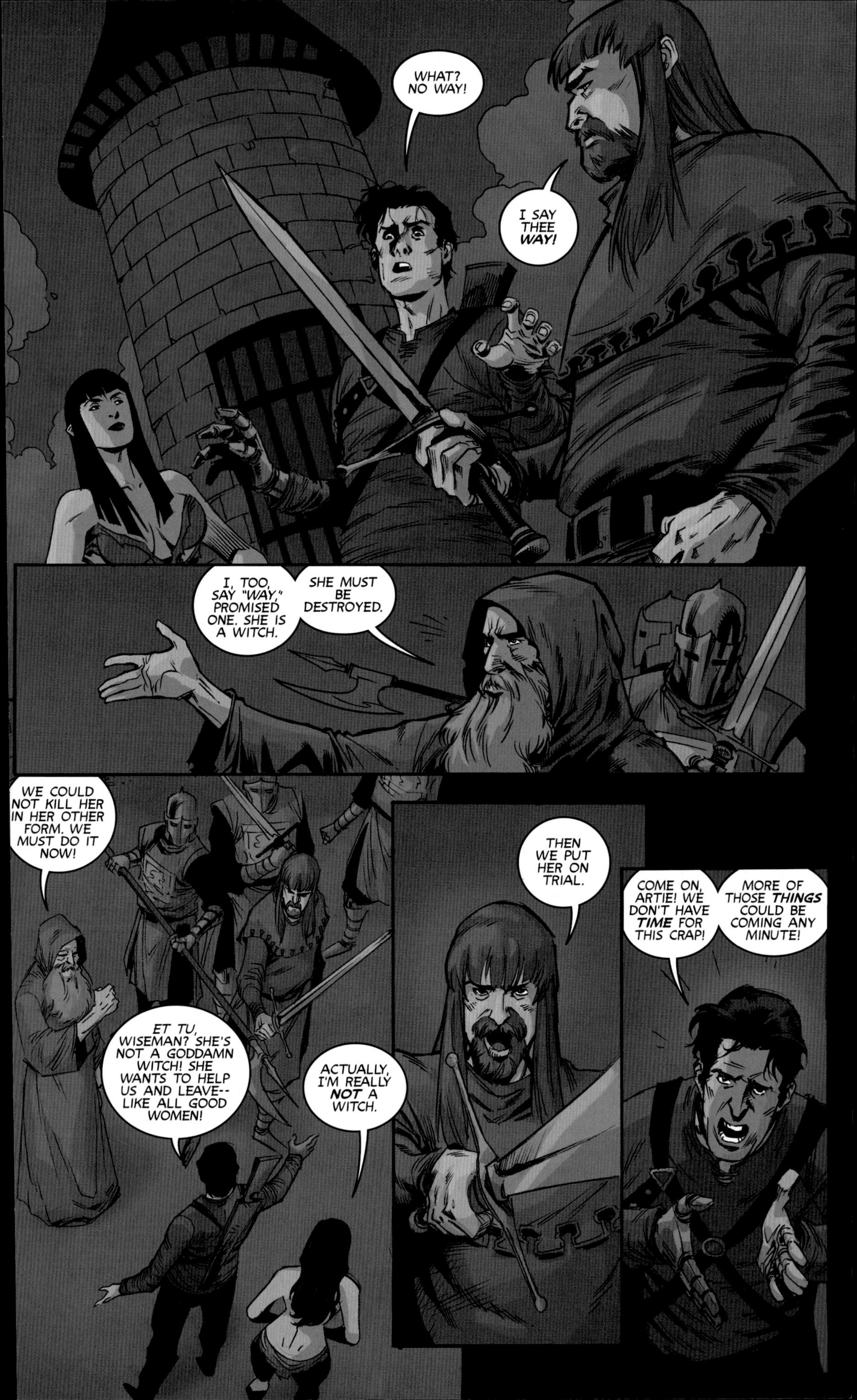
WHAT? NO WAY!
I SAY THEE *WAY!*
I, TOO, SAY "*WAY*," PROMISED ONE. SHE IS A WITCH.
SHE MUST BE DESTROYED.
WE COULD NOT KILL HER IN HER OTHER FORM. WE MUST DO IT NOW!
ET TU, WISEMAN? SHE'S NOT A GODDAMN WITCH! SHE WANTS TO HELP US AND LEAVE-- LIKE ALL GOOD WOMEN!
ACTUALLY, I'M REALLY *NOT* A WITCH.
THEN WE PUT HER ON TRIAL.
COME ON, ARTIE! WE DON'T HAVE *TIME* FOR THIS CRAP!
MORE OF THOSE *THINGS* COULD BE COMING ANY MINUTE!

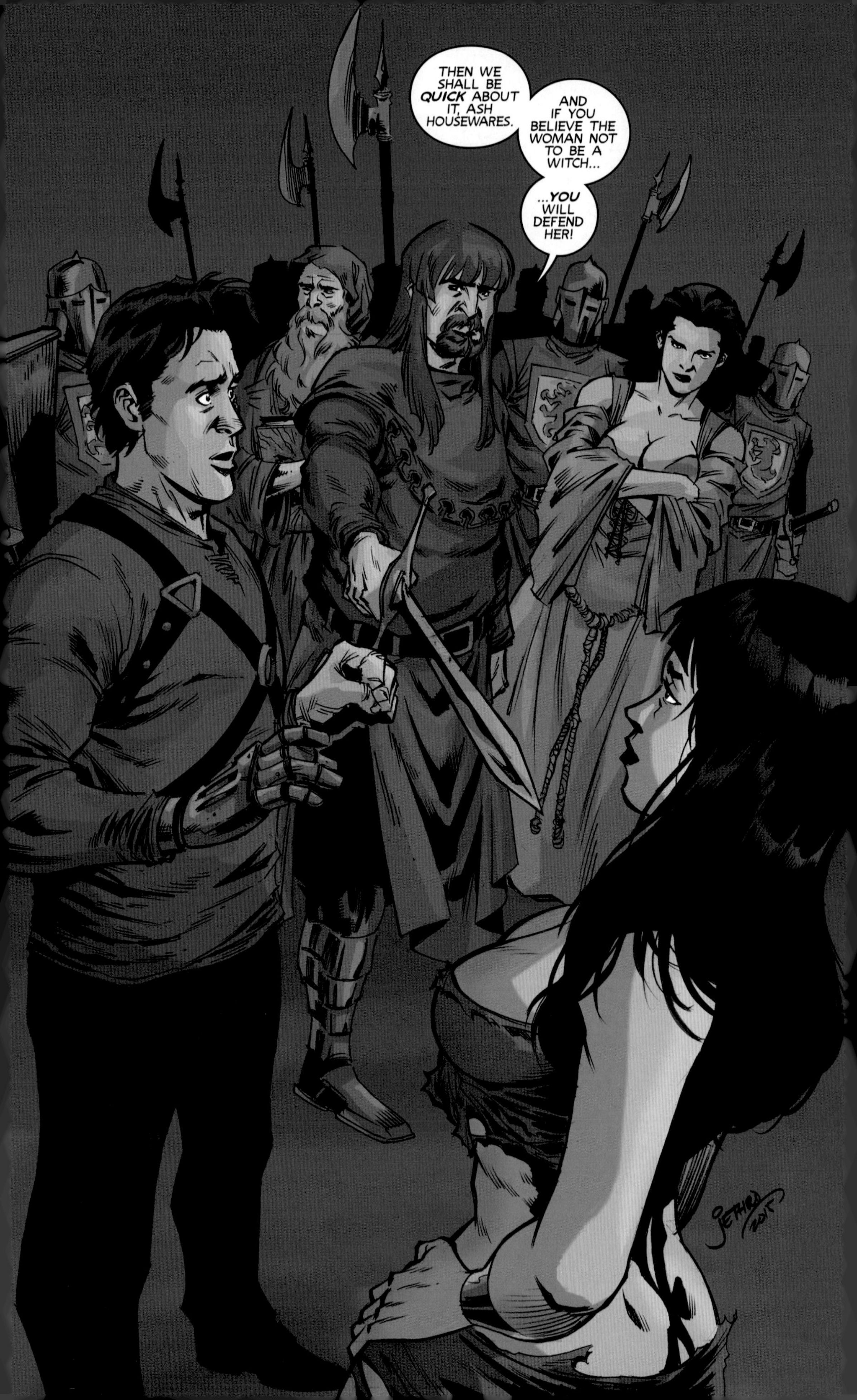
THEN WE SHALL BE QUICK ABOUT IT, ASH HOUSEWARES.
AND IF YOU BELIEVE THE WOMAN NOT TO BE A WITCH...
...YOU WILL DEFEND HER!
JETHRO 2015

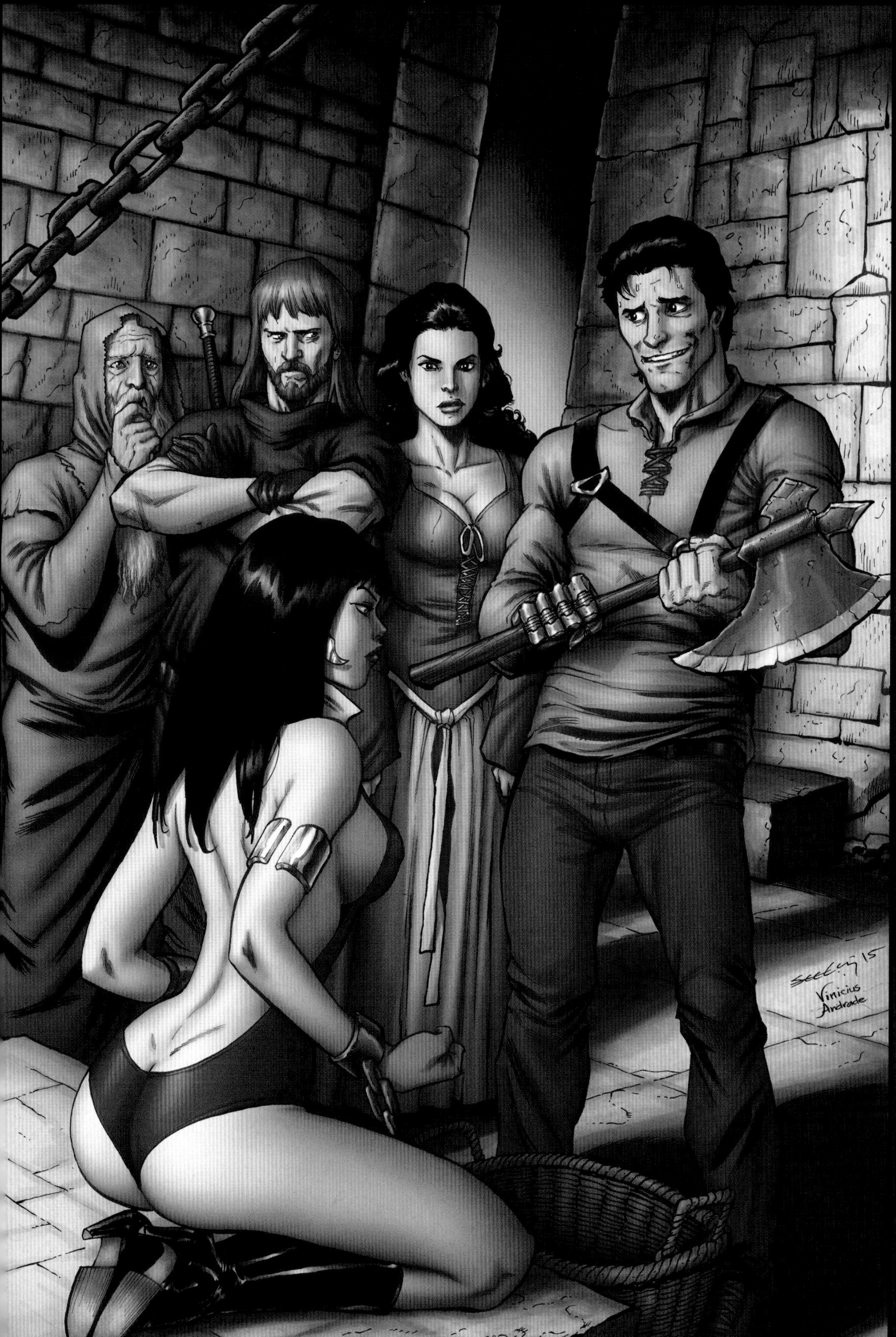
Vinicius Andrade

ISSUE #3 COVER ART BY TIM SEELEY COLORS BY VINICIUS ANDRADE

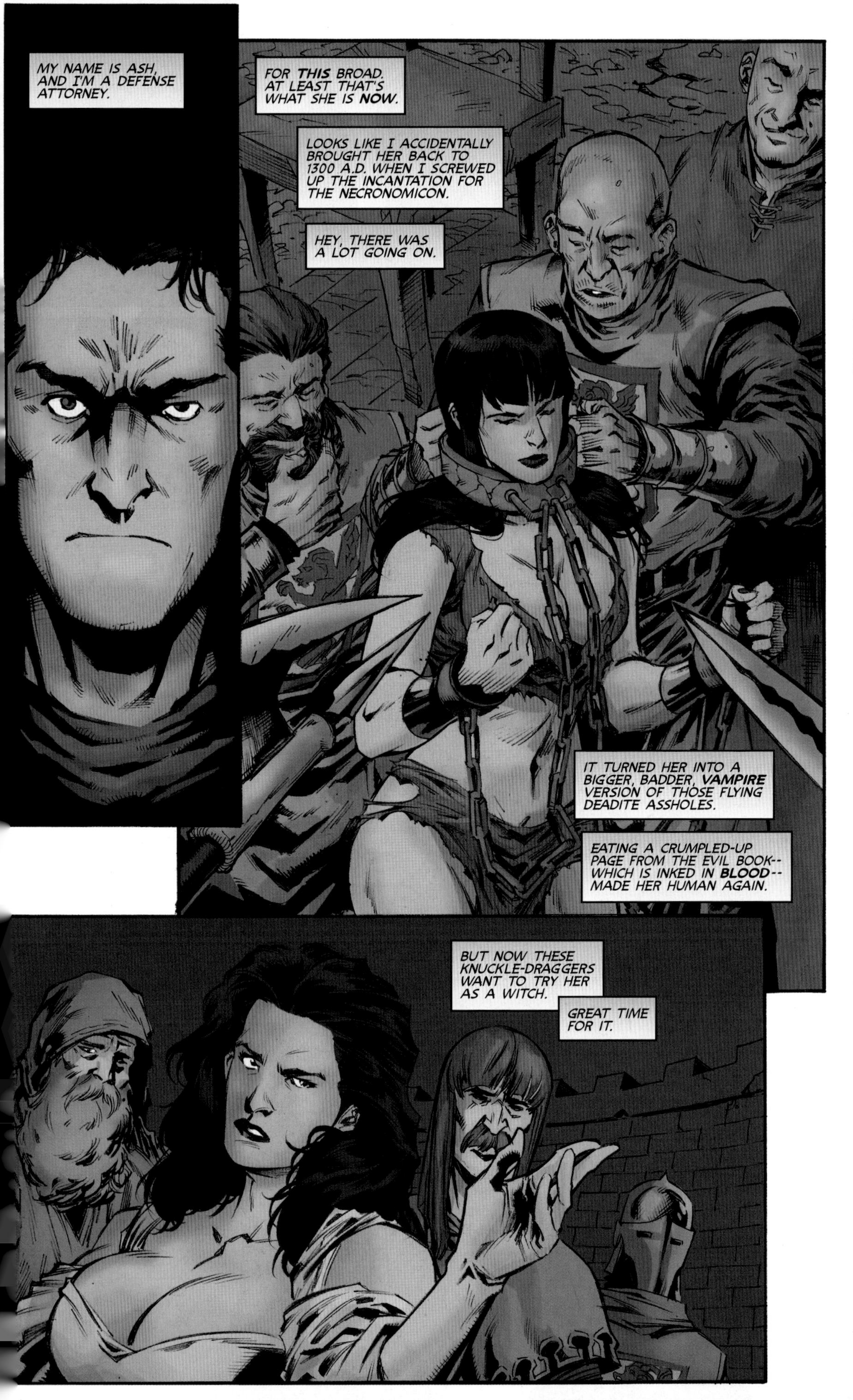
MY NAME IS ASH, AND I'M A DEFENSE ATTORNEY.
FOR THIS BROAD. AT LEAST THAT'S WHAT SHE IS NOW.
LOOKS LIKE I ACCIDENTALLY BROUGHT HER BACK TO 1300 A.D. WHEN I SCREWED UP THE INCANTATION FOR THE NECRONOMICON.
HEY, THERE WAS A LOT GOING ON.
IT TURNED HER INTO A BIGGER, BADDER, VAMPIRE VERSION OF THOSE FLYING DEADITE ASSHOLES.
EATING A CRUMPLED-UP PAGE FROM THE EVIL BOOK--WHICH IS INKED IN BLOOD--MADE HER HUMAN AGAIN.
BUT NOW THESE KNUCKLE-DRAGGERS WANT TO TRY HER AS A WITCH.
GREAT TIME FOR IT.

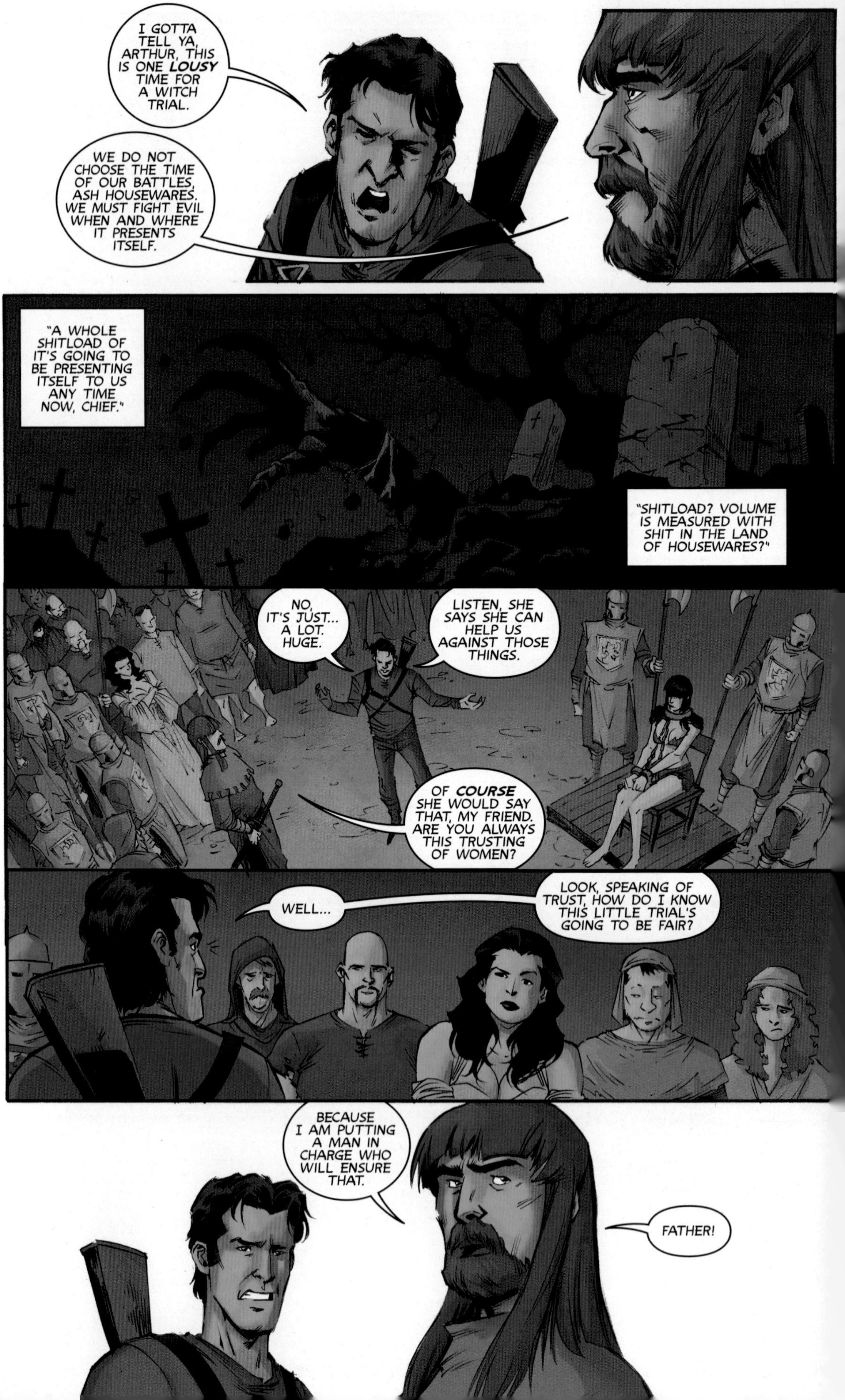
I GOTTA TELL YA, ARTHUR, THIS IS ONE LOUSY TIME FOR A WITCH TRIAL.
WE DO NOT CHOOSE THE TIME OF OUR BATTLES, ASH HOUSEWARES. WE MUST FIGHT EVIL WHEN AND WHERE IT PRESENTS ITSELF.
"A WHOLE SHITLOAD OF IT'S GOING TO BE PRESENTING ITSELF TO US ANY TIME NOW, CHIEF."
"SHITLOAD? VOLUME IS MEASURED WITH SHIT IN THE LAND OF HOUSEWARES?"
NO, IT'S JUST... A LOT. HUGE.
LISTEN, SHE SAYS SHE CAN HELP US AGAINST THOSE THINGS.
OF COURSE SHE WOULD SAY THAT, MY FRIEND. ARE YOU ALWAYS THIS TRUSTING OF WOMEN?
WELL...
LOOK, SPEAKING OF TRUST, HOW DO I KNOW THIS LITTLE TRIAL'S GOING TO BE FAIR?
BECAUSE I AM PUTTING A MAN IN CHARGE WHO WILL ENSURE THAT.
FATHER!

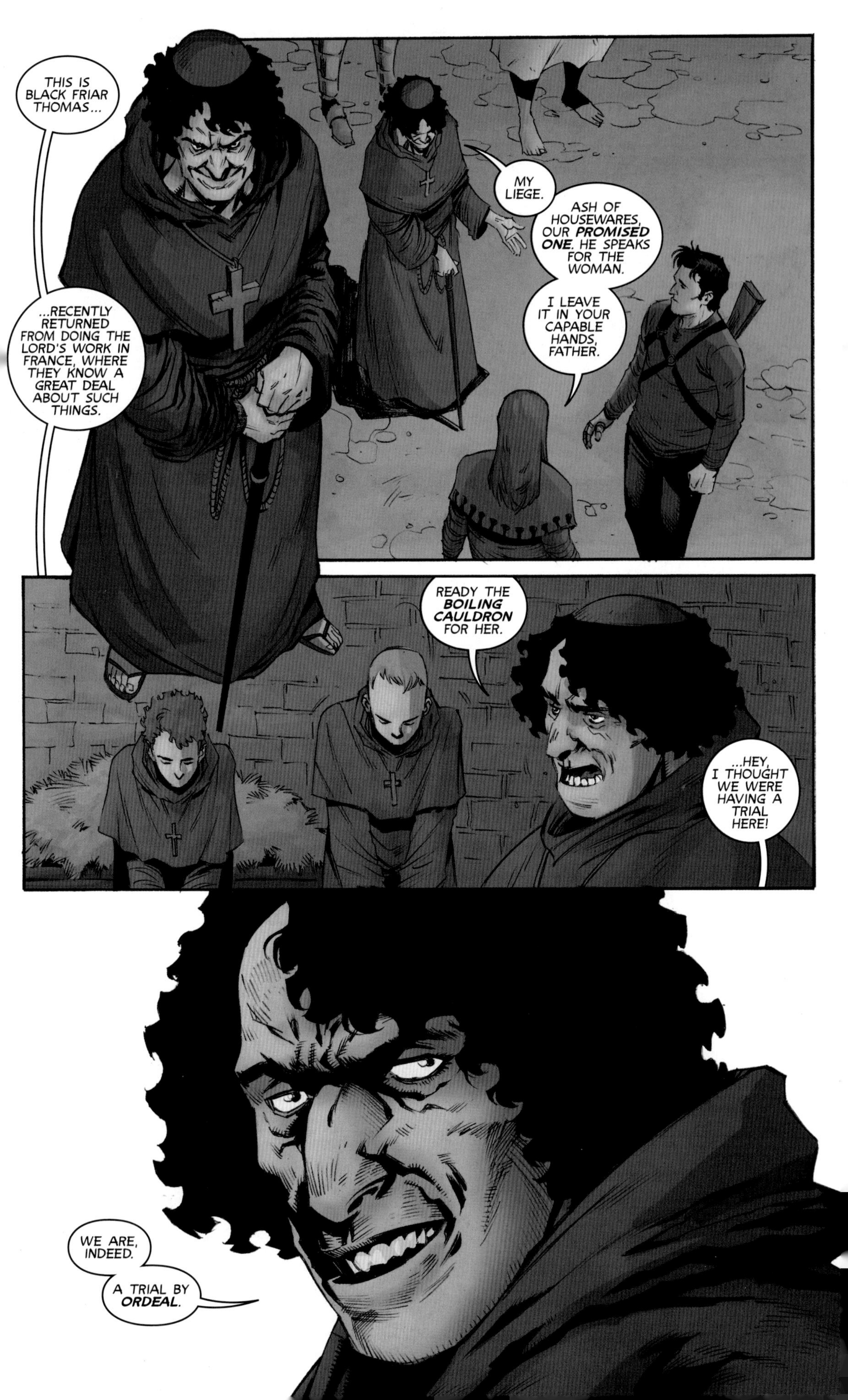
THIS IS BLACK FRIAR THOMAS...
...RECENTLY RETURNED FROM DOING THE LORD'S WORK IN FRANCE, WHERE THEY KNOW A GREAT DEAL ABOUT SUCH THINGS.
MY LIEGE.
ASH OF HOUSEWARES, OUR **PROMISED ONE**. HE SPEAKS FOR THE WOMAN.
I LEAVE IT IN YOUR CAPABLE HANDS, FATHER.
READY THE **BOILING CAULDRON** FOR HER.
...HEY, I THOUGHT WE WERE HAVING A TRIAL HERE!
WE ARE, INDEED.
A TRIAL BY **ORDEAL**.

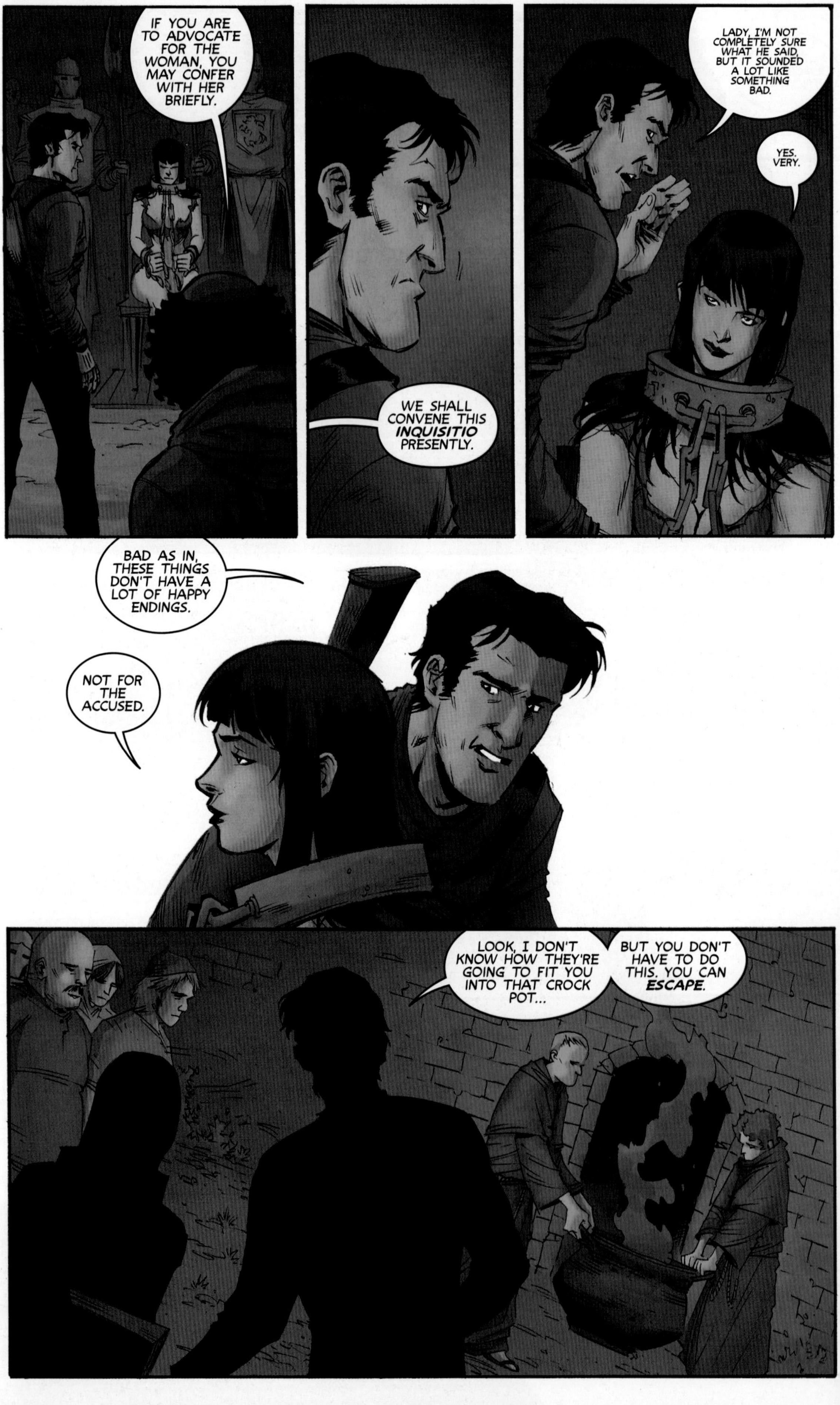
IF YOU ARE TO ADVOCATE FOR THE WOMAN, YOU MAY CONFER WITH HER BRIEFLY.
WE SHALL CONVENE THIS *INQUISITIO* PRESENTLY.
LADY, I'M NOT COMPLETELY SURE WHAT HE SAID, BUT IT SOUNDED A LOT LIKE SOMETHING BAD.
YES. VERY.
BAD AS IN, THESE THINGS DON'T HAVE A LOT OF HAPPY ENDINGS.
NOT FOR THE ACCUSED.
LOOK, I DON'T KNOW HOW THEY'RE GOING TO FIT YOU INTO THAT CROCK POT...
BUT YOU DON'T HAVE TO DO THIS. YOU CAN *ESCAPE*.

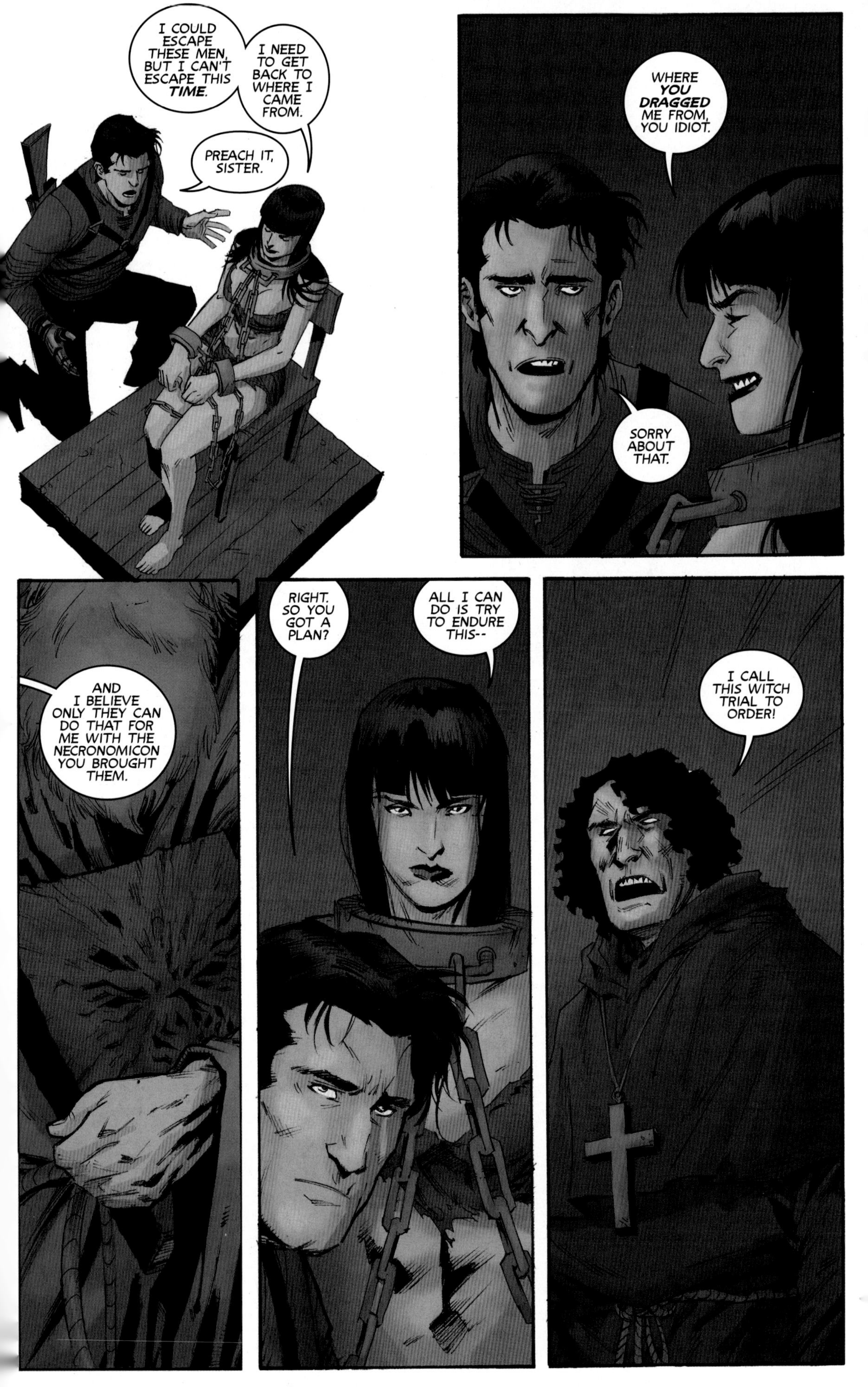
I COULD ESCAPE THESE MEN, BUT I CAN'T ESCAPE THIS TIME.
I NEED TO GET BACK TO WHERE I CAME FROM.
PREACH IT, SISTER.
WHERE YOU DRAGGED ME FROM, YOU IDIOT.
SORRY ABOUT THAT.
AND I BELIEVE ONLY THEY CAN DO THAT FOR ME WITH THE NECRONOMICON YOU BROUGHT THEM.
RIGHT. SO YOU GOT A PLAN?
ALL I CAN DO IS TRY TO ENDURE THIS--
I CALL THIS WITCH TRIAL TO ORDER!

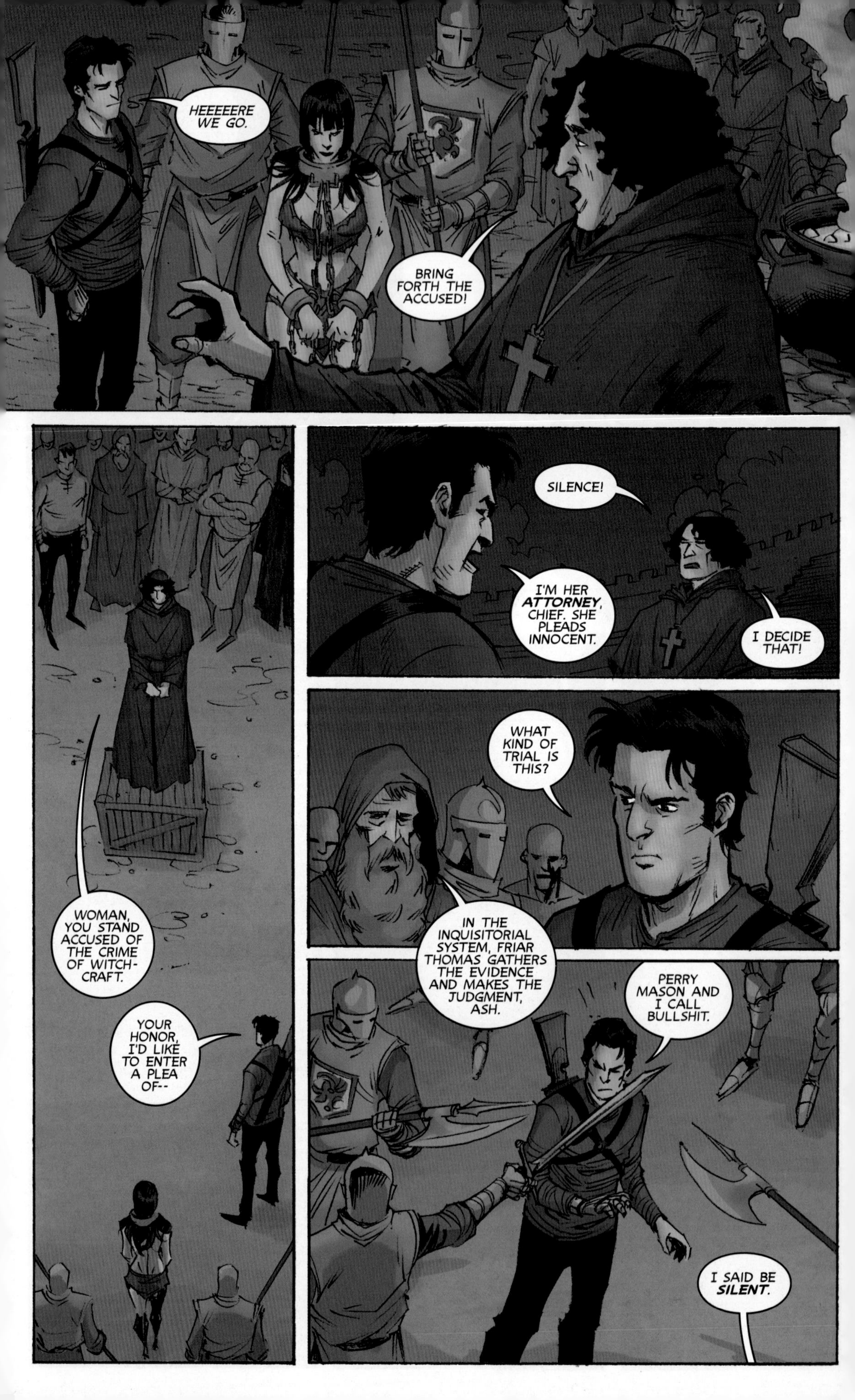
HEEEEERE WE GO.
BRING FORTH THE ACCUSED!
WOMAN, YOU STAND ACCUSED OF THE CRIME OF WITCH-CRAFT.
YOUR HONOR, I'D LIKE TO ENTER A PLEA OF--
SILENCE!
I'M HER ATTORNEY, CHIEF. SHE PLEADS INNOCENT.
I DECIDE THAT!
WHAT KIND OF TRIAL IS THIS?
IN THE INQUISITORIAL SYSTEM, FRIAR THOMAS GATHERS THE EVIDENCE AND MAKES THE JUDGMENT, ASH.
PERRY MASON AND I CALL BULLSHIT.
I SAID BE SILENT.

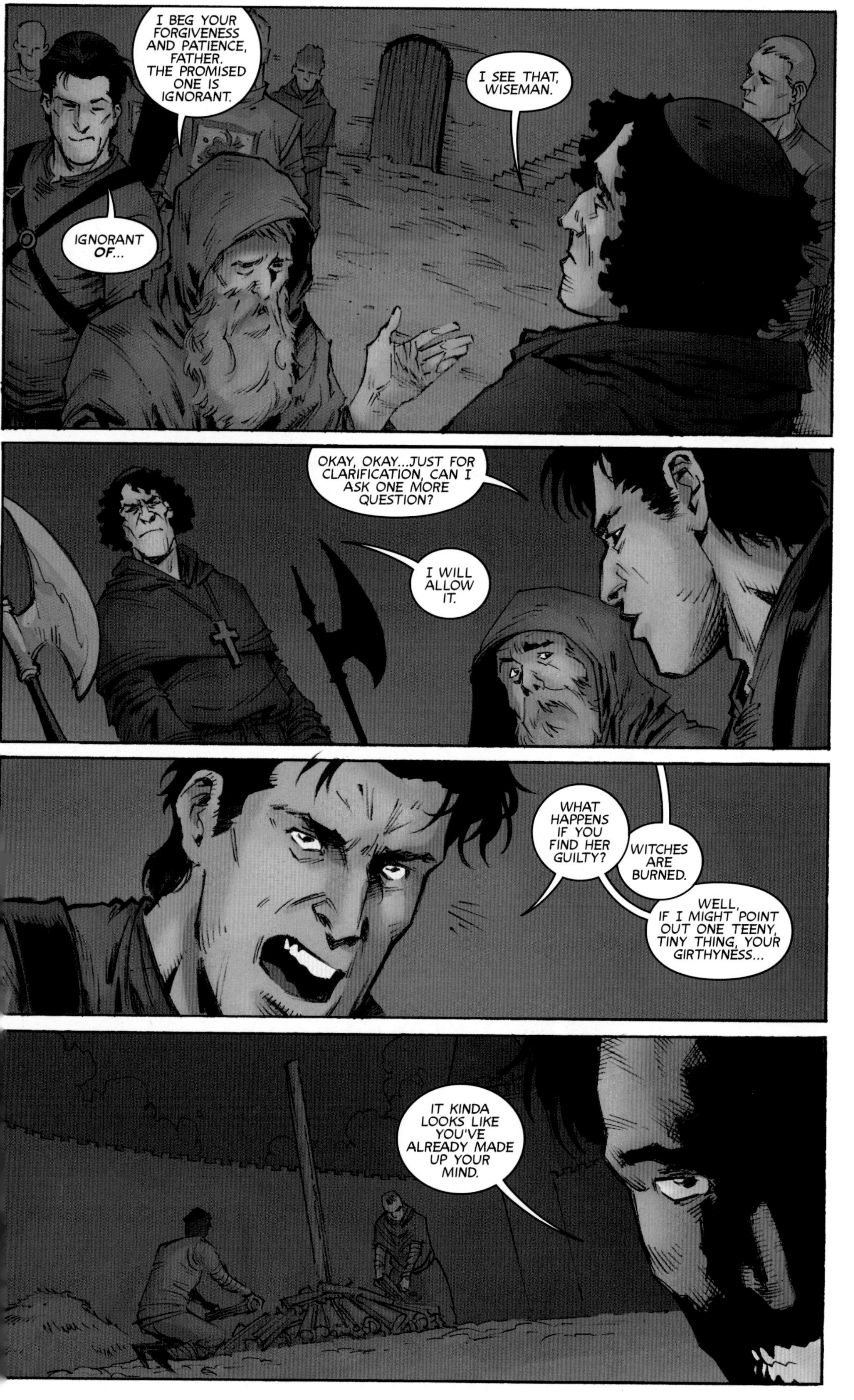
I BEG YOUR FORGIVENESS AND PATIENCE, FATHER. THE PROMISED ONE IS IGNORANT.
IGNORANT OF...
I SEE THAT, WISEMAN.
OKAY, OKAY...JUST FOR CLARIFICATION, CAN I ASK ONE MORE QUESTION?
I WILL ALLOW IT.
WHAT HAPPENS IF YOU FIND HER GUILTY?
WITCHES ARE BURNED.
WELL, IF I MIGHT POINT OUT ONE TEENY, TINY THING, YOUR GIRTHYNESS...
IT KINDA LOOKS LIKE YOU'VE ALREADY MADE UP YOUR MIND.

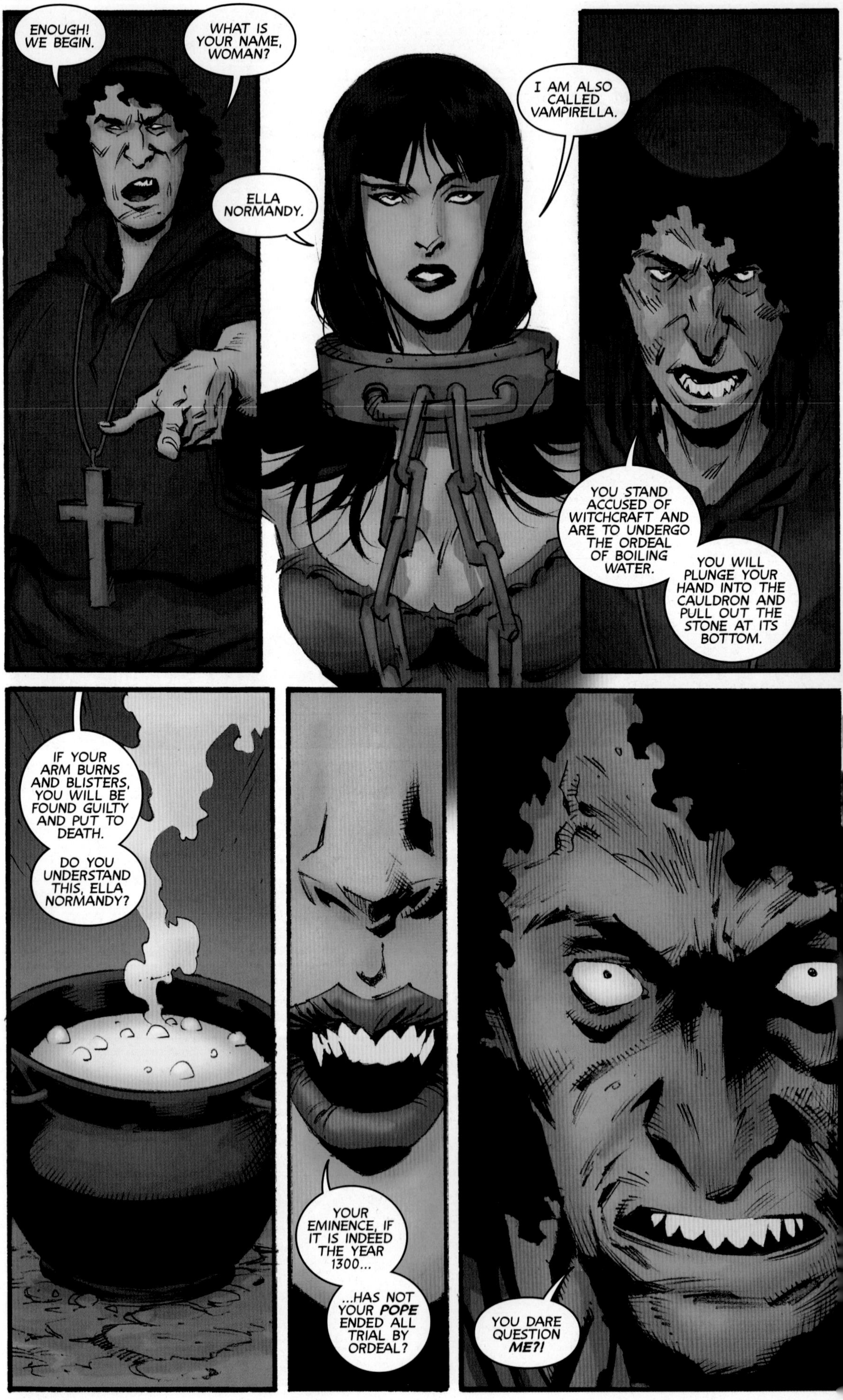
ENOUGH! WE BEGIN.
WHAT IS YOUR NAME, WOMAN?
ELLA NORMANDY.
I AM ALSO CALLED VAMPIRELLA.
YOU STAND ACCUSED OF WITCHCRAFT AND ARE TO UNDERGO THE ORDEAL OF BOILING WATER.
YOU WILL PLUNGE YOUR HAND INTO THE CAULDRON AND PULL OUT THE STONE AT ITS BOTTOM.
IF YOUR ARM BURNS AND BLISTERS, YOU WILL BE FOUND GUILTY AND PUT TO DEATH.
DO YOU UNDERSTAND THIS, ELLA NORMANDY?
YOUR EMINENCE, IF IT IS INDEED THE YEAR 1300...
...HAS NOT YOUR *POPE* ENDED ALL TRIAL BY ORDEAL?
YOU DARE QUESTION *ME?!*

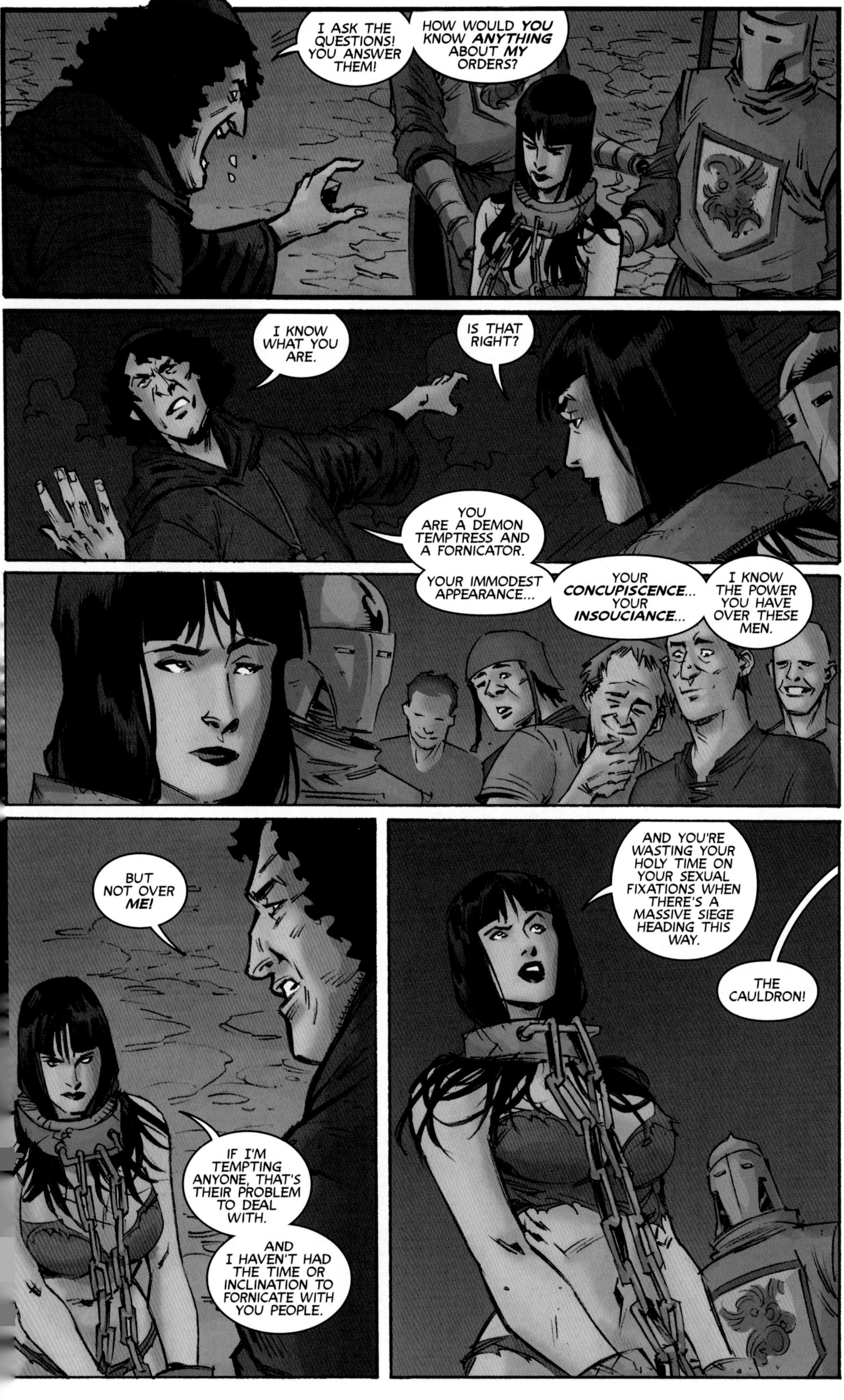
I ASK THE QUESTIONS! YOU ANSWER THEM!
HOW WOULD *YOU* KNOW *ANYTHING* ABOUT *MY* ORDERS?
I KNOW WHAT YOU ARE.
IS THAT RIGHT?
YOU ARE A DEMON TEMPTRESS AND A FORNICATOR.
YOUR IMMODEST APPEARANCE...
YOUR *CONCUPISCENCE*... YOUR *INSOUCIANCE*...
I KNOW THE POWER YOU HAVE OVER THESE MEN.
BUT NOT OVER *ME!*
IF I'M TEMPTING ANYONE, THAT'S THEIR PROBLEM TO DEAL WITH.
AND I HAVEN'T HAD THE TIME OR INCLINATION TO FORNICATE WITH YOU PEOPLE.
AND YOU'RE WASTING YOUR HOLY TIME ON YOUR SEXUAL FIXATIONS WHEN THERE'S A MASSIVE SIEGE HEADING THIS WAY.
THE CAULDRON!

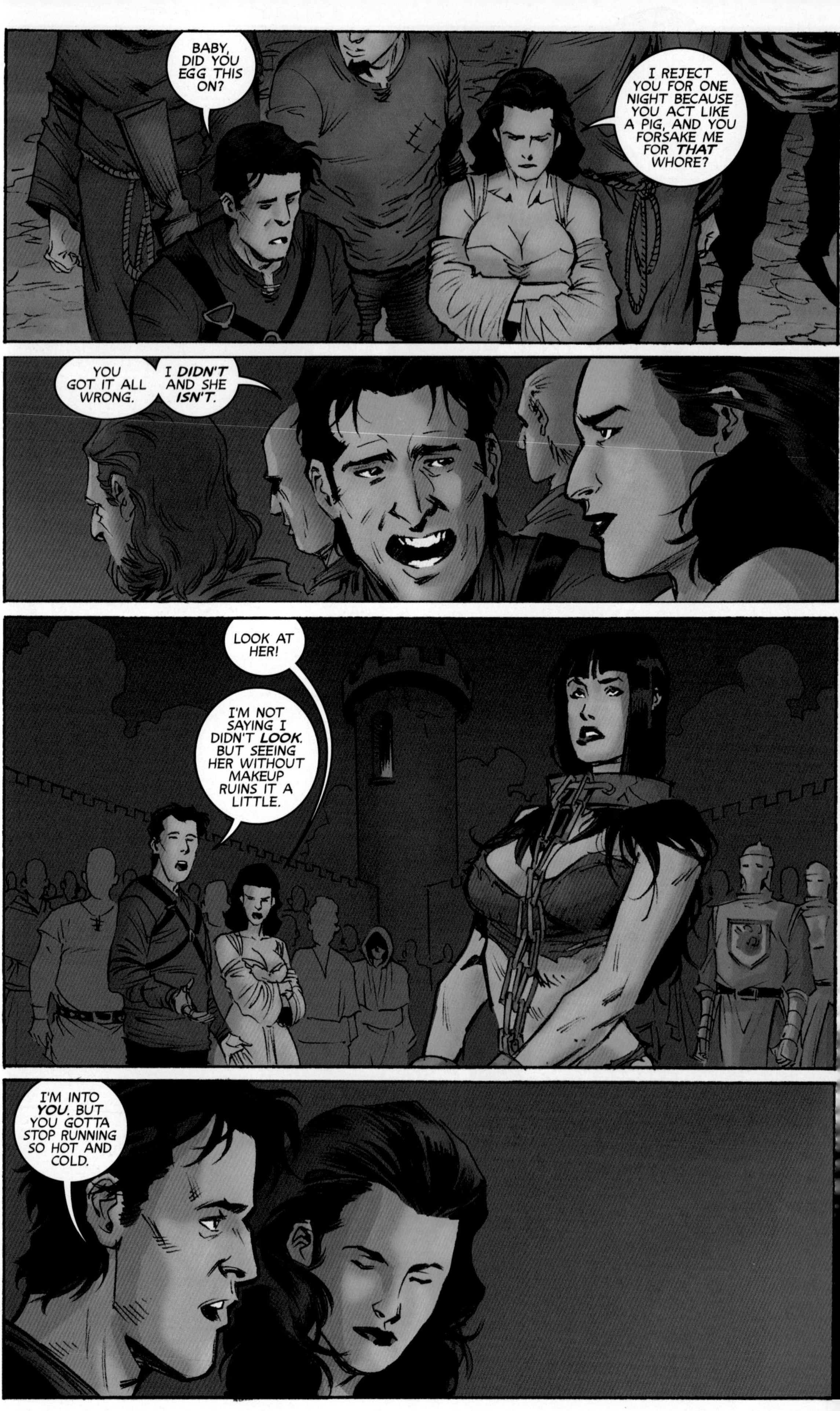
BABY, DID YOU EGG THIS ON?
I REJECT YOU FOR ONE NIGHT BECAUSE YOU ACT LIKE A PIG, AND YOU FORSAKE ME FOR *THAT* WHORE?
YOU GOT IT ALL WRONG.
I *DIDN'T* AND SHE *ISN'T*.
LOOK AT HER!
I'M NOT SAYING I DIDN'T *LOOK*. BUT SEEING HER WITHOUT MAKEUP RUINS IT A LITTLE.
I'M INTO *YOU*. BUT YOU GOTTA STOP RUNNING SO HOT AND COLD.

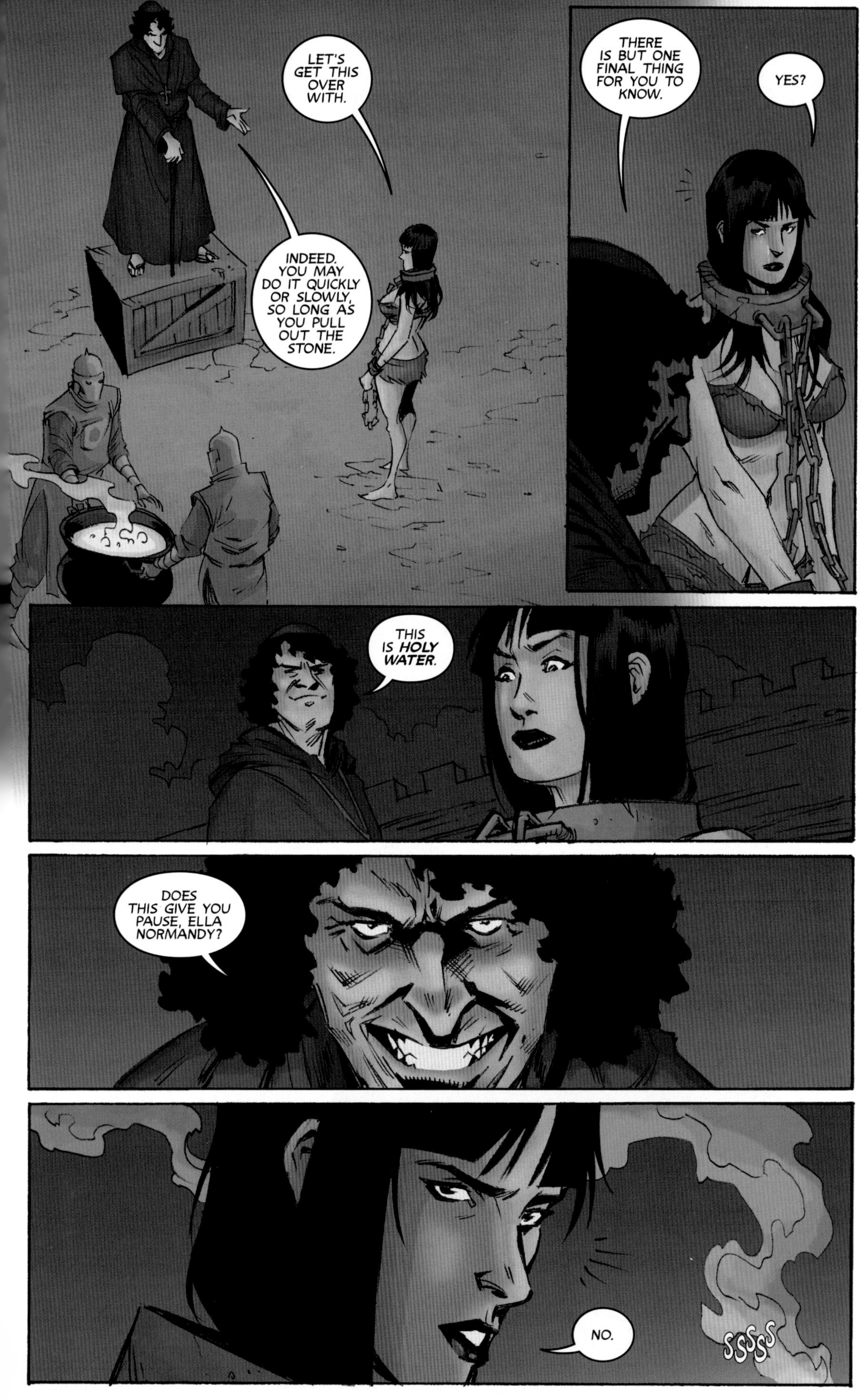
LET'S GET THIS OVER WITH.
INDEED. YOU MAY DO IT QUICKLY OR SLOWLY, SO LONG AS YOU PULL OUT THE STONE.
THERE IS BUT ONE FINAL THING FOR YOU TO KNOW.
YES?
THIS IS **HOLY WATER**.
DOES THIS GIVE YOU PAUSE, ELLA NORMANDY?
NO.
SSSSS

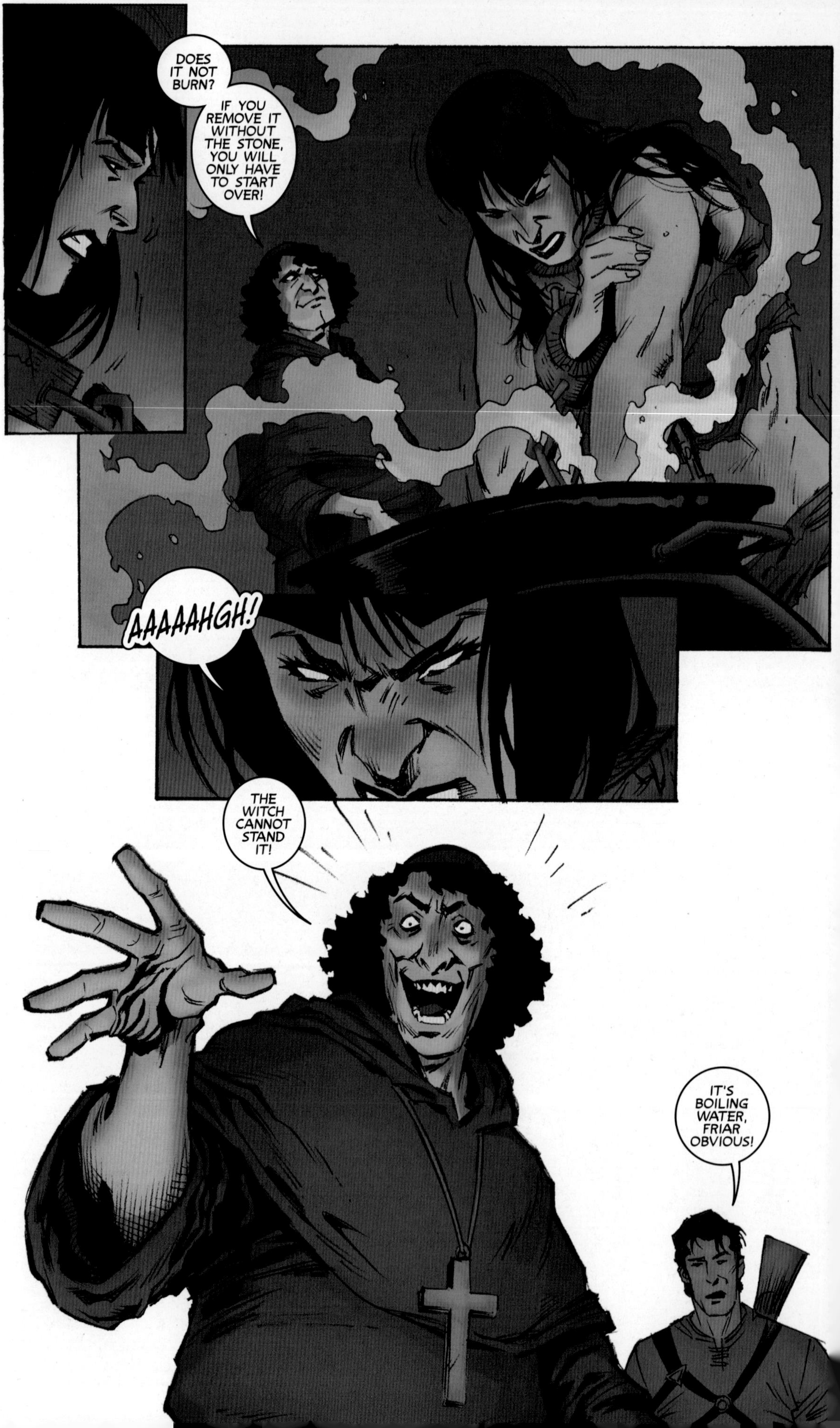
DOES IT NOT BURN?
IF YOU REMOVE IT WITHOUT THE STONE, YOU WILL ONLY HAVE TO START OVER!
AAAAAHGH!
THE WITCH CANNOT STAND IT!
IT'S BOILING WATER, FRIAR OBVIOUS!

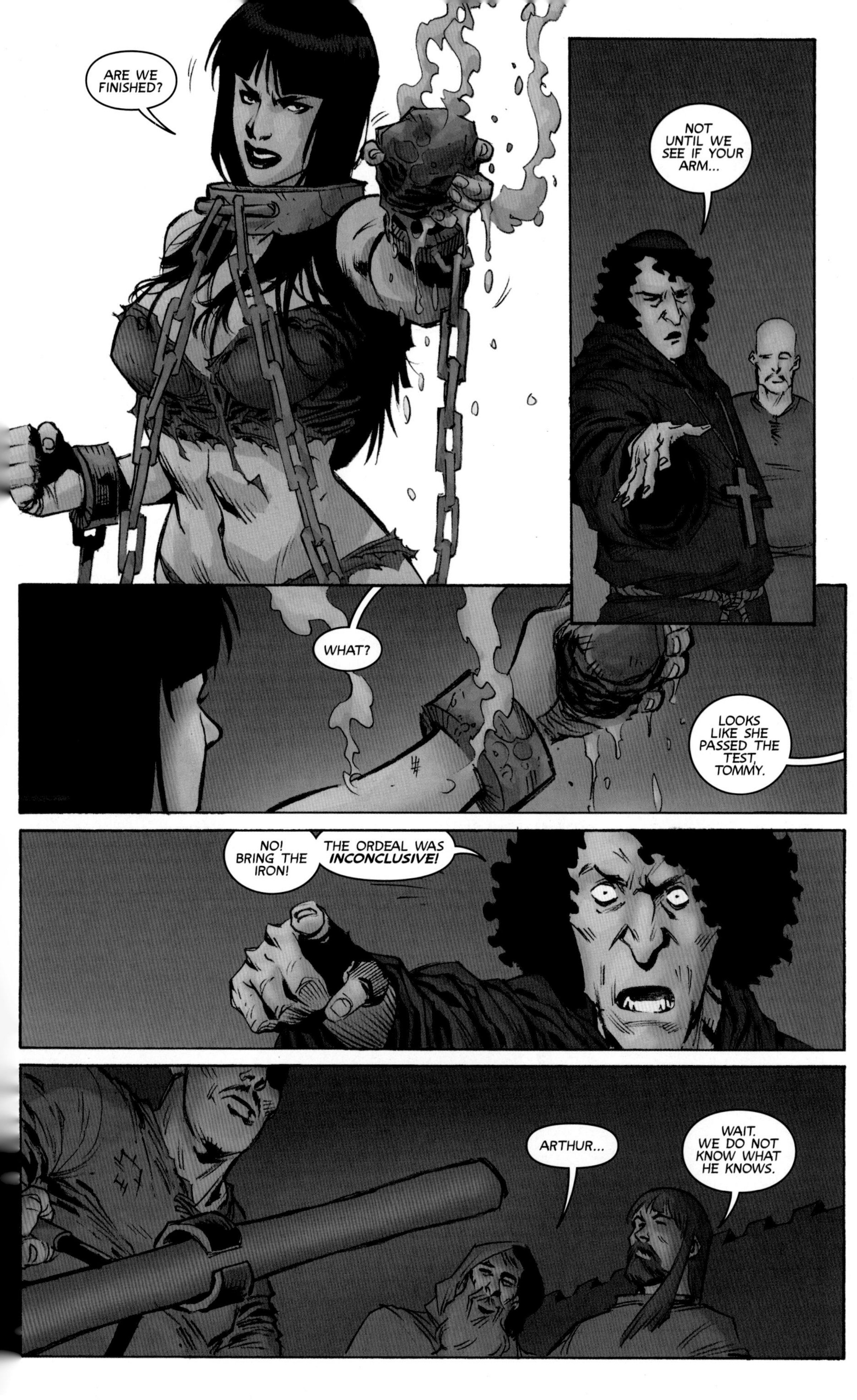
ARE WE FINISHED?
NOT UNTIL WE SEE IF YOUR ARM...
WHAT?
LOOKS LIKE SHE PASSED THE TEST, TOMMY.
NO! BRING THE IRON!
THE ORDEAL WAS *INCONCLUSIVE!*
ARTHUR...
WAIT. WE DO NOT KNOW WHAT HE KNOWS.

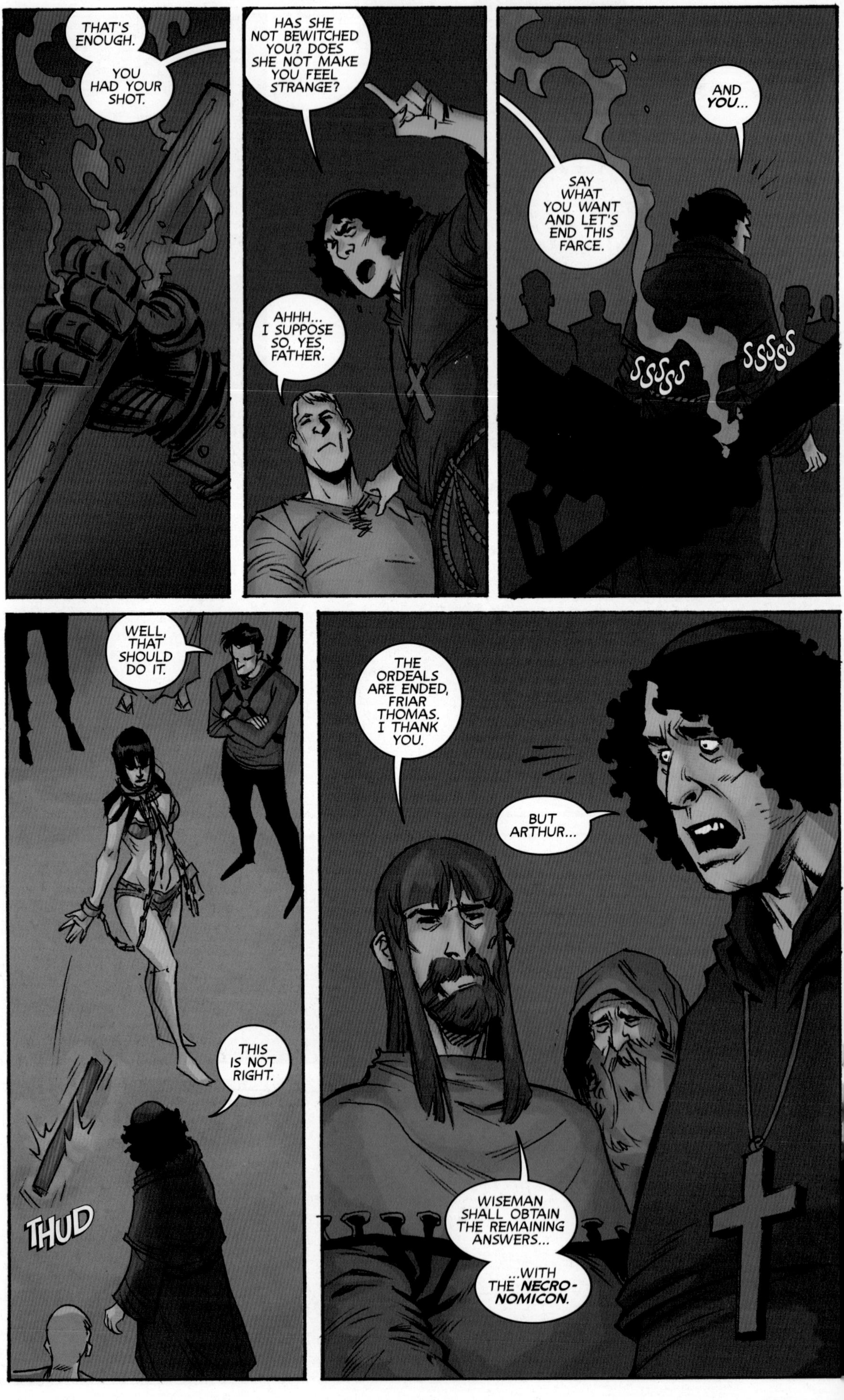
THAT'S ENOUGH.
YOU HAD YOUR SHOT.
HAS SHE NOT BEWITCHED YOU? DOES SHE NOT MAKE YOU FEEL STRANGE?
AHHH... I SUPPOSE SO, YES, FATHER.
AND YOU...
SAY WHAT YOU WANT AND LET'S END THIS FARCE.
SSSSS
SSSSS
WELL, THAT SHOULD DO IT.
THIS IS NOT RIGHT.
THUD
THE ORDEALS ARE ENDED, FRIAR THOMAS. I THANK YOU.
BUT ARTHUR...
WISEMAN SHALL OBTAIN THE REMAINING ANSWERS...
...WITH THE NECRONOMICON.

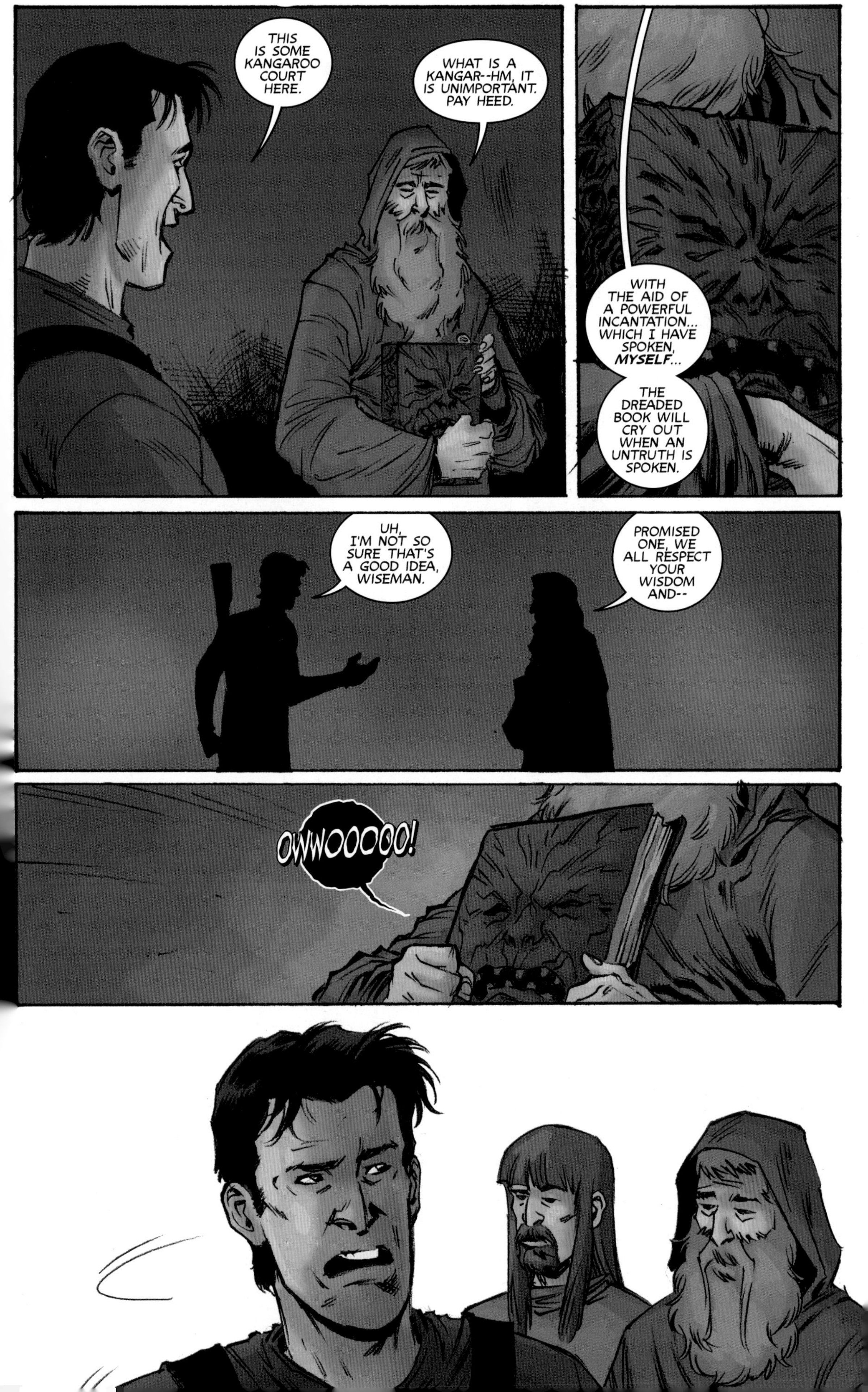
THIS IS SOME KANGAROO COURT HERE.
WHAT IS A KANGAR--HM, IT IS UNIMPORTANT. PAY HEED.
WITH THE AID OF A POWERFUL INCANTATION... WHICH I HAVE SPOKEN, MYSELF...
THE DREADED BOOK WILL CRY OUT WHEN AN UNTRUTH IS SPOKEN.
UH, I'M NOT SO SURE THAT'S A GOOD IDEA, WISEMAN.
PROMISED ONE, WE ALL RESPECT YOUR WISDOM AND--
OWWOOOOO!

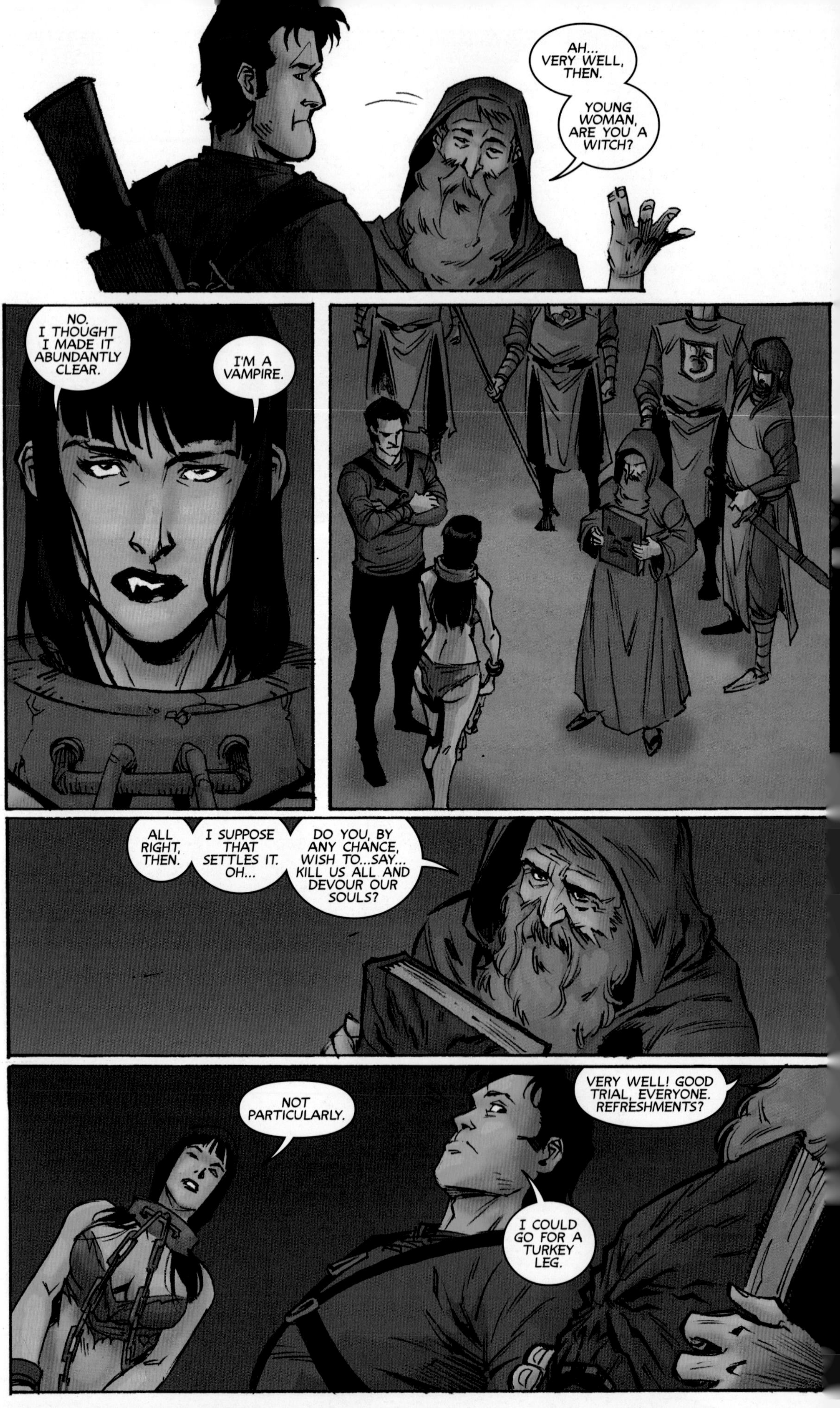
AH... VERY WELL, THEN.
YOUNG WOMAN, ARE YOU A WITCH?
NO. I THOUGHT I MADE IT ABUNDANTLY CLEAR.
I'M A VAMPIRE.
ALL RIGHT, THEN.
I SUPPOSE THAT SETTLES IT. OH...
DO YOU, BY ANY CHANCE, WISH TO...SAY... KILL US ALL AND DEVOUR OUR SOULS?
NOT PARTICULARLY.
VERY WELL! GOOD TRIAL, EVERYONE. REFRESHMENTS?
I COULD GO FOR A TURKEY LEG.

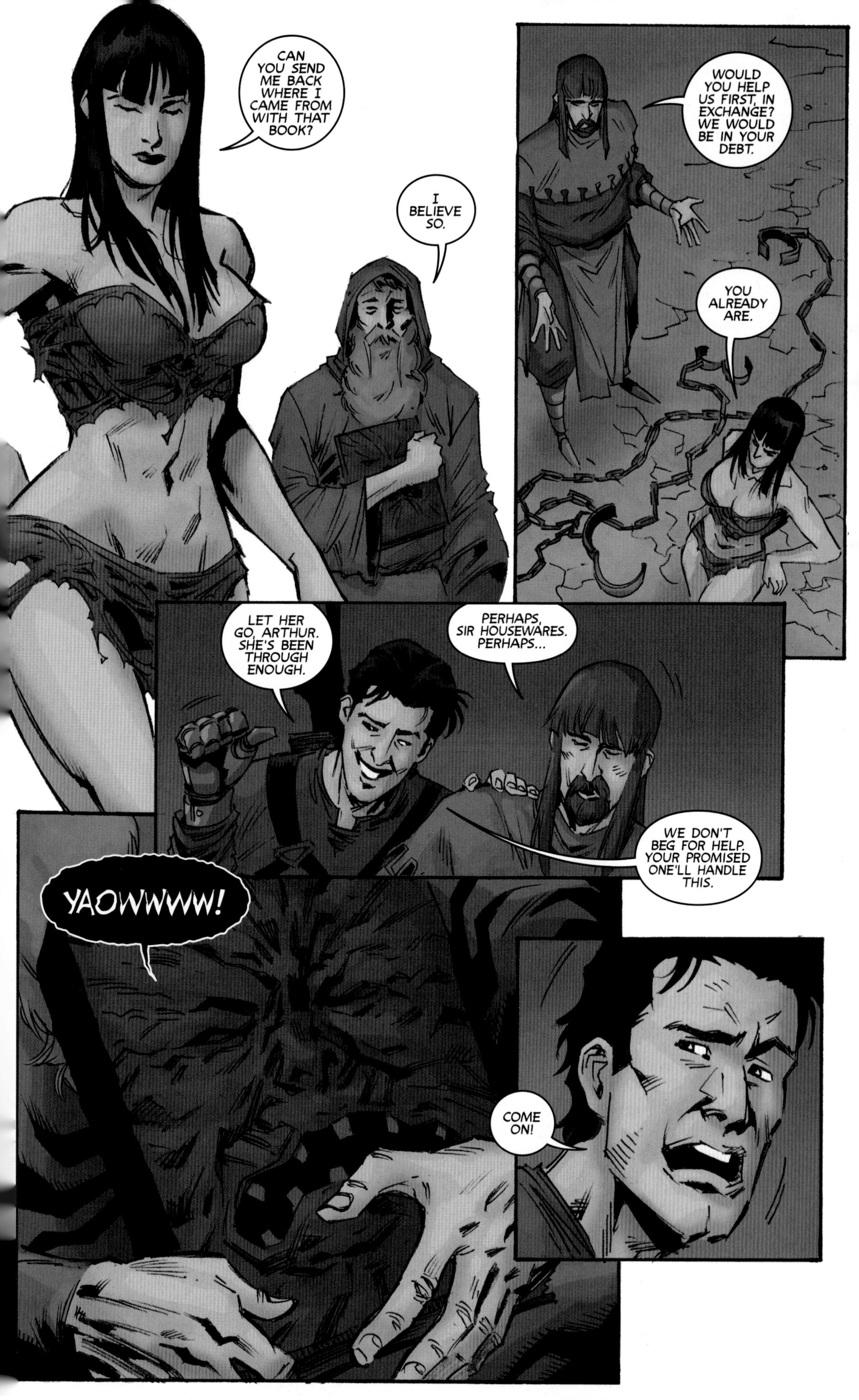
CAN YOU SEND ME BACK WHERE I CAME FROM WITH THAT BOOK?
I BELIEVE SO.
WOULD YOU HELP US FIRST, IN EXCHANGE? WE WOULD BE IN YOUR DEBT.
YOU ALREADY ARE.
LET HER GO, ARTHUR. SHE'S BEEN THROUGH ENOUGH.
PERHAPS, SIR HOUSEWARES. PERHAPS...
WE DON'T BEG FOR HELP. YOUR PROMISED ONE'LL HANDLE THIS.
YAOWWWW!
COME ON!

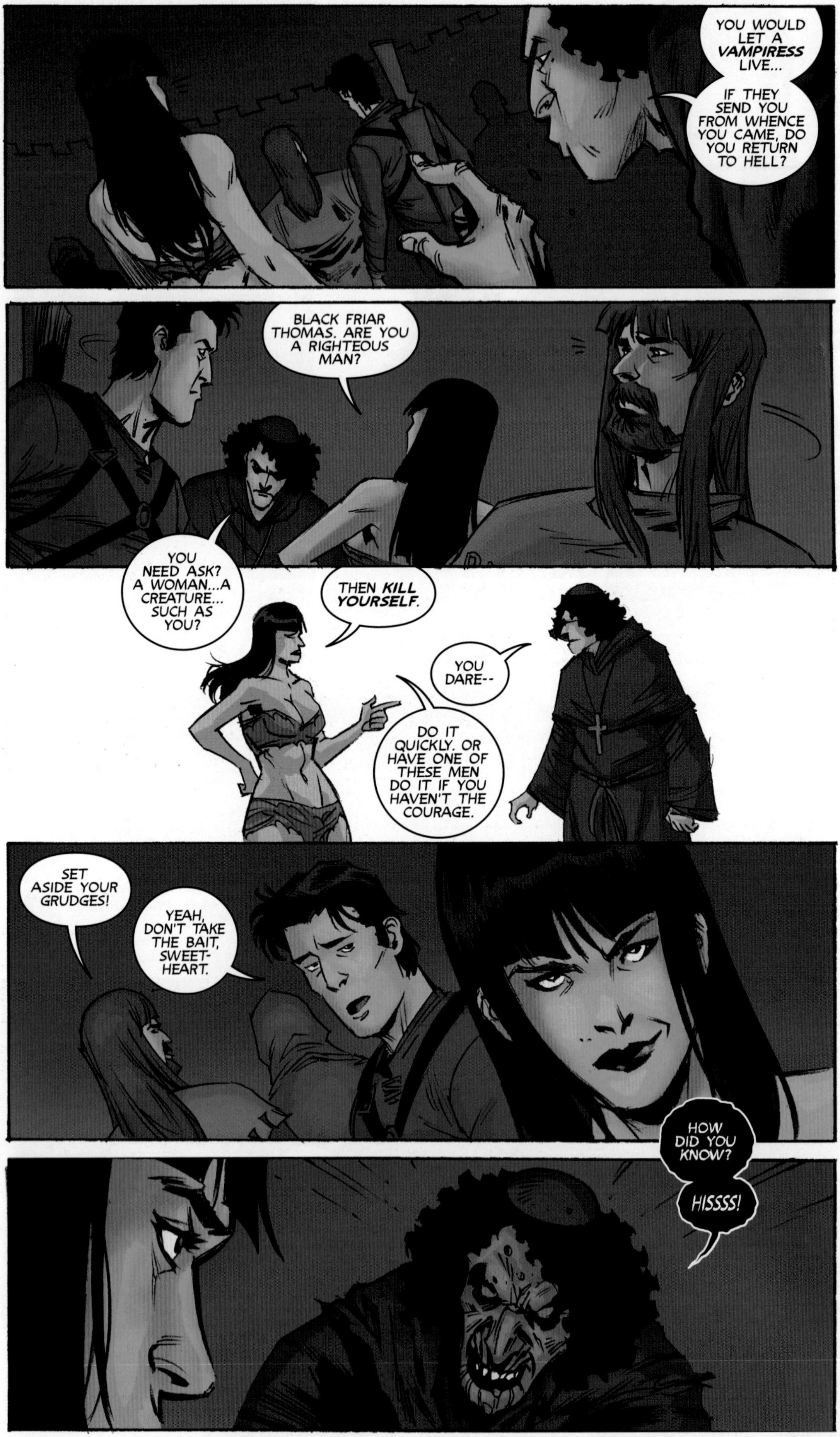
YOU WOULD LET A VAMPIRESS LIVE...
IF THEY SEND YOU FROM WHENCE YOU CAME, DO YOU RETURN TO HELL?
BLACK FRIAR THOMAS. ARE YOU A RIGHTEOUS MAN?
YOU NEED ASK? A WOMAN...A CREATURE... SUCH AS YOU?
THEN KILL YOURSELF.
YOU DARE--
DO IT QUICKLY. OR HAVE ONE OF THESE MEN DO IT IF YOU HAVEN'T THE COURAGE.
SET ASIDE YOUR GRUDGES!
YEAH, DON'T TAKE THE BAIT, SWEET-HEART.
HOW DID YOU KNOW?
HISSSS!

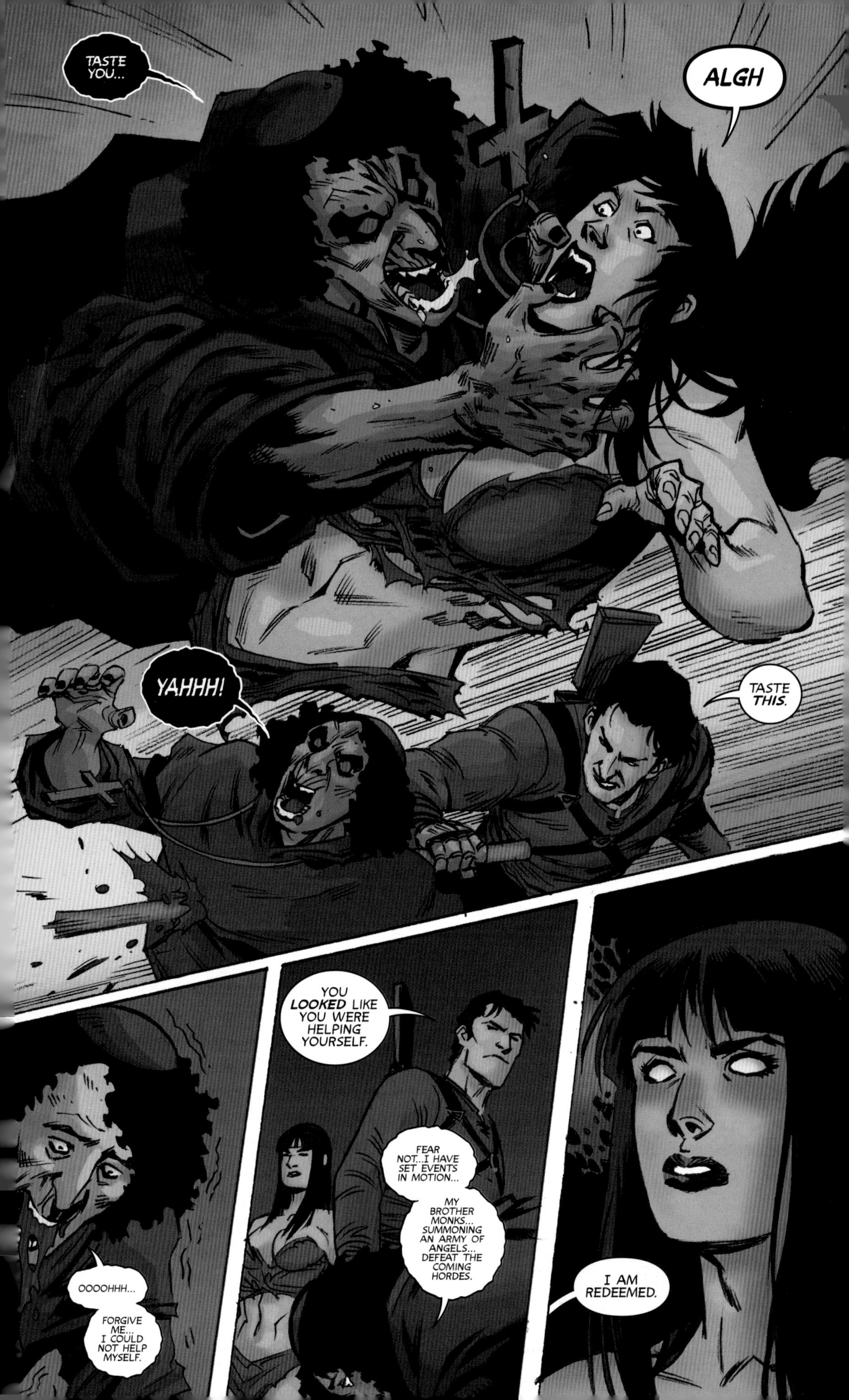
TASTE YOU...
ALGH
YAHHH!
TASTE THIS.
OOOOHHH...
FORGIVE ME... I COULD NOT HELP MYSELF.
YOU LOOKED LIKE YOU WERE HELPING YOURSELF.
FEAR NOT...I HAVE SET EVENTS IN MOTION...
MY BROTHER MONKS... SUMMONING AN ARMY OF ANGELS... DEFEAT THE COMING HORDES.
I AM REDEEMED.

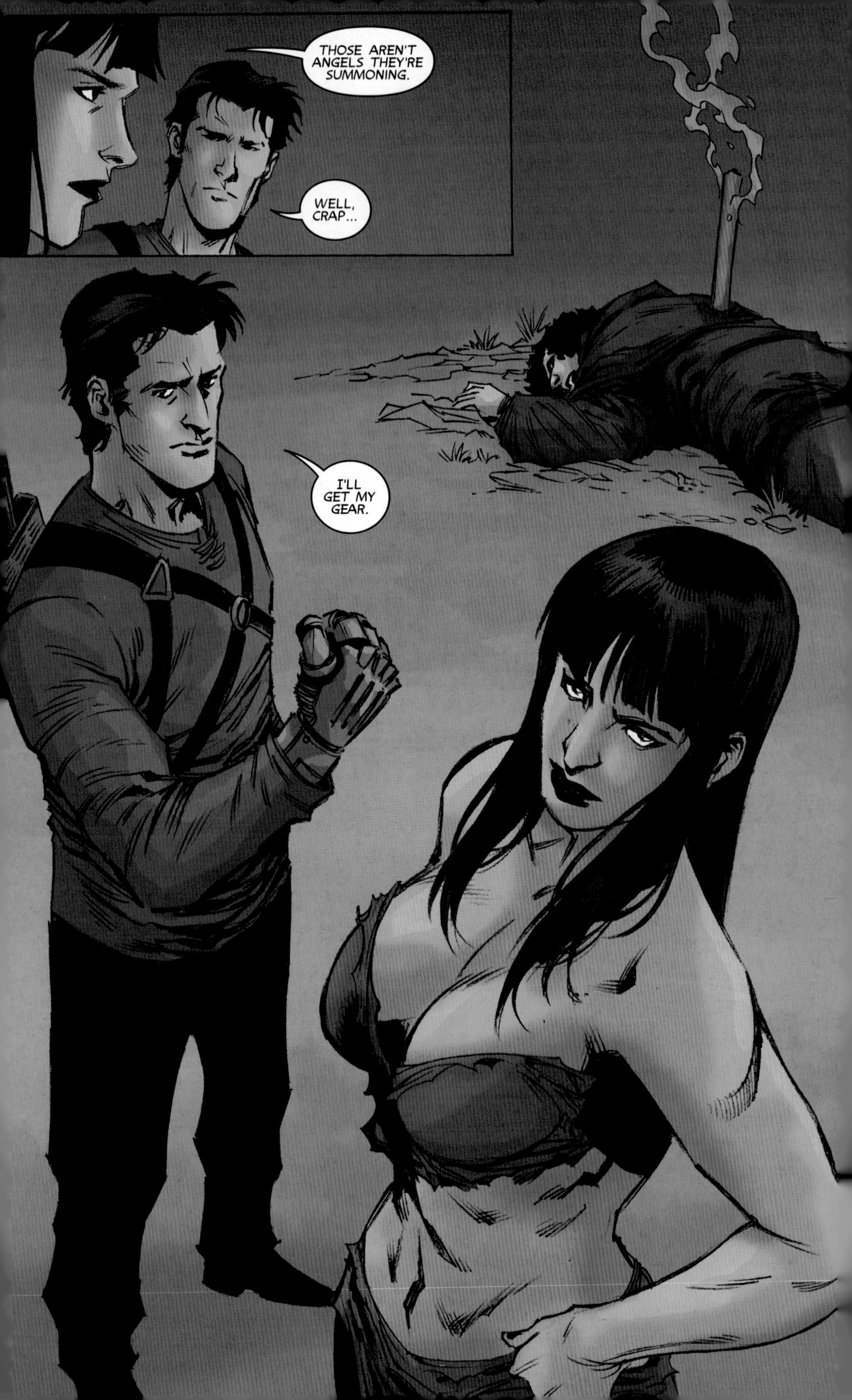
THOSE AREN'T ANGELS THEY'RE SUMMONING.
WELL, CRAP...
I'LL GET MY GEAR.

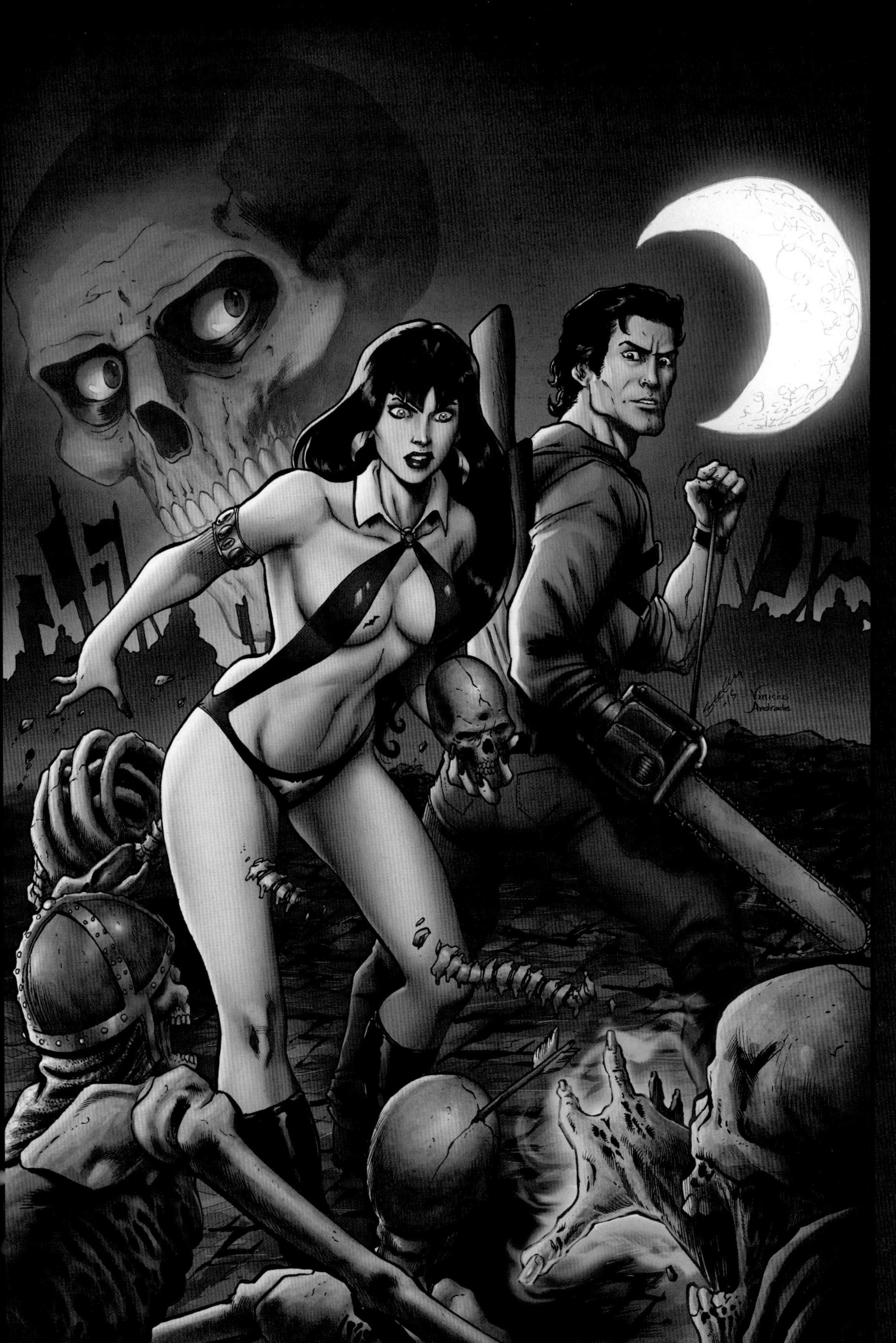
Vinicius
Andrade

ISSUE #4 COVER ART BY TIM SEELEY COLORS BY VINICIUS ANDRADE

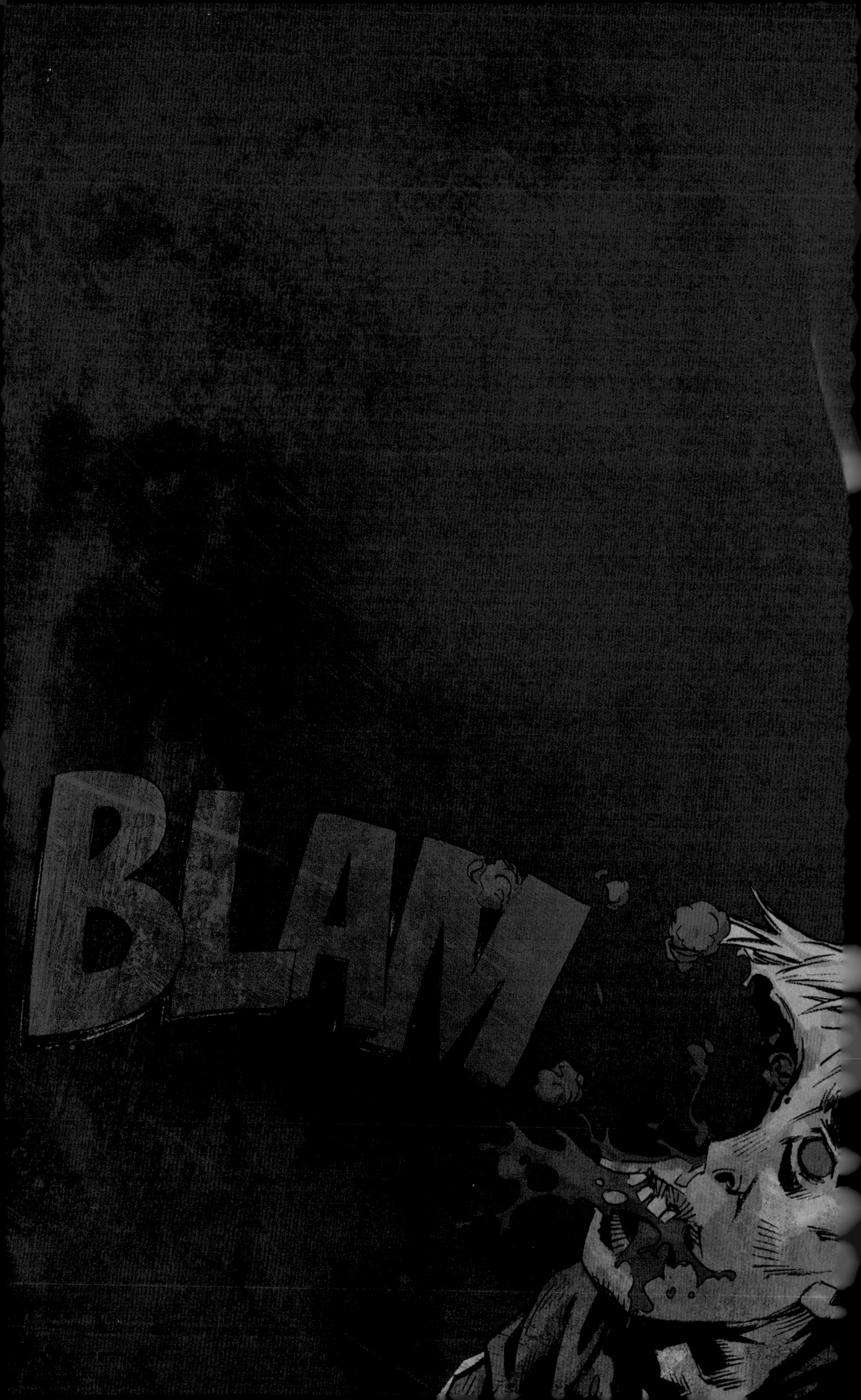
BLAM

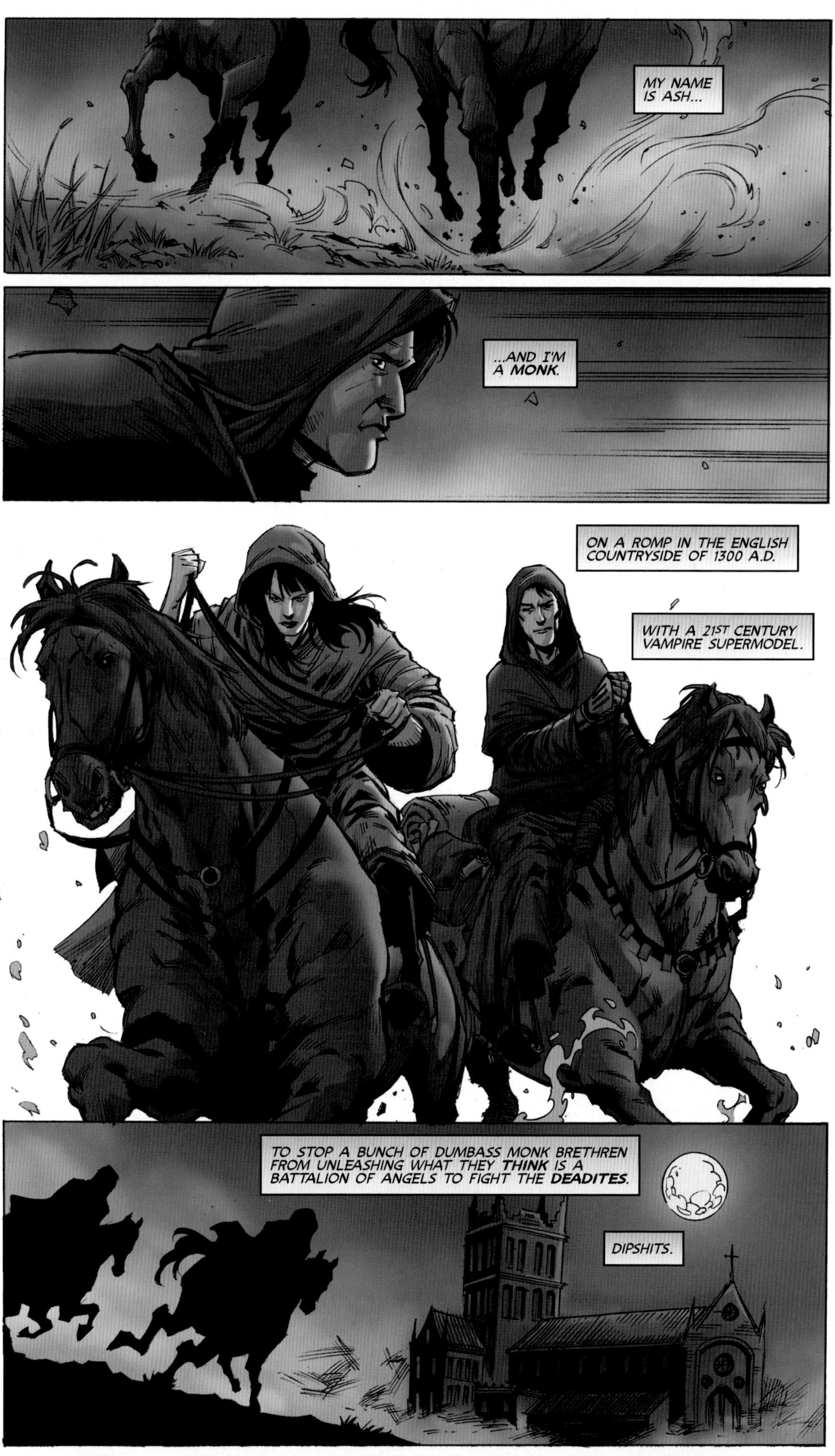
MY NAME IS ASH...
...AND I'M A MONK.
ON A ROMP IN THE ENGLISH COUNTRYSIDE OF 1300 A.D.
WITH A 21ST CENTURY VAMPIRE SUPERMODEL.
TO STOP A BUNCH OF DUMBASS MONK BRETHREN FROM UNLEASHING WHAT THEY **THINK** IS A BATTALION OF ANGELS TO FIGHT THE **DEADITES**.
DIPSHITS.

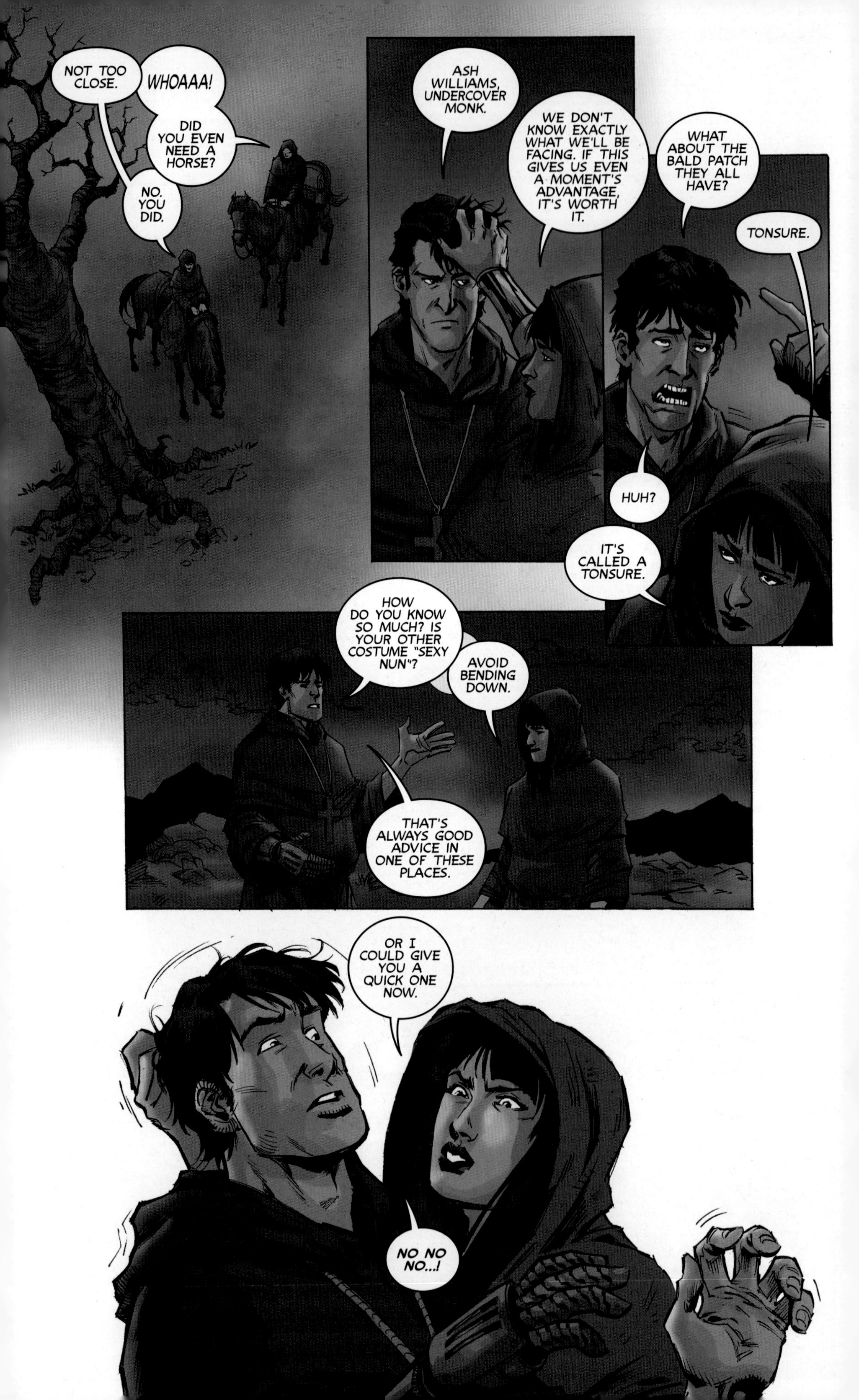
NOT TOO CLOSE.
WHOAAA!
DID YOU EVEN NEED A HORSE?
NO. YOU DID.
ASH WILLIAMS, UNDERCOVER MONK.
WE DON'T KNOW EXACTLY WHAT WE'LL BE FACING. IF THIS GIVES US EVEN A MOMENT'S ADVANTAGE, IT'S WORTH IT.
WHAT ABOUT THE BALD PATCH THEY ALL HAVE?
TONSURE.
HUH?
IT'S CALLED A TONSURE.
HOW DO YOU KNOW SO MUCH? IS YOUR OTHER COSTUME "SEXY NUN"?
AVOID BENDING DOWN.
THAT'S ALWAYS GOOD ADVICE IN ONE OF THESE PLACES.
OR I COULD GIVE YOU A QUICK ONE NOW.
NO NO NO...!

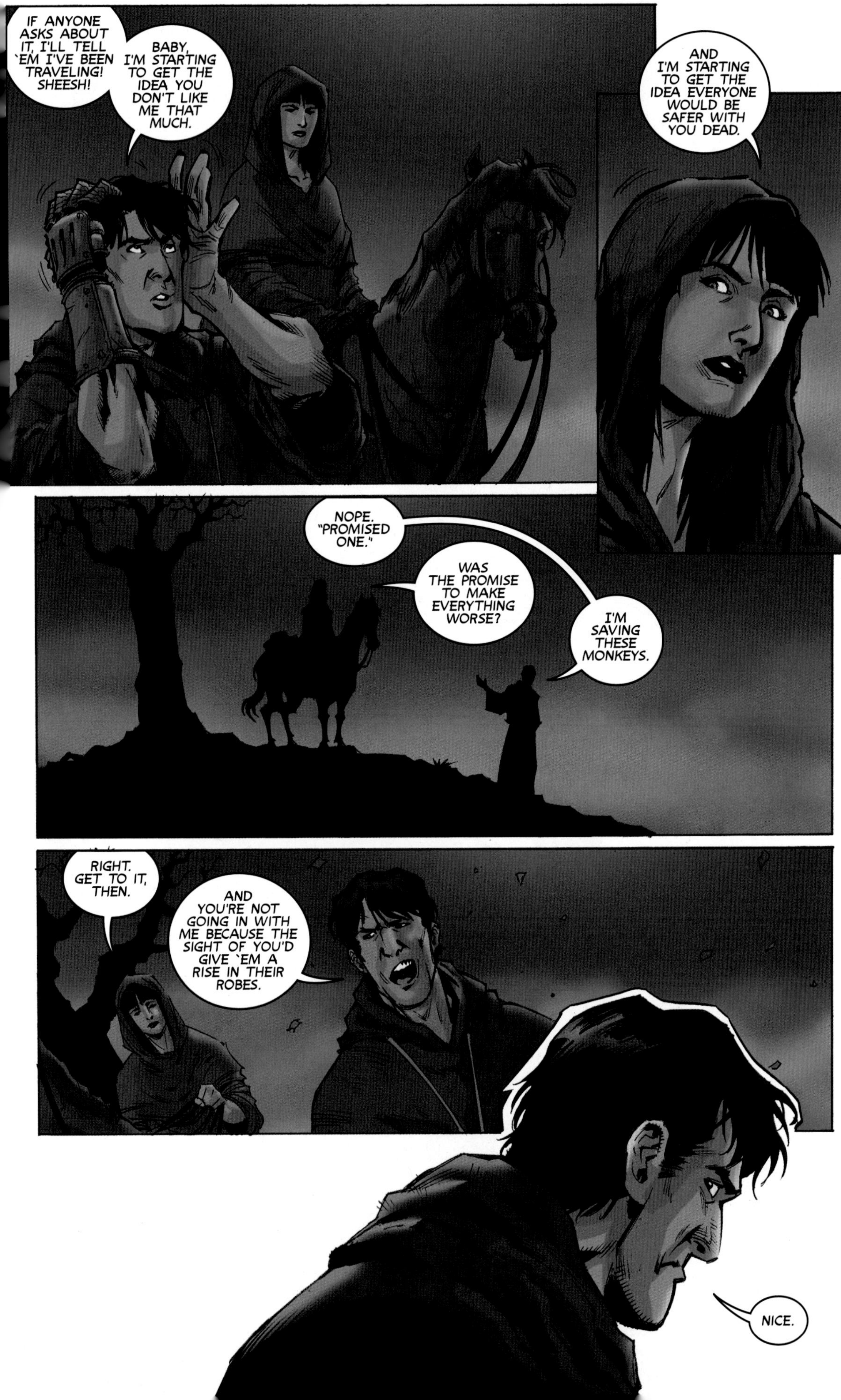
IF ANYONE ASKS ABOUT IT, I'LL TELL `EM I'VE BEEN TRAVELING! SHEESH!
BABY, I'M STARTING TO GET THE IDEA YOU DON'T LIKE ME THAT MUCH.
AND I'M STARTING TO GET THE IDEA EVERYONE WOULD BE SAFER WITH YOU DEAD.
NOPE. "PROMISED ONE."
WAS THE PROMISE TO MAKE EVERYTHING WORSE?
I'M SAVING THESE MONKEYS.
RIGHT. GET TO IT, THEN.
AND YOU'RE NOT GOING IN WITH ME BECAUSE THE SIGHT OF YOU'D GIVE `EM A RISE IN THEIR ROBES.
NICE.

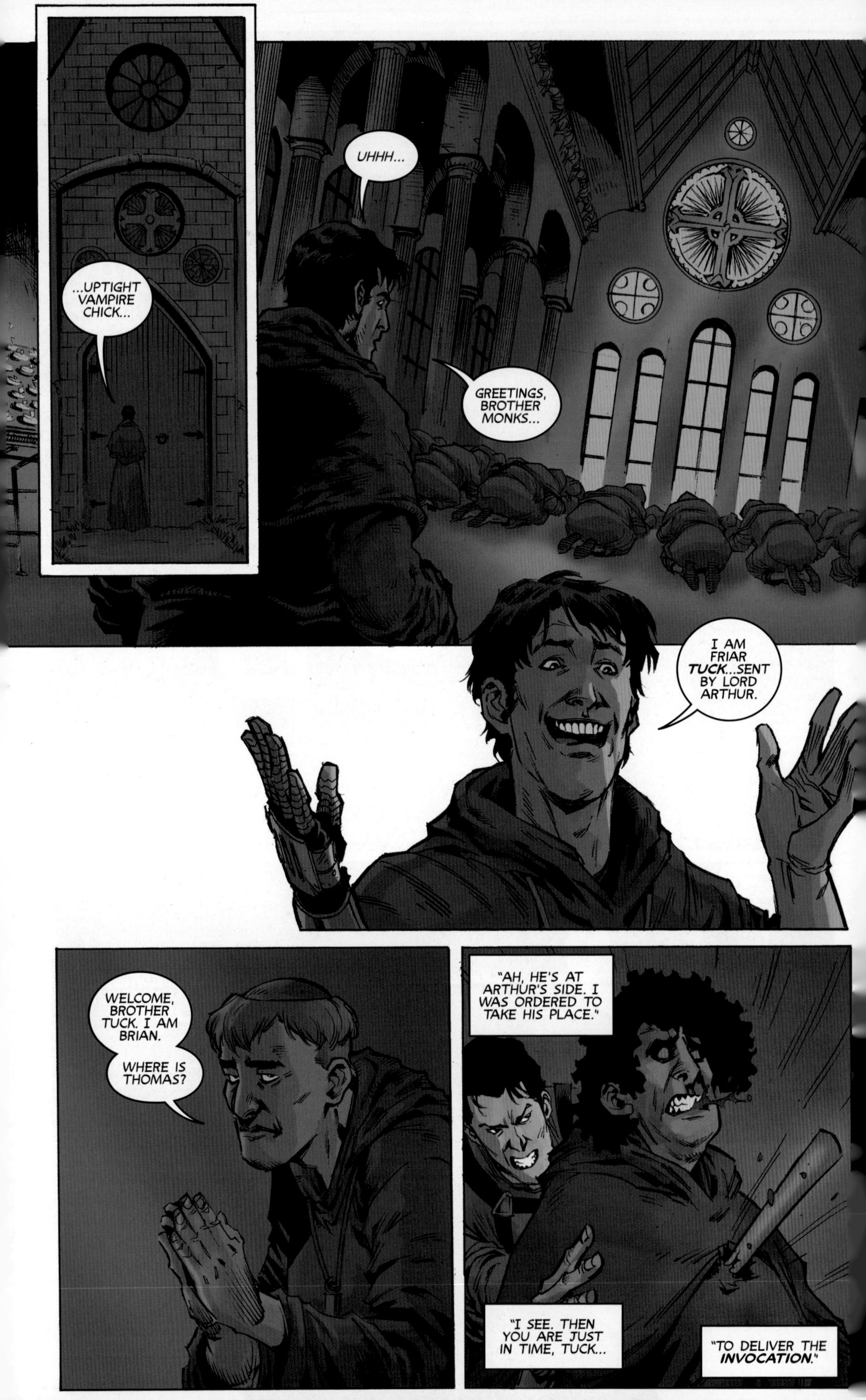
...UPTIGHT VAMPIRE CHICK...
UHHH...
GREETINGS, BROTHER MONKS...
I AM FRIAR TUCK...SENT BY LORD ARTHUR.
WELCOME, BROTHER TUCK. I AM BRIAN.
WHERE IS THOMAS?
"AH, HE'S AT ARTHUR'S SIDE. I WAS ORDERED TO TAKE HIS PLACE."
"I SEE. THEN YOU ARE JUST IN TIME, TUCK...
"TO DELIVER THE INVOCATION."

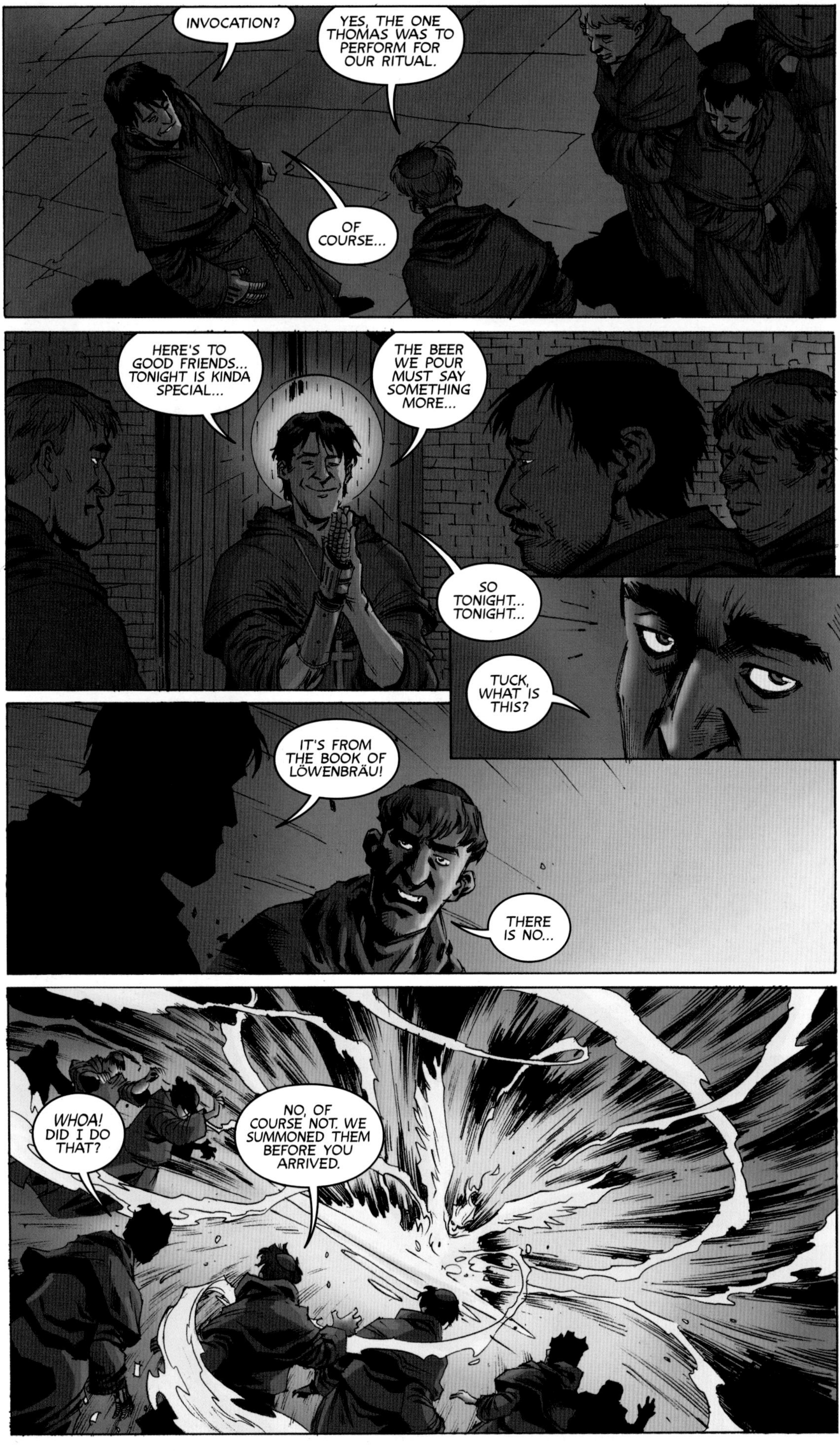
INVOCATION?
YES, THE ONE THOMAS WAS TO PERFORM FOR OUR RITUAL.
OF COURSE...
HERE'S TO GOOD FRIENDS... TONIGHT IS KINDA SPECIAL...
THE BEER WE POUR MUST SAY SOMETHING MORE...
SO TONIGHT... TONIGHT...
TUCK, WHAT IS THIS?
IT'S FROM THE BOOK OF LÖWENBRÄU!
THERE IS NO...
WHOA! DID I DO THAT?
NO, OF COURSE NOT. WE SUMMONED THEM BEFORE YOU ARRIVED.

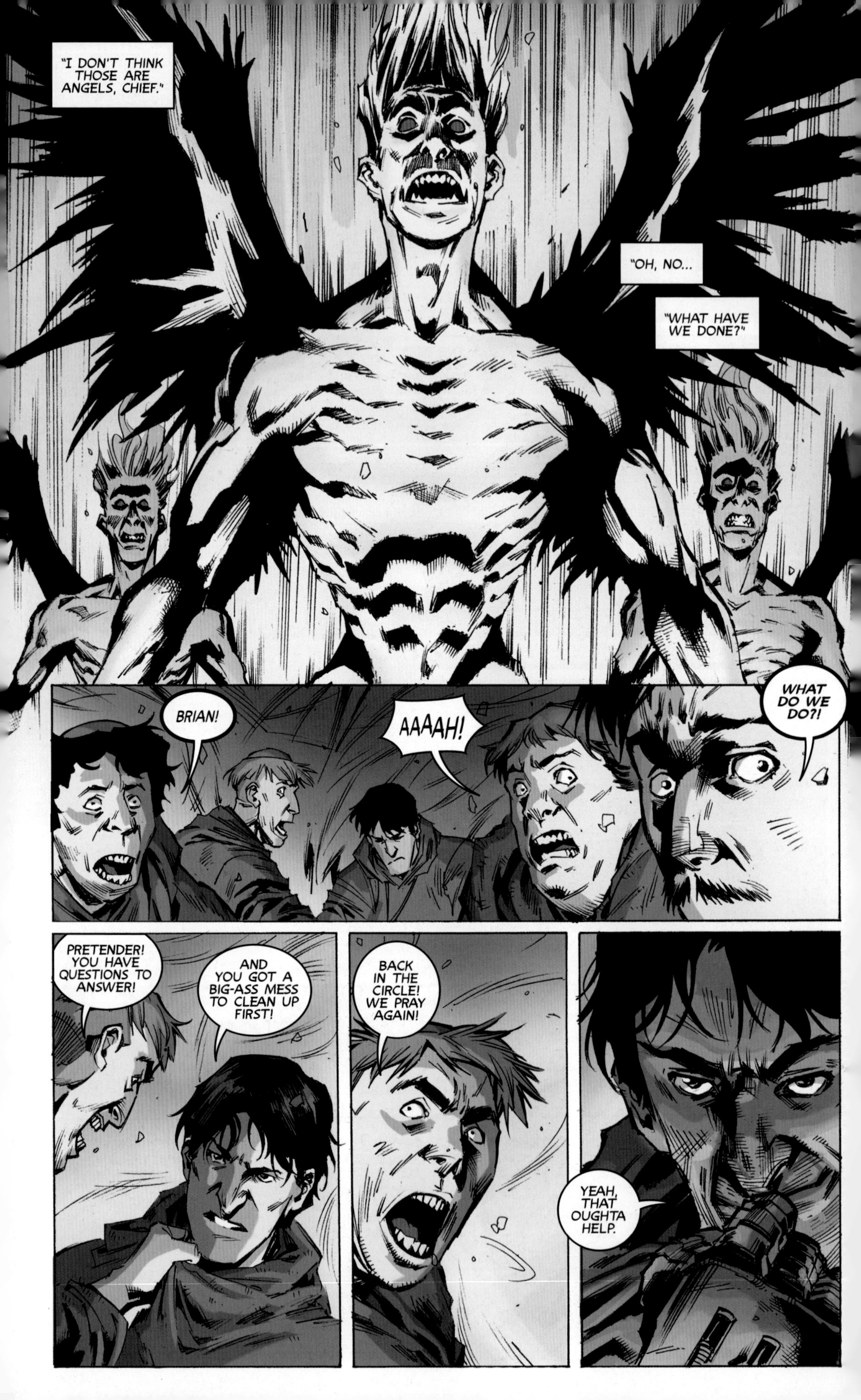
"I DON'T THINK THOSE ARE ANGELS, CHIEF."
"OH, NO...
"WHAT HAVE WE DONE?"
BRIAN!
AAAAH!
WHAT DO WE DO?!
PRETENDER! YOU HAVE QUESTIONS TO ANSWER!
AND YOU GOT A BIG-ASS MESS TO CLEAN UP FIRST!
BACK IN THE CIRCLE! WE PRAY AGAIN!
YEAH, THAT OUGHTA HELP.

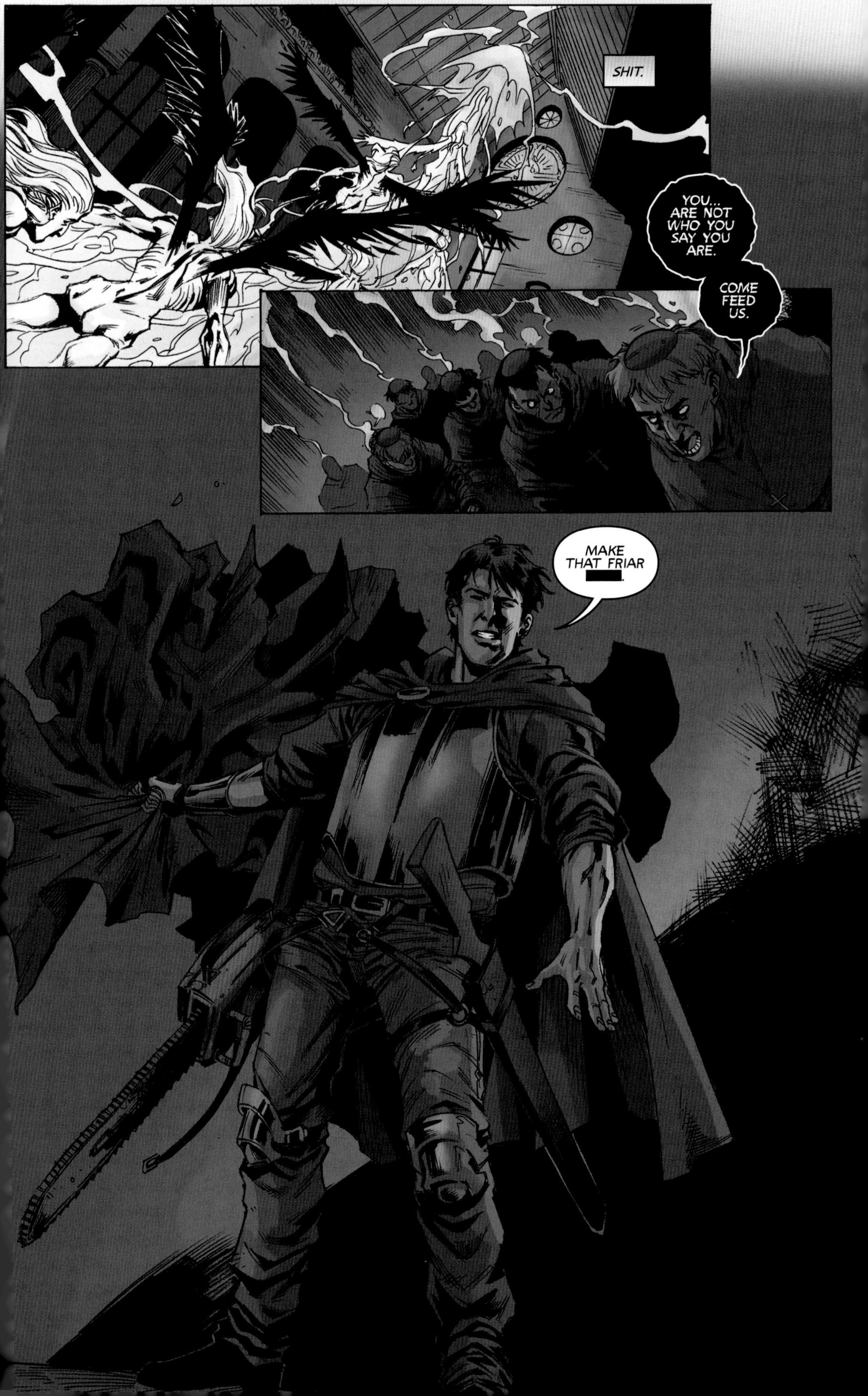
SHIT.
YOU... ARE NOT WHO YOU SAY YOU ARE.
COME FEED US.
MAKE THAT FRIAR [redacted].

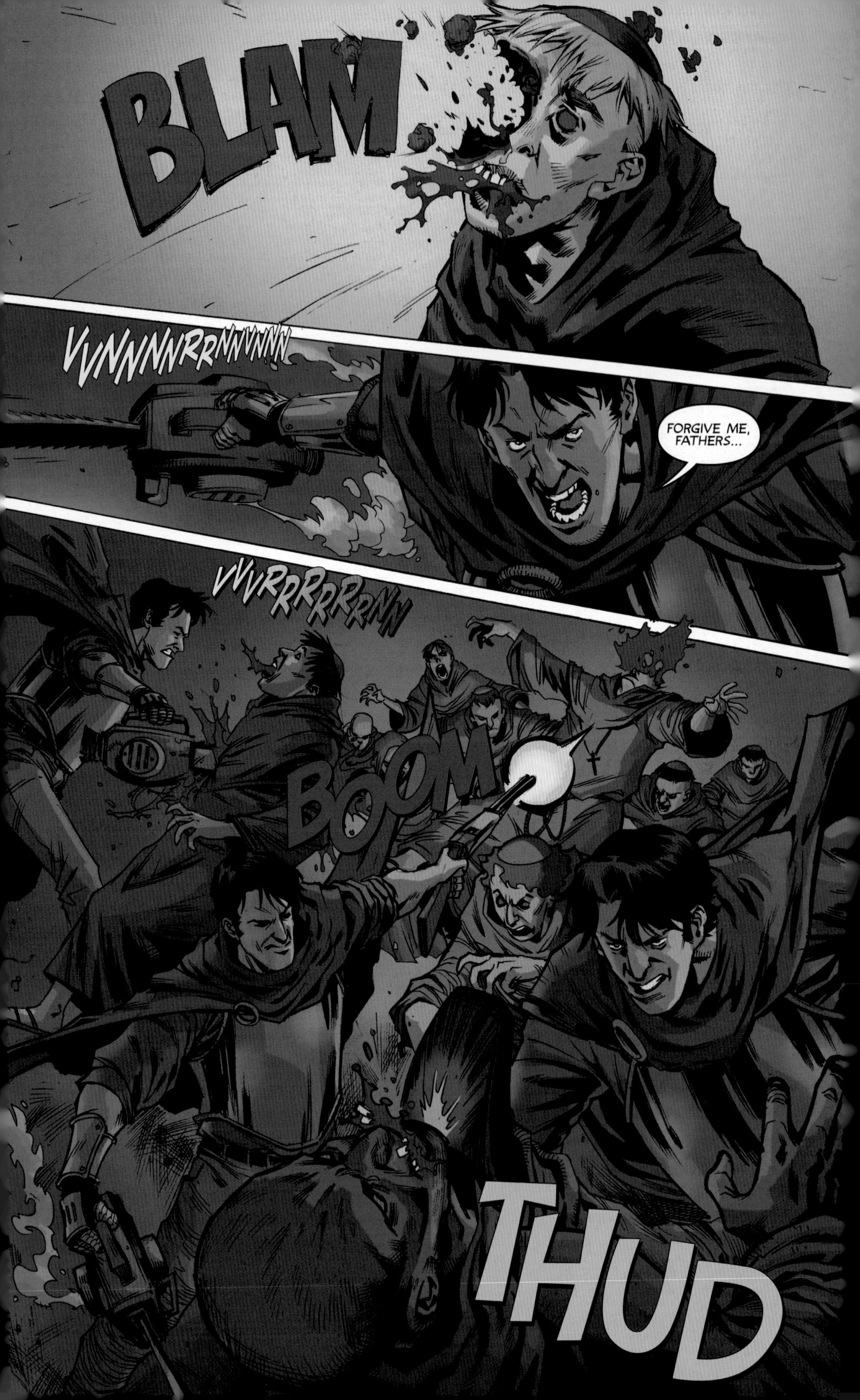
BLAM
VVNNNNRRNNVNNN
FORGIVE ME, FATHERS...
VVVRRRRRRNN
BOOM
THUD

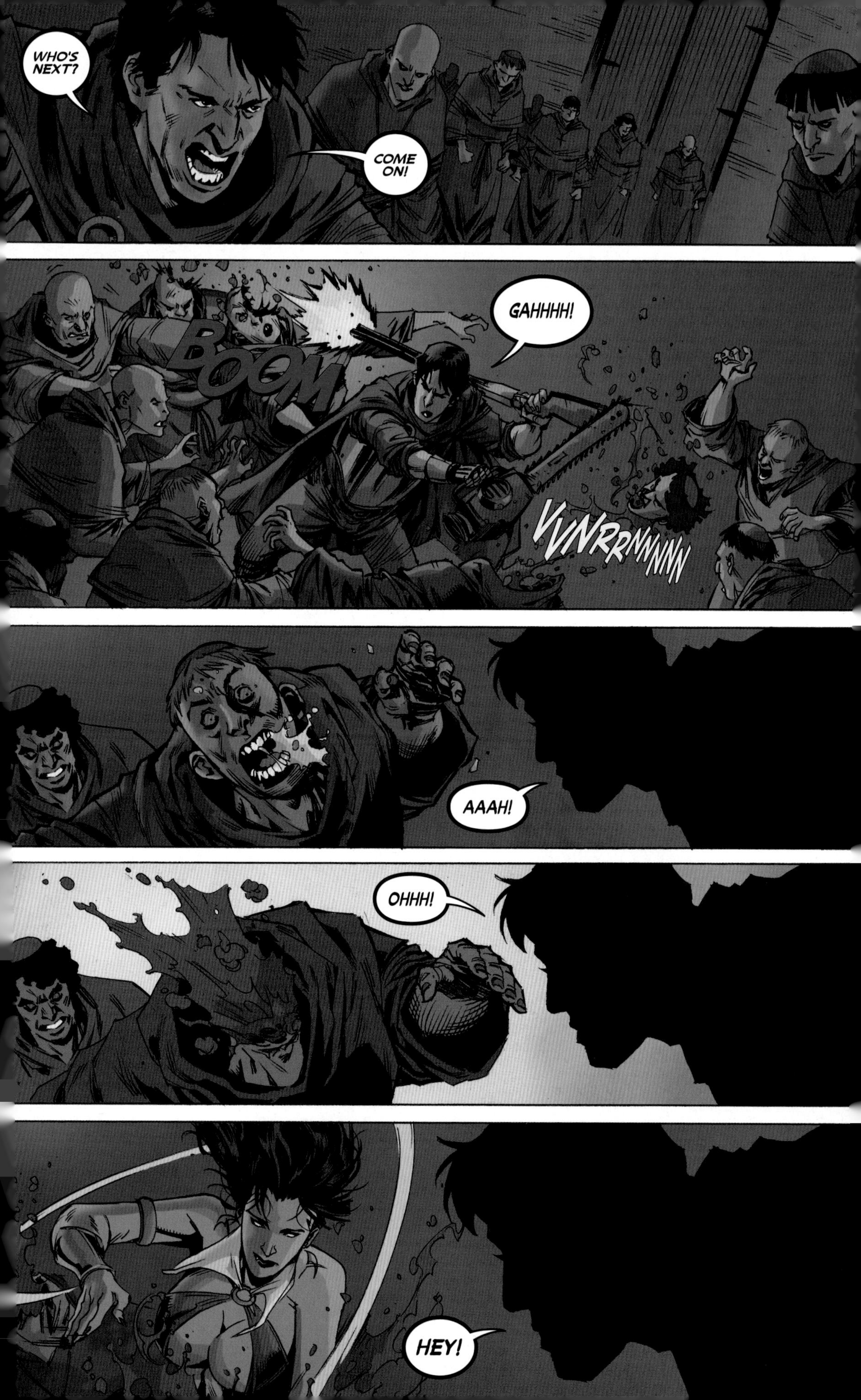
WHO'S NEXT?
COME ON!
BOOM
GAHHHH!
VVNRRNNNNN
AAAH!
OHHH!
HEY!

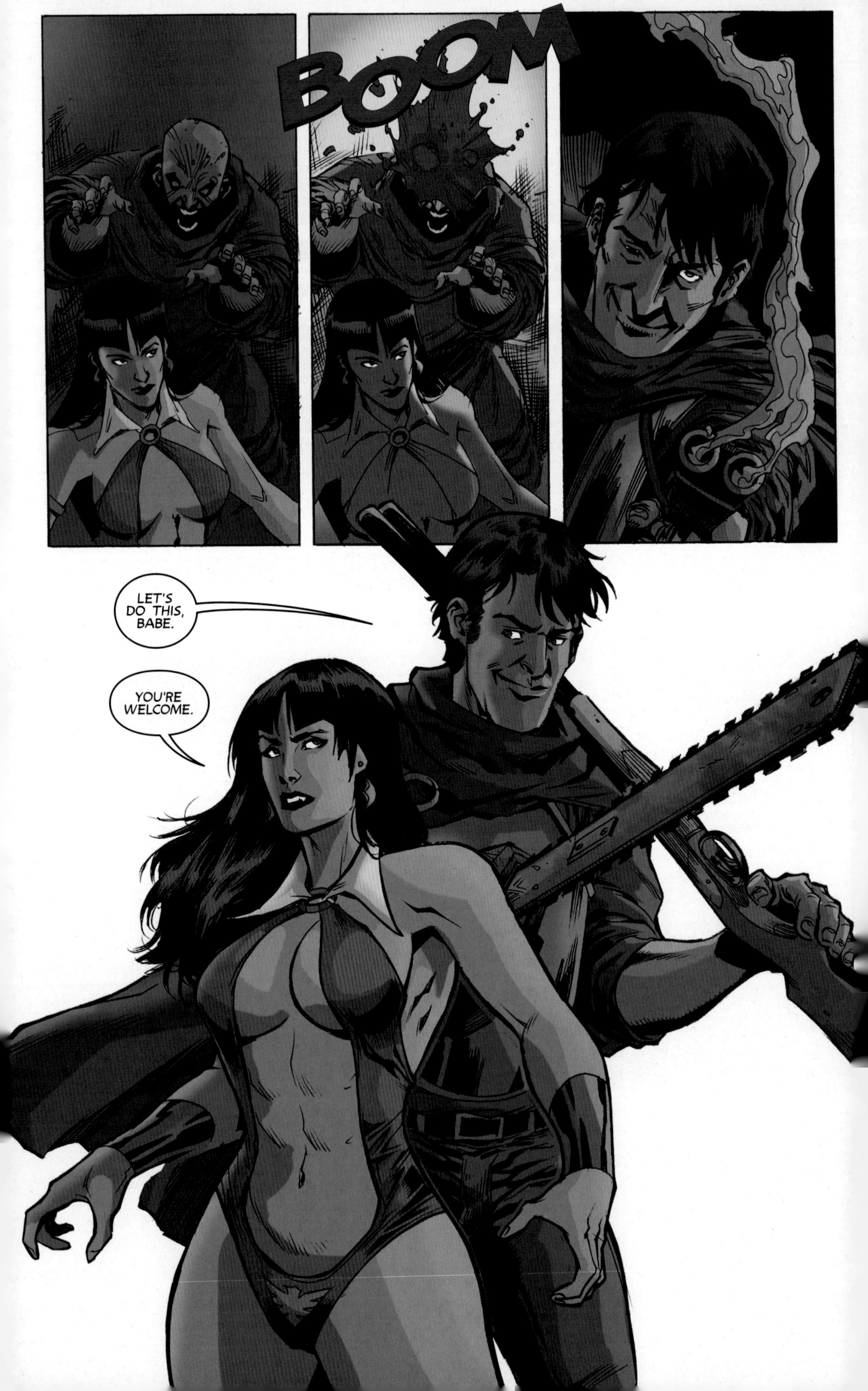
BOOM
LET'S DO THIS, BABE.
YOU'RE WELCOME.

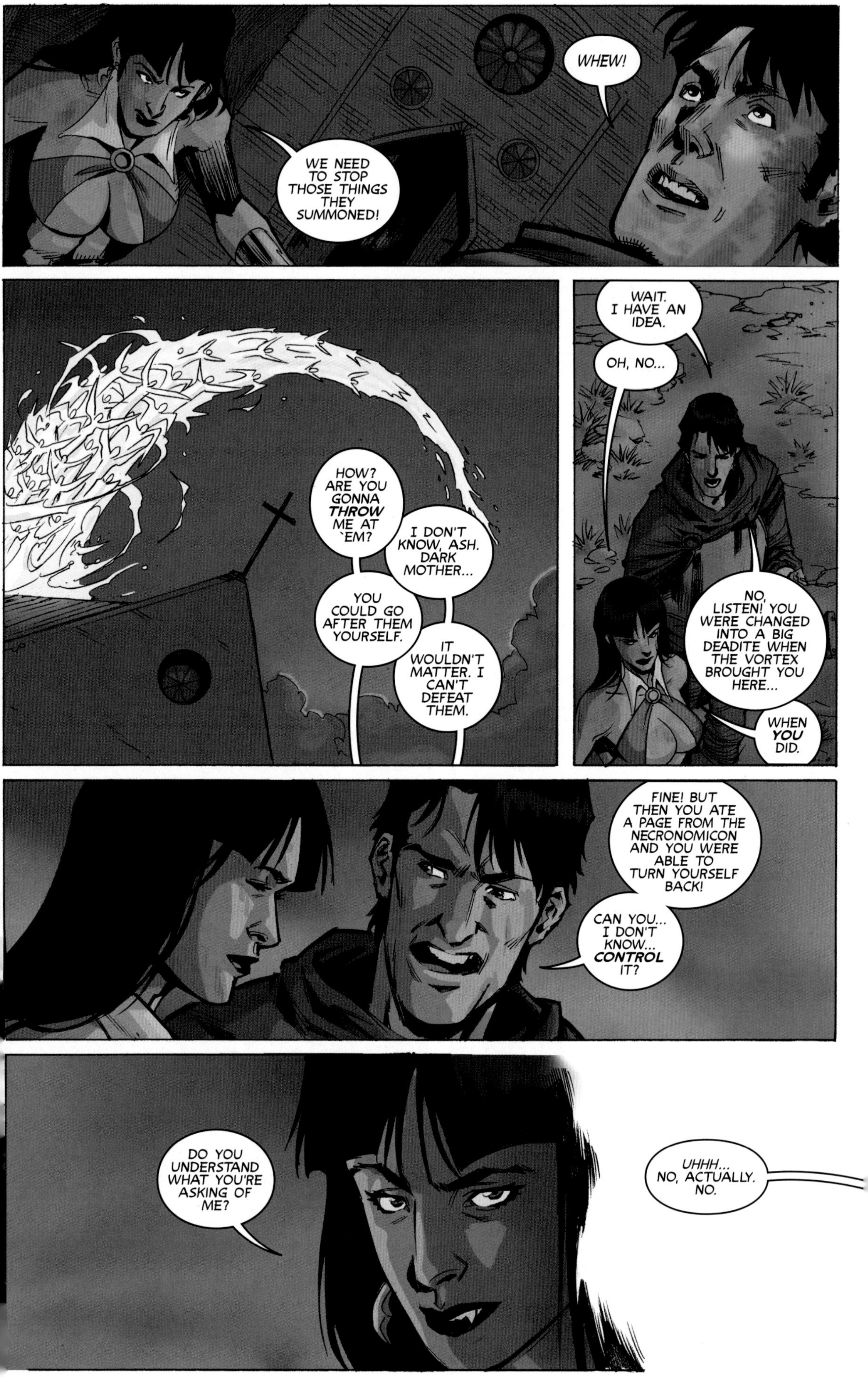
WHEW!
WE NEED TO STOP THOSE THINGS THEY SUMMONED!
HOW? ARE YOU GONNA THROW ME AT `EM?
I DON'T KNOW, ASH. DARK MOTHER...
YOU COULD GO AFTER THEM YOURSELF.
IT WOULDN'T MATTER. I CAN'T DEFEAT THEM.
WAIT. I HAVE AN IDEA.
OH, NO...
NO, LISTEN! YOU WERE CHANGED INTO A BIG DEADITE WHEN THE VORTEX BROUGHT YOU HERE...
WHEN YOU DID.
FINE! BUT THEN YOU ATE A PAGE FROM THE NECRONOMICON AND YOU WERE ABLE TO TURN YOURSELF BACK!
CAN YOU... I DON'T KNOW... CONTROL IT?
DO YOU UNDERSTAND WHAT YOU'RE ASKING OF ME?
UHHH... NO, ACTUALLY. NO.

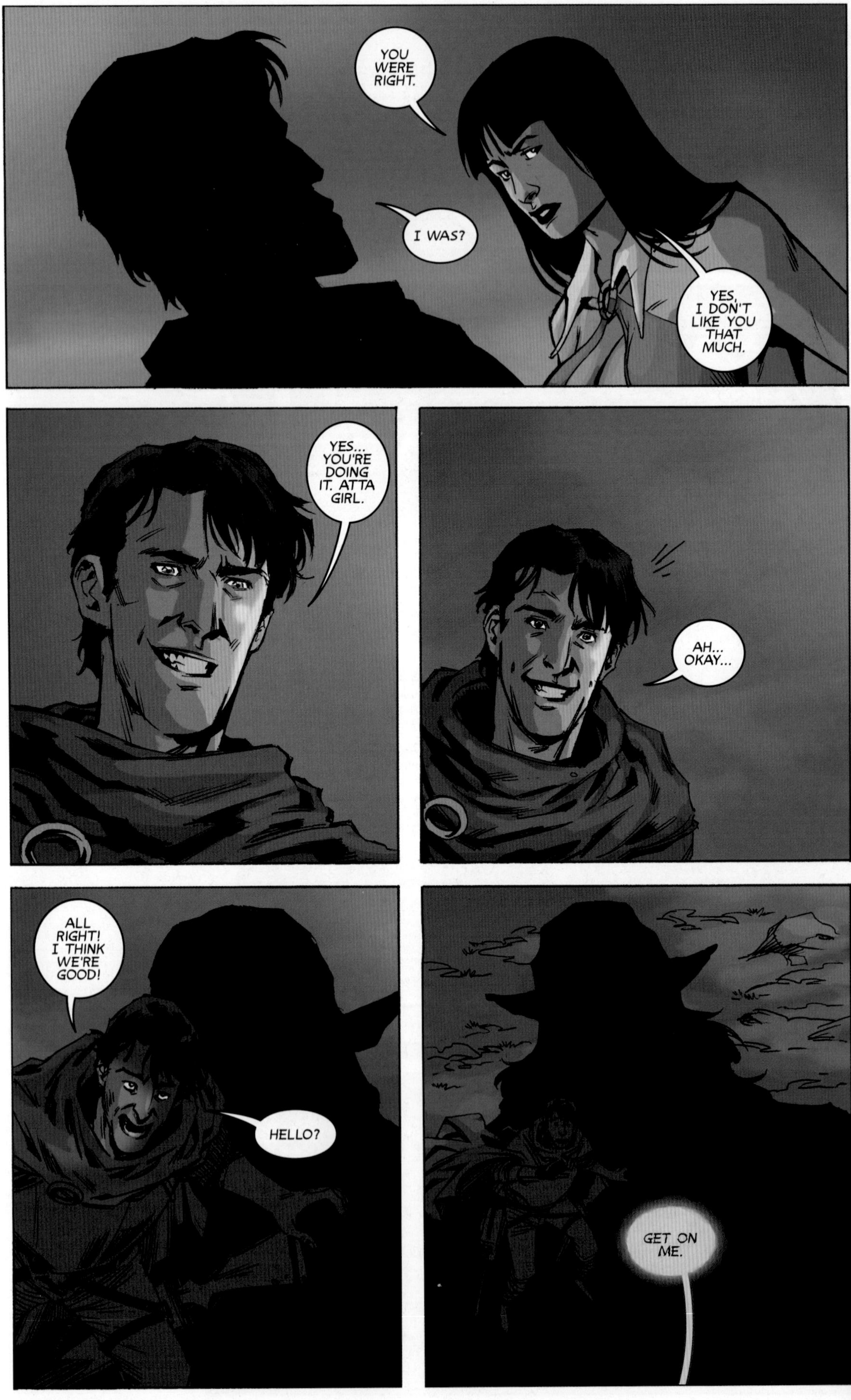
YOU WERE RIGHT.
I WAS?
YES, I DON'T LIKE YOU THAT MUCH.
YES... YOU'RE DOING IT. ATTA GIRL.
AH... OKAY...
ALL RIGHT! I THINK WE'RE GOOD!
HELLO?
GET ON ME.

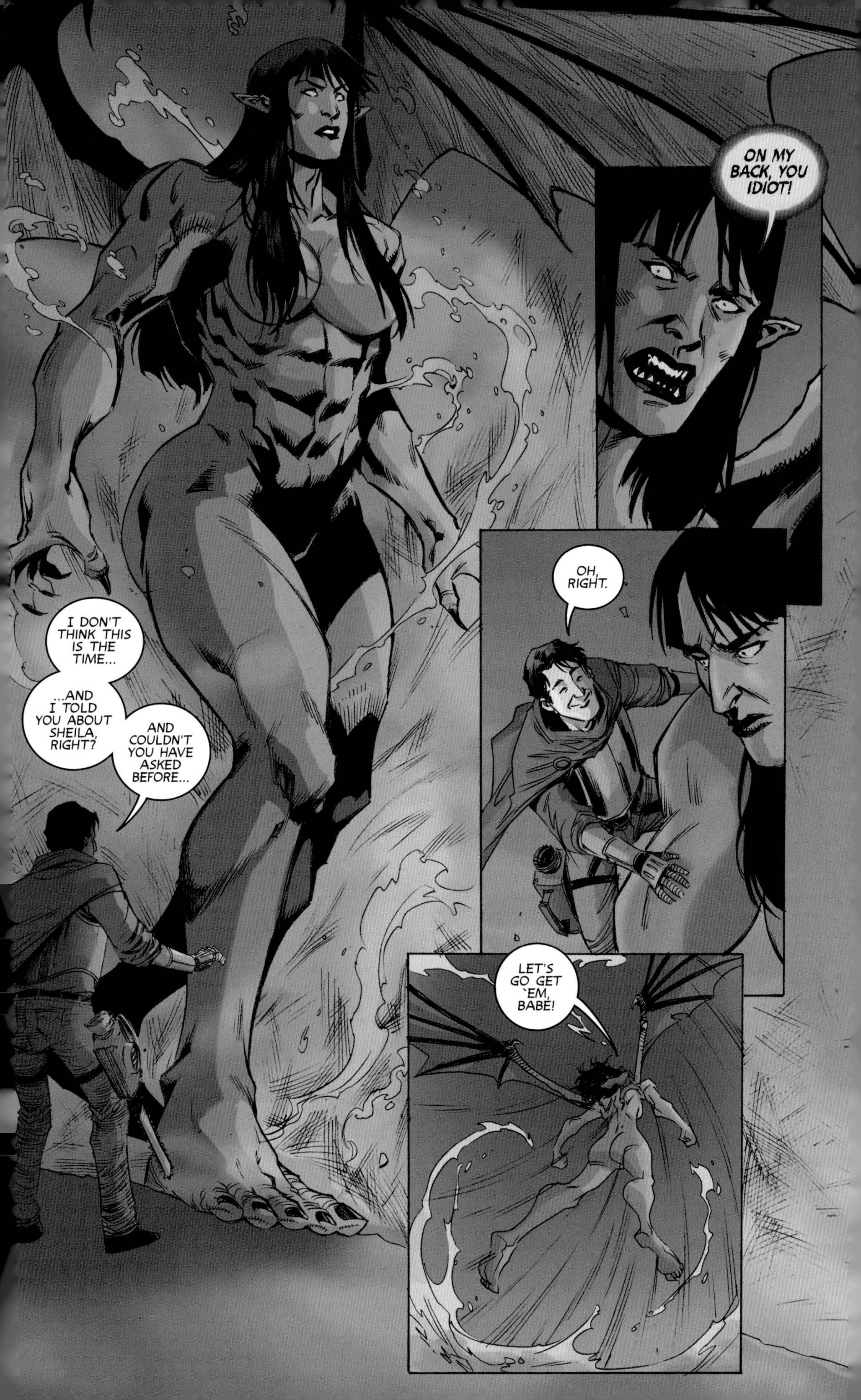
ON MY BACK, YOU IDIOT!
I DON'T THINK THIS IS THE TIME...
...AND I TOLD YOU ABOUT SHEILA, RIGHT?
AND COULDN'T YOU HAVE ASKED BEFORE...
OH, RIGHT.
LET'S GO GET `EM, BABE!

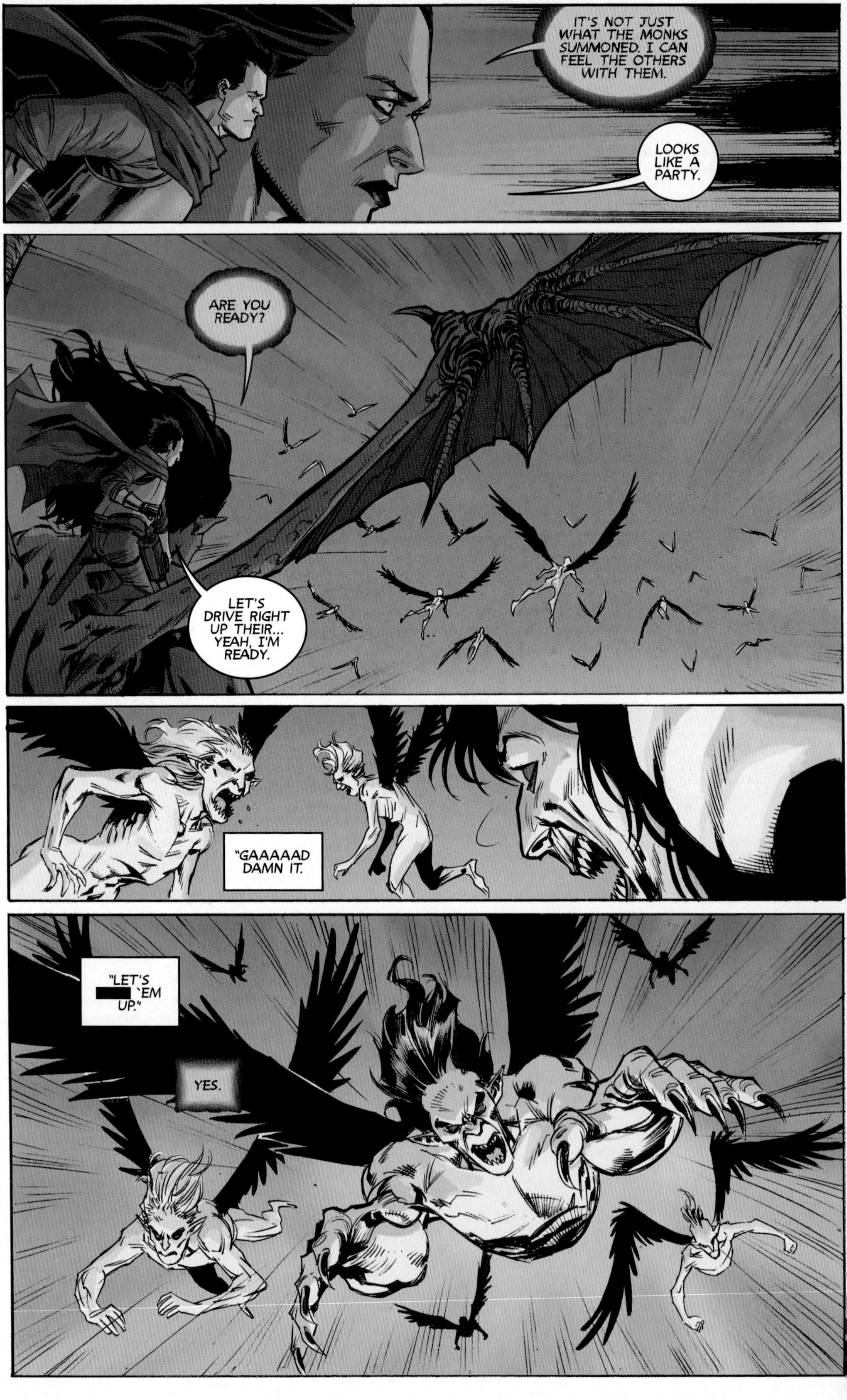
IT'S NOT JUST WHAT THE MONKS SUMMONED. I CAN FEEL THE OTHERS WITH THEM.
LOOKS LIKE A PARTY.
ARE YOU READY?
LET'S DRIVE RIGHT UP THEIR... YEAH, I'M READY.
"GAAAAAD DAMN IT.
"LET'S [redacted] `EM UP."
YES.

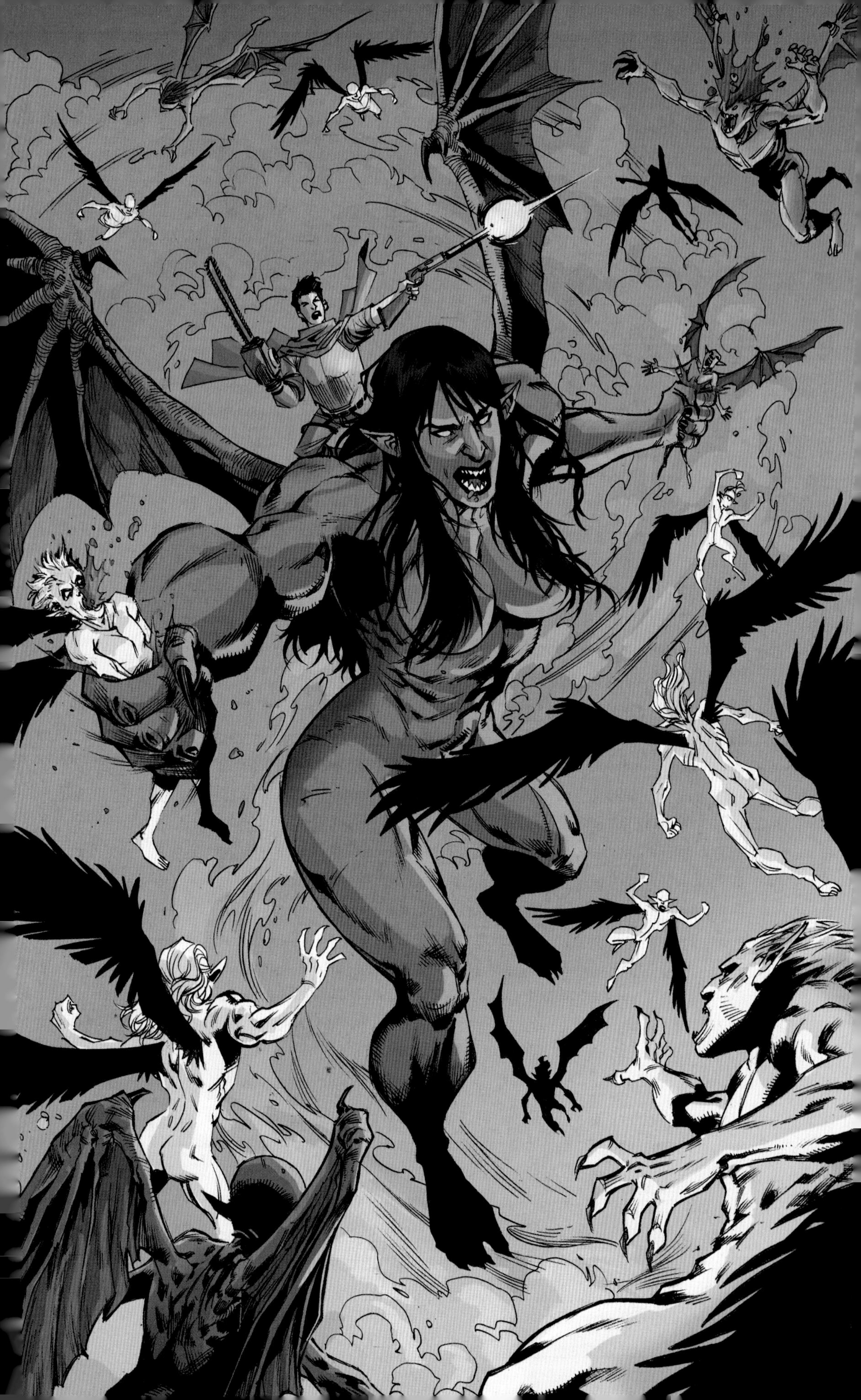

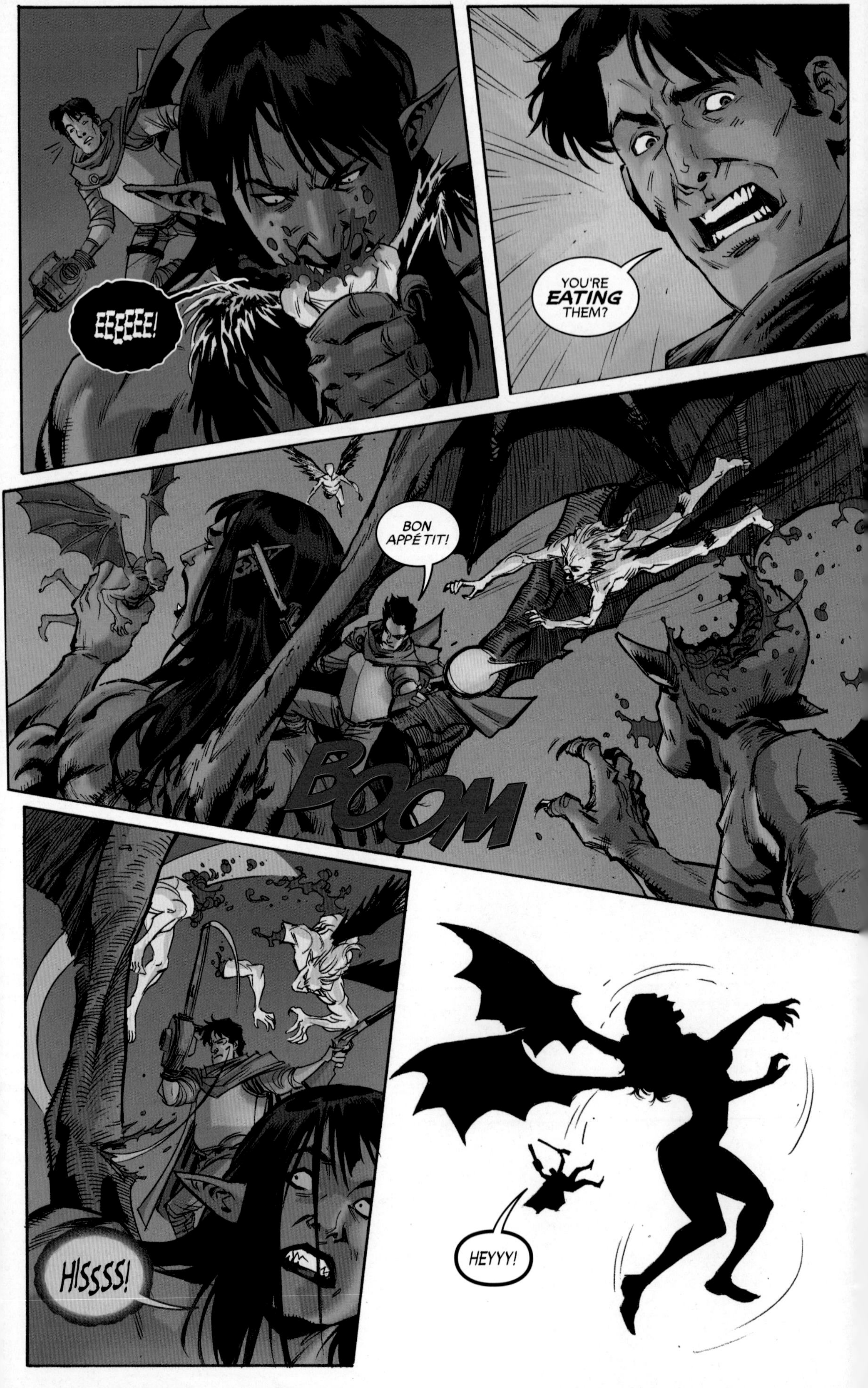
EEEEEE!
YOU'RE EATING THEM?
BON APPÉTIT!
BOOM
HISSSS!
HEYYY!

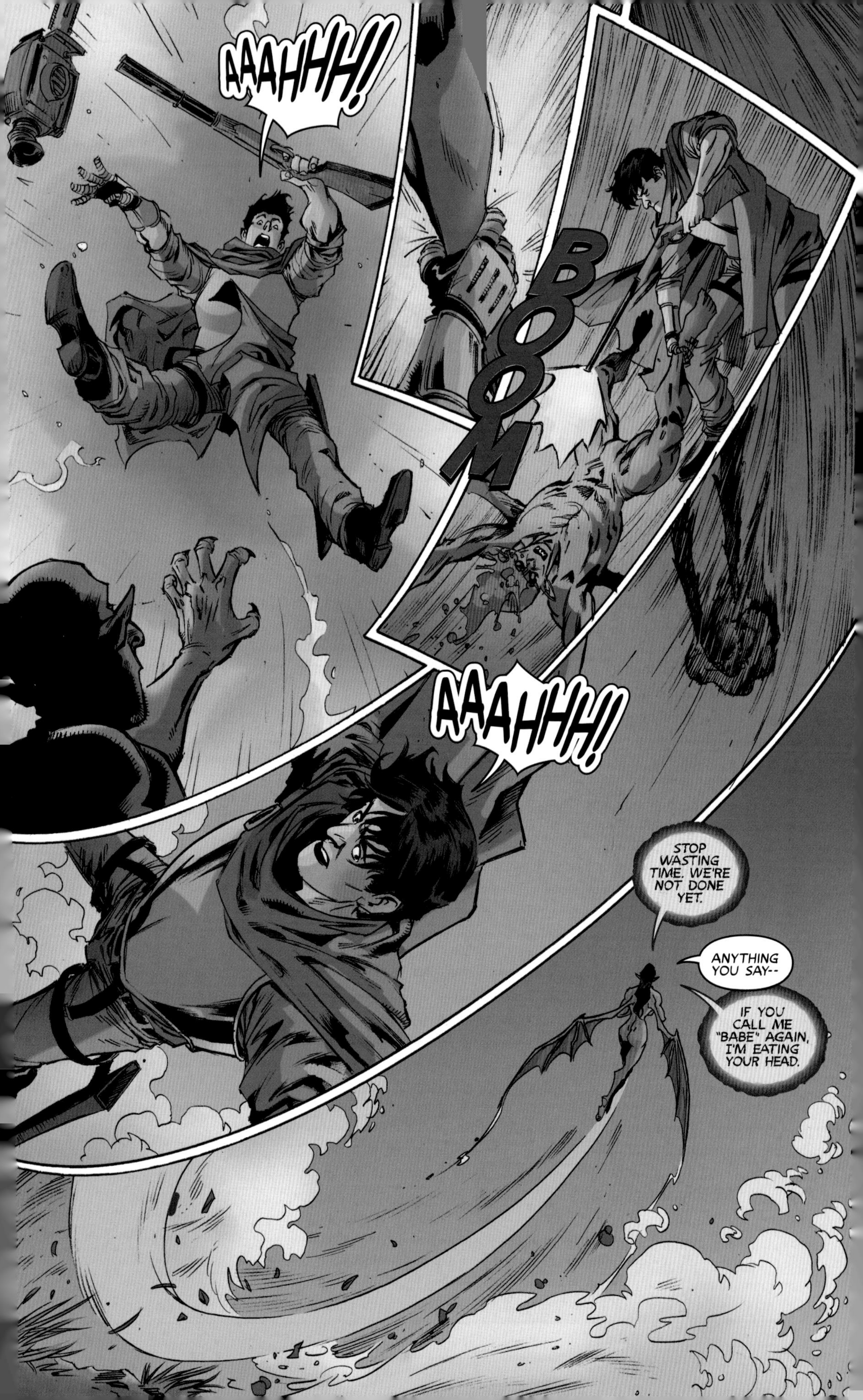
AAAHHH!!
BOOOM
AAAHHH!!
STOP WASTING TIME. WE'RE NOT DONE YET.
ANYTHING YOU SAY--
IF YOU CALL ME "BABE" AGAIN, I'M EATING YOUR HEAD.

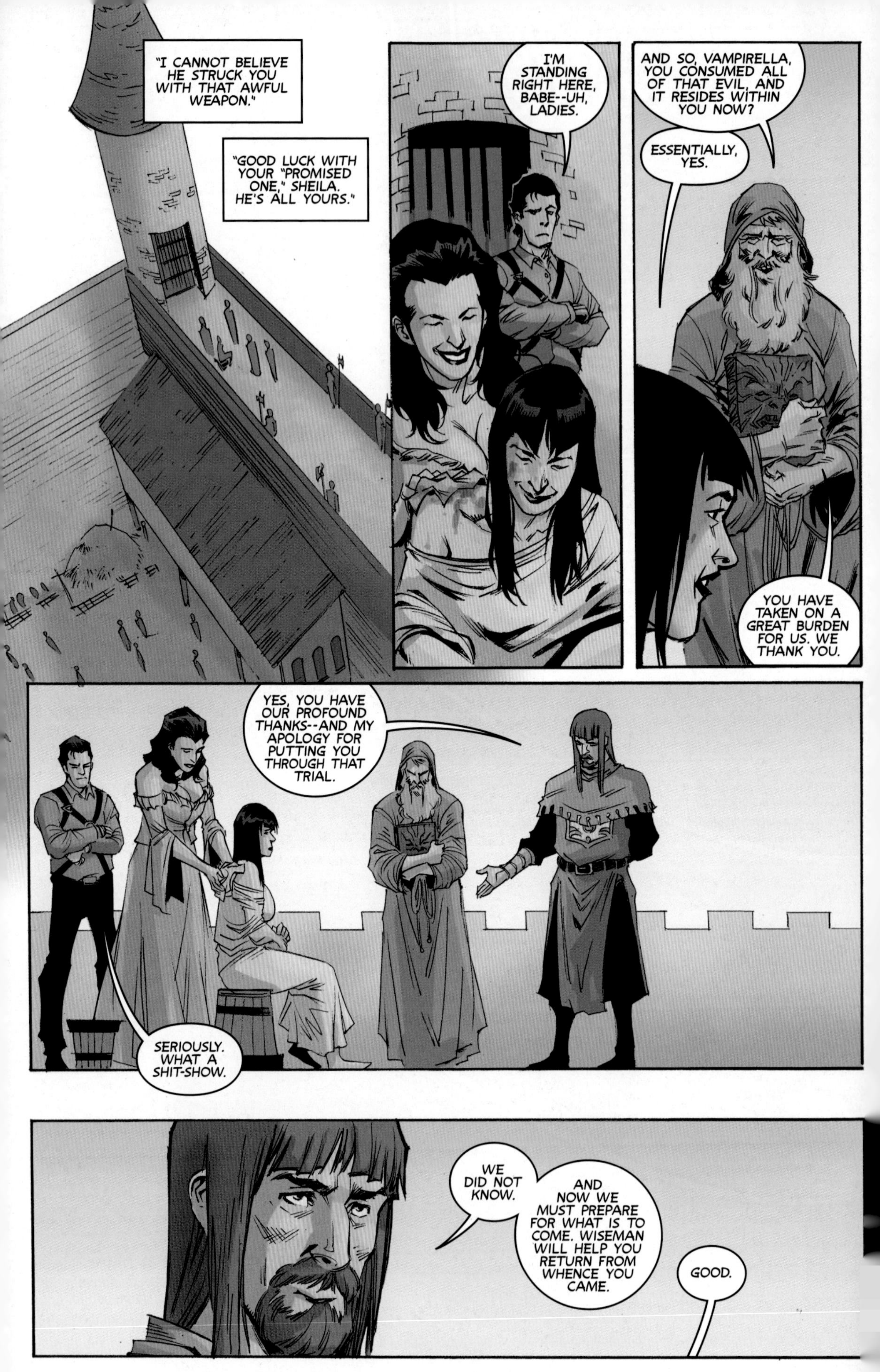
"I CANNOT BELIEVE HE STRUCK YOU WITH THAT AWFUL WEAPON."
"GOOD LUCK WITH YOUR "PROMISED ONE," SHEILA. HE'S ALL YOURS."
I'M STANDING RIGHT HERE, BABE--UH, LADIES.
AND SO, VAMPIRELLA, YOU CONSUMED ALL OF THAT EVIL, AND IT RESIDES WITHIN YOU NOW?
ESSENTIALLY, YES.
YOU HAVE TAKEN ON A GREAT BURDEN FOR US. WE THANK YOU.
YES, YOU HAVE OUR PROFOUND THANKS--AND MY APOLOGY FOR PUTTING YOU THROUGH THAT TRIAL.
SERIOUSLY. WHAT A SHIT-SHOW.
WE DID NOT KNOW.
AND NOW WE MUST PREPARE FOR WHAT IS TO COME. WISEMAN WILL HELP YOU RETURN FROM WHENCE YOU CAME.
GOOD.

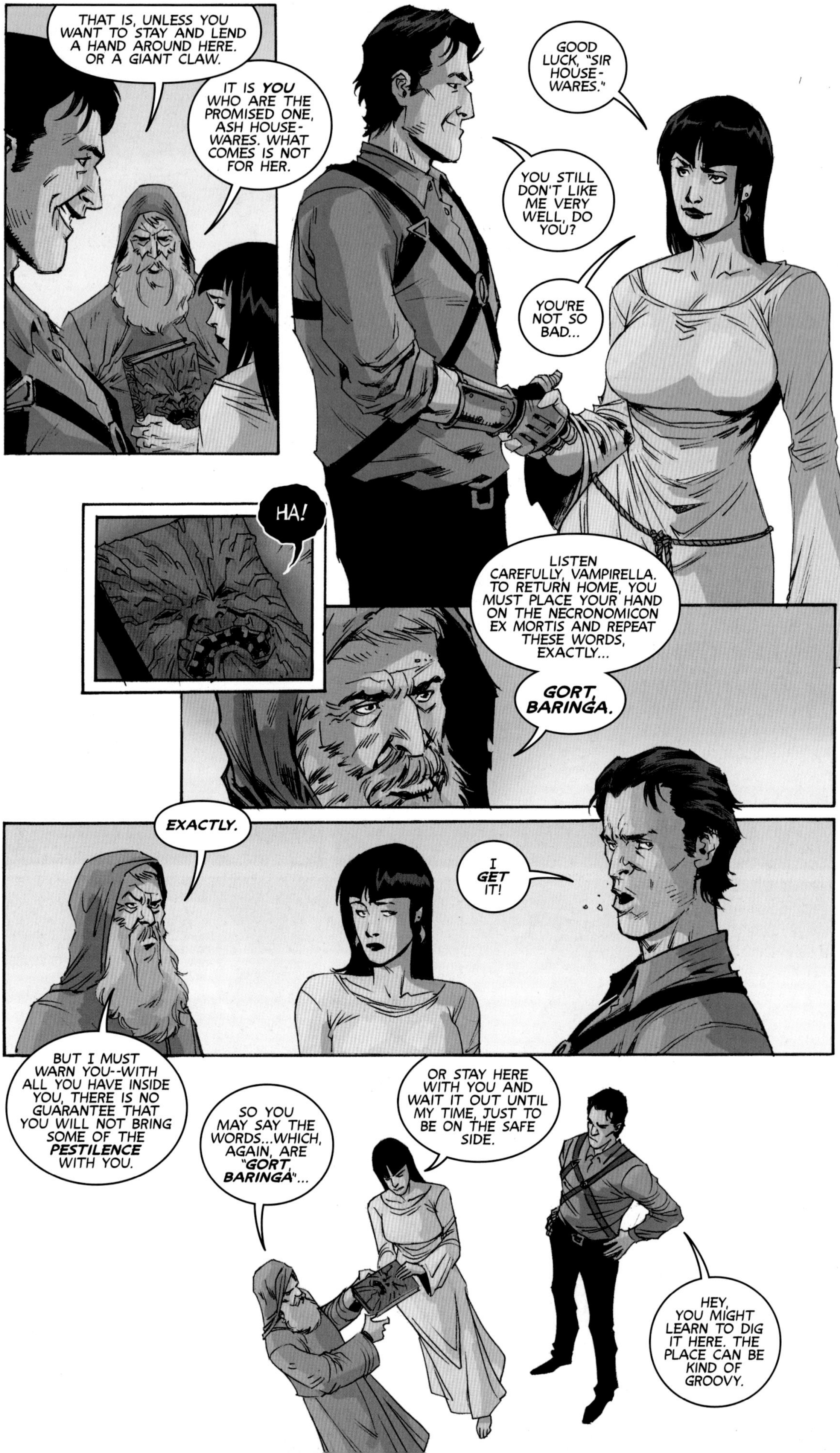

THAT IS, UNLESS YOU WANT TO STAY AND LEND A HAND AROUND HERE. OR A GIANT CLAW.
IT IS YOU WHO ARE THE PROMISED ONE, ASH HOUSE-WARES. WHAT COMES IS NOT FOR HER.
GOOD LUCK, "SIR HOUSE-WARES."
YOU STILL DON'T LIKE ME VERY WELL, DO YOU?
YOU'RE NOT SO BAD...
HA!
LISTEN CAREFULLY, VAMPIRELLA. TO RETURN HOME, YOU MUST PLACE YOUR HAND ON THE NECRONOMICON EX MORTIS AND REPEAT THESE WORDS, EXACTLY...
GORT, BARINGA.
EXACTLY.
I GET IT!
BUT I MUST WARN YOU--WITH ALL YOU HAVE INSIDE YOU, THERE IS NO GUARANTEE THAT YOU WILL NOT BRING SOME OF THE PESTILENCE WITH YOU.
SO YOU MAY SAY THE WORDS...WHICH, AGAIN, ARE "GORT, BARINGA"...
OR STAY HERE WITH YOU AND WAIT IT OUT UNTIL MY TIME, JUST TO BE ON THE SAFE SIDE.
HEY, YOU MIGHT LEARN TO DIG IT HERE. THE PLACE CAN BE KIND OF GROOVY.

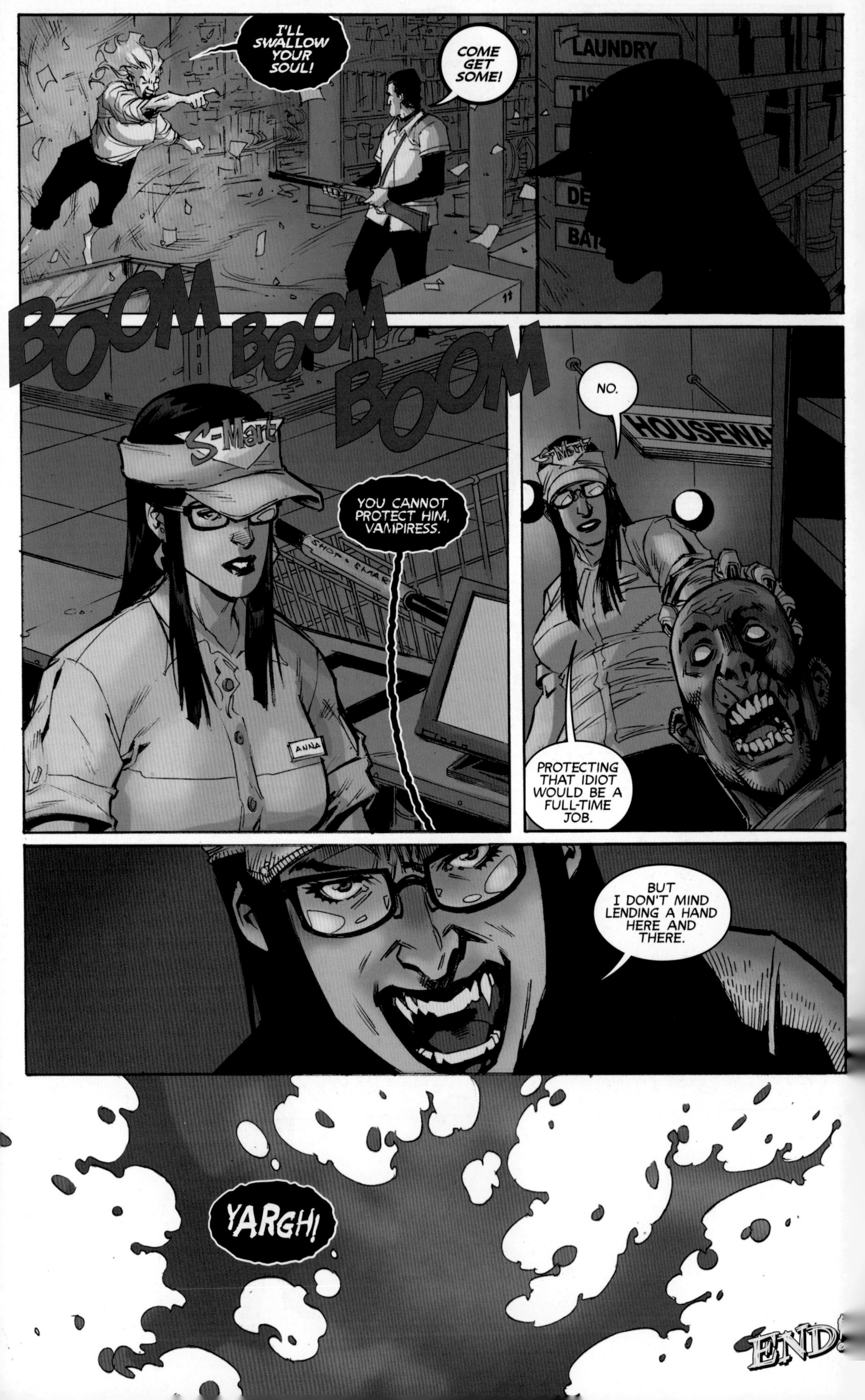
I'LL SWALLOW YOUR SOUL!
COME GET SOME!
LAUNDRY
BOOM BOOM BOOM
S-Mart
YOU CANNOT PROTECT HIM, VAMPIRESS.
ANNA
NO.
HOUSEWA
PROTECTING THAT IDIOT WOULD BE A FULL-TIME JOB.
BUT I DON'T MIND LENDING A HAND HERE AND THERE.
YARGH!
END!

COVER
GALLERY

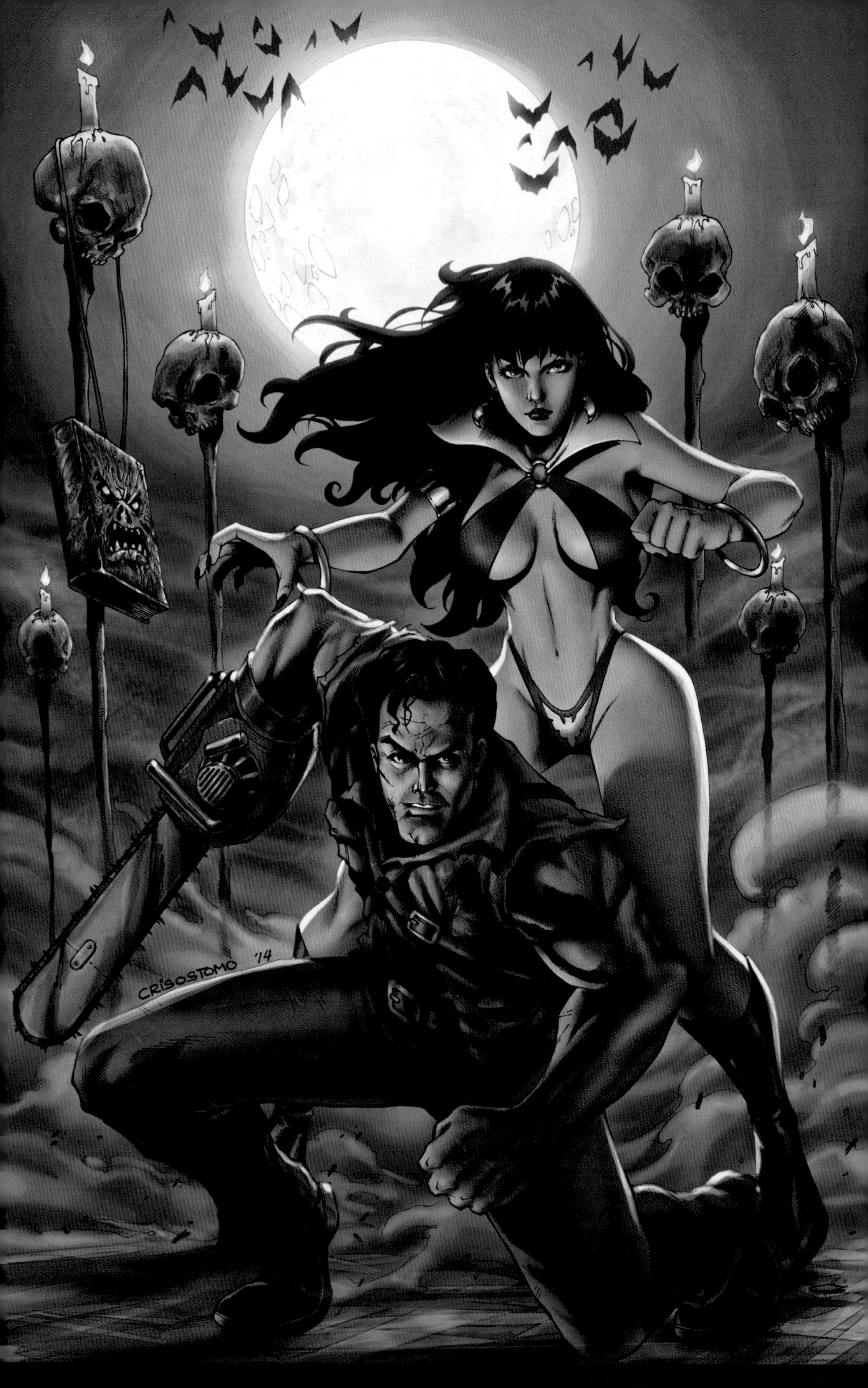
CRISOSTOMO '14

ISSUE #1 SECOND PRINT COVER ART BY DENNIS CRISOSTOMO

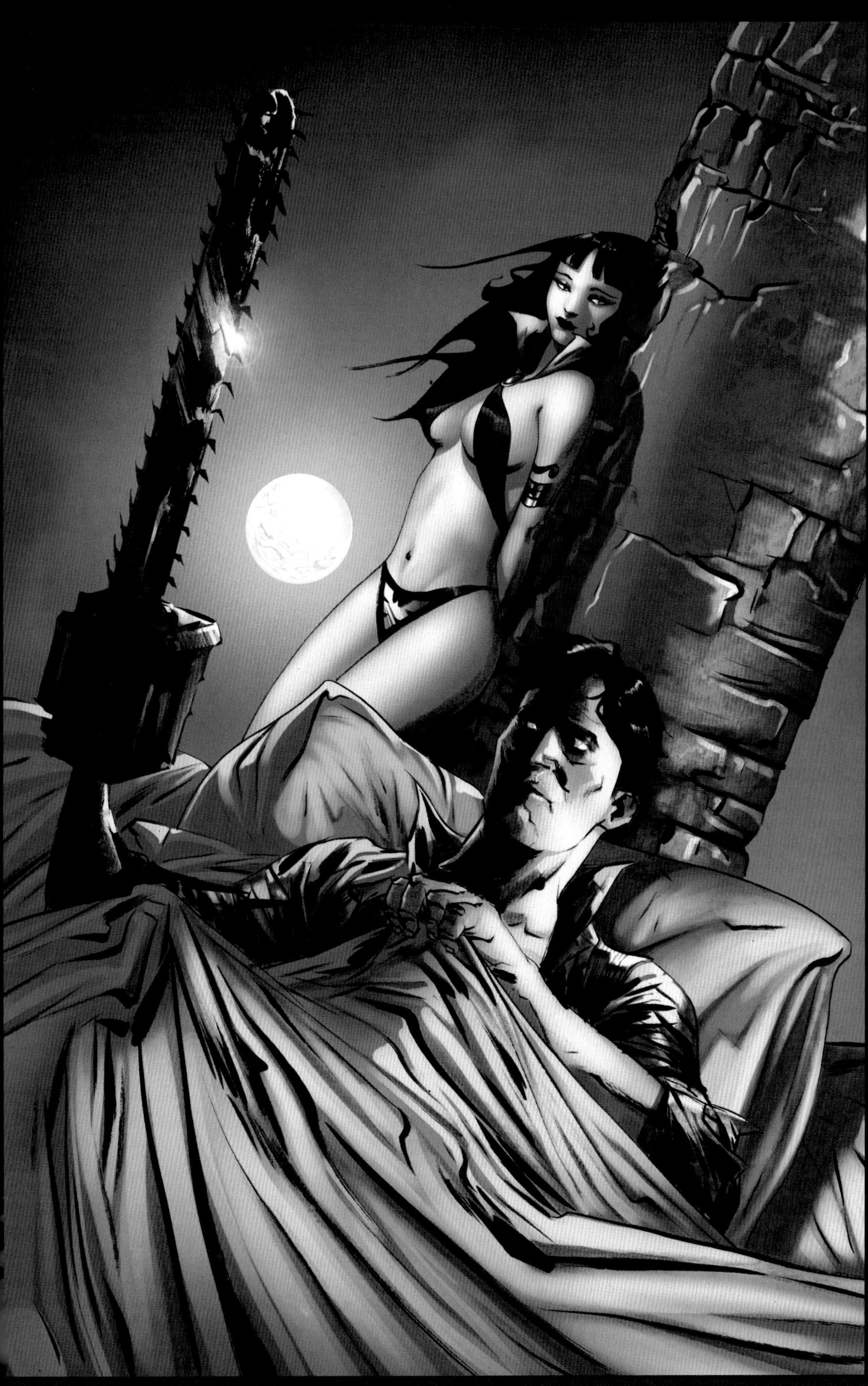

ISSUE #1 COVER ART BY JAE LEE COLORS BY IVAN NUNES

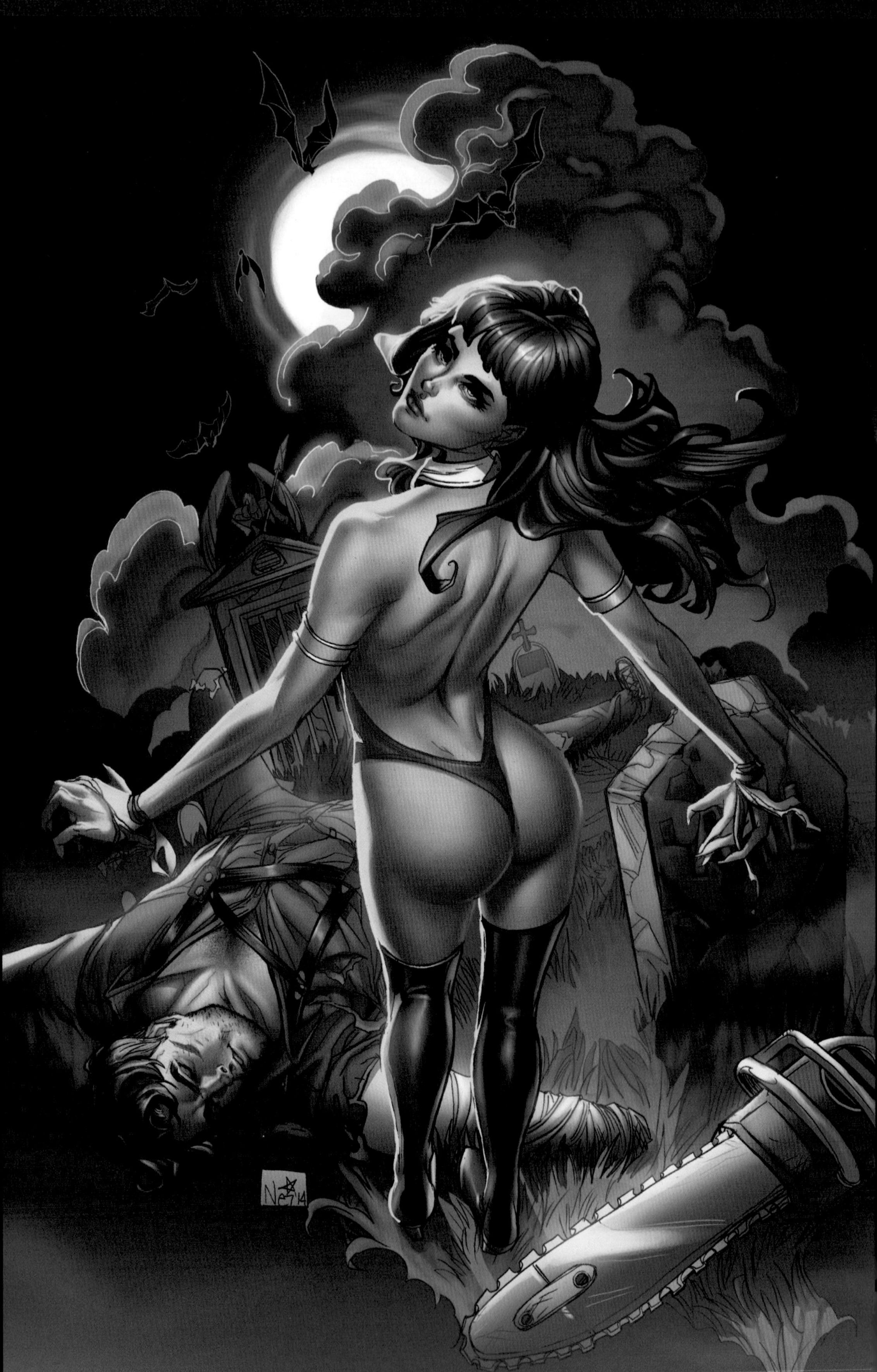

ISSUE #1 CONNECTICUT COMICONN EXCLUSIVE COVER ART BY NEI RUFFINO

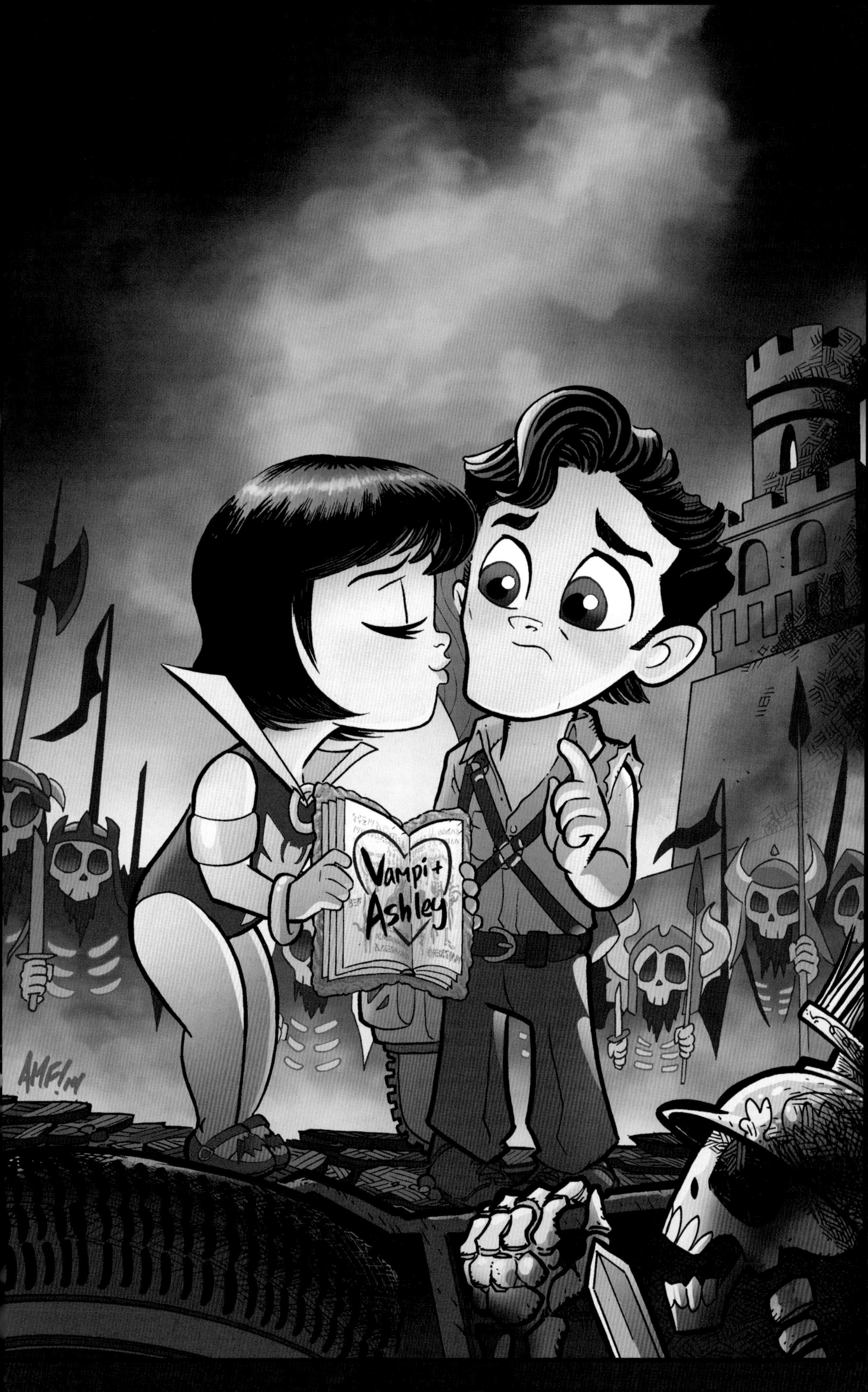
Vampi + Ashley
AMF! '14

ISSUE #1 COVER ART BY TONY FLEECS

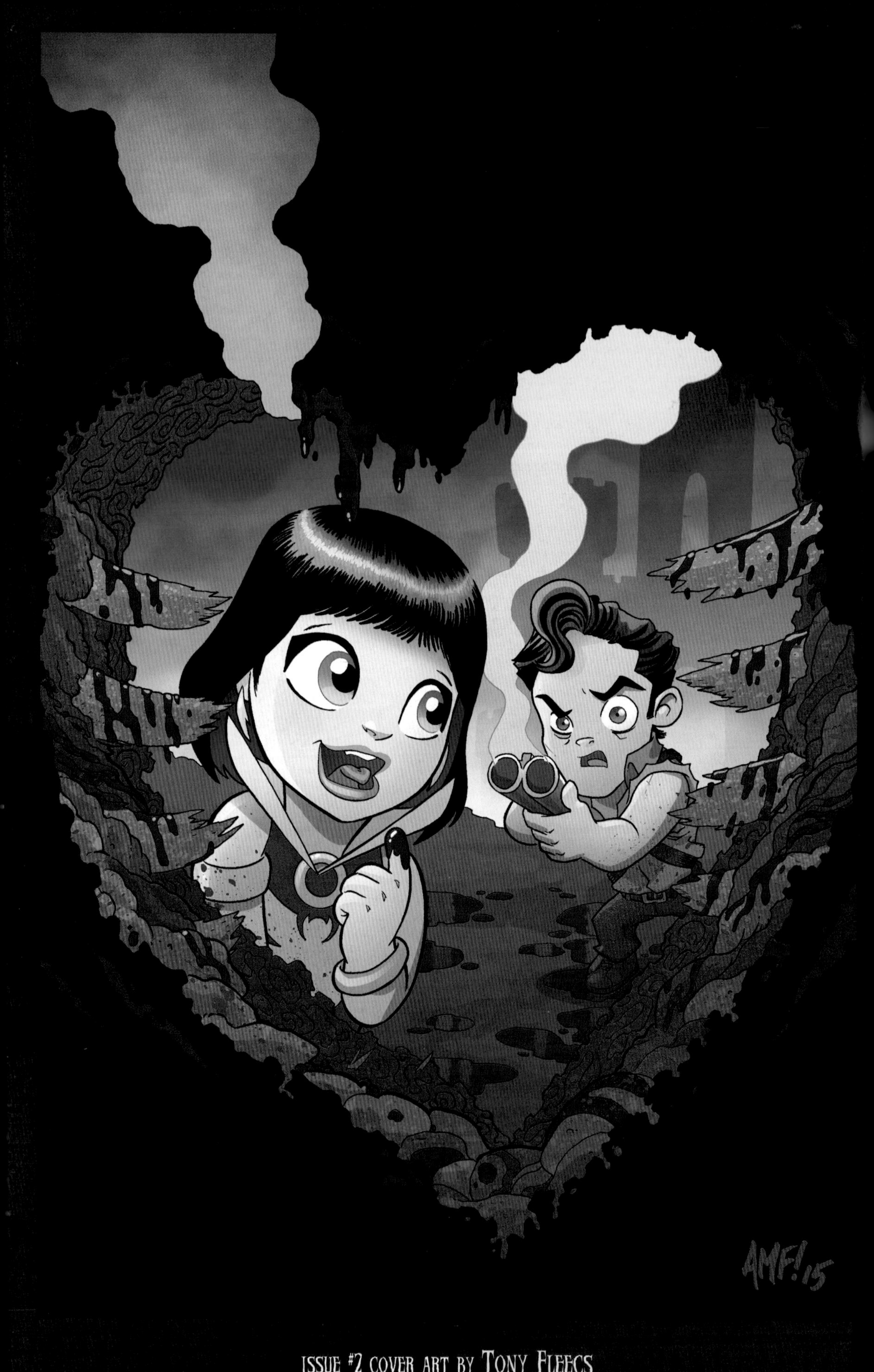

ISSUE #2 COVER ART BY TONY FLEECS

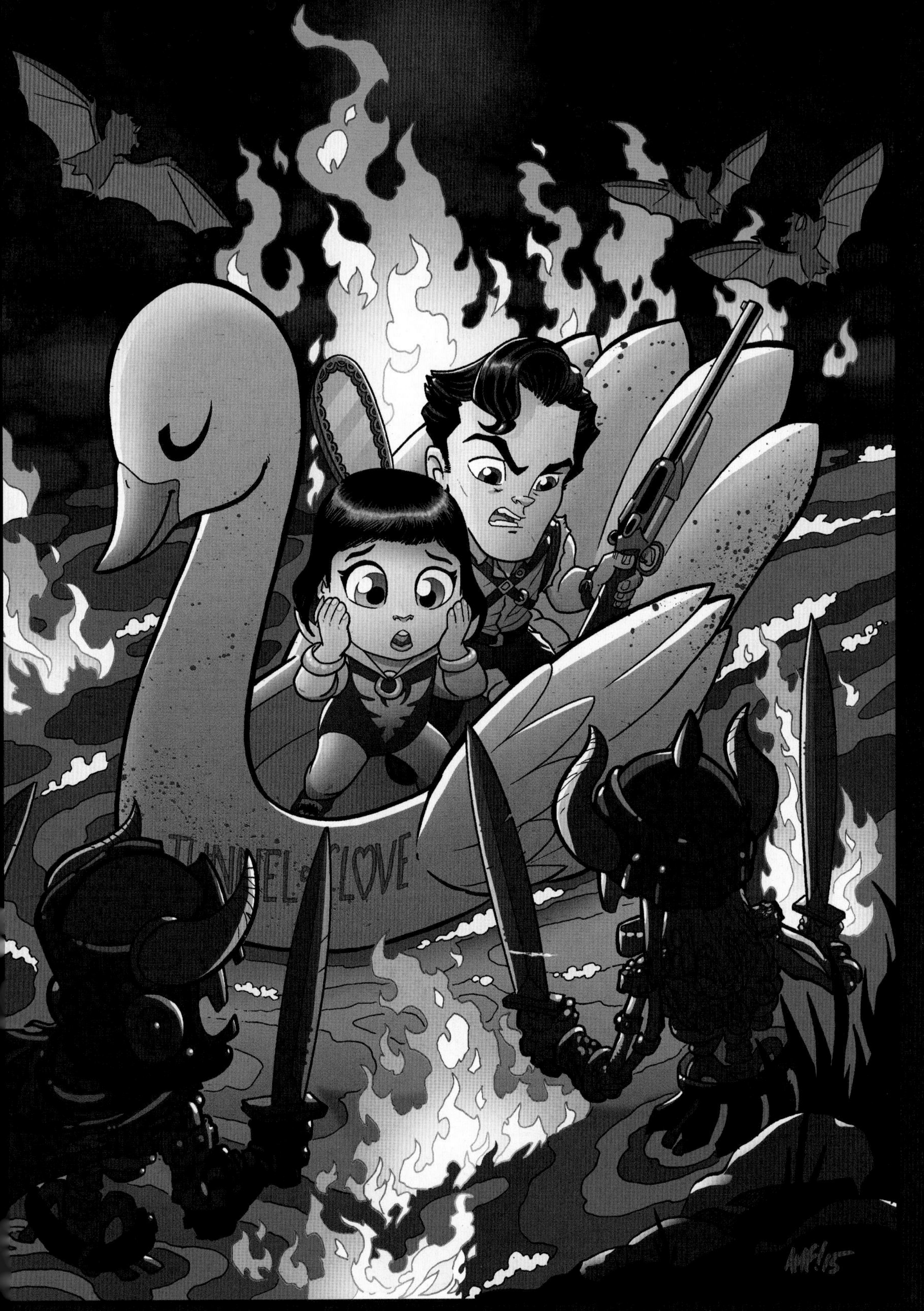
TUNNEL LOVE

ISSUE #3 COVER ART BY TONY FLEECS

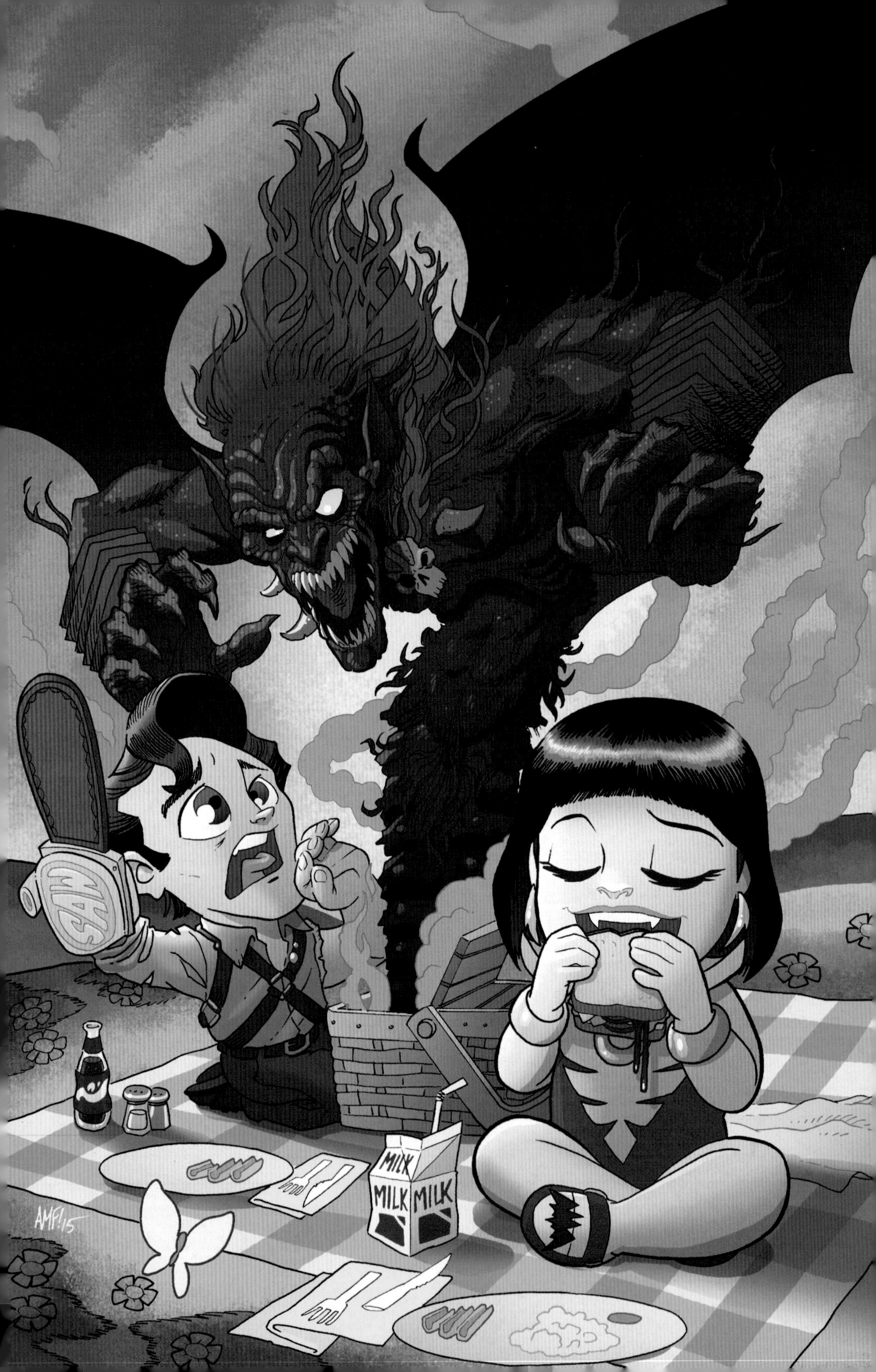
SAM
MILK
MILK MILK
AMF!15

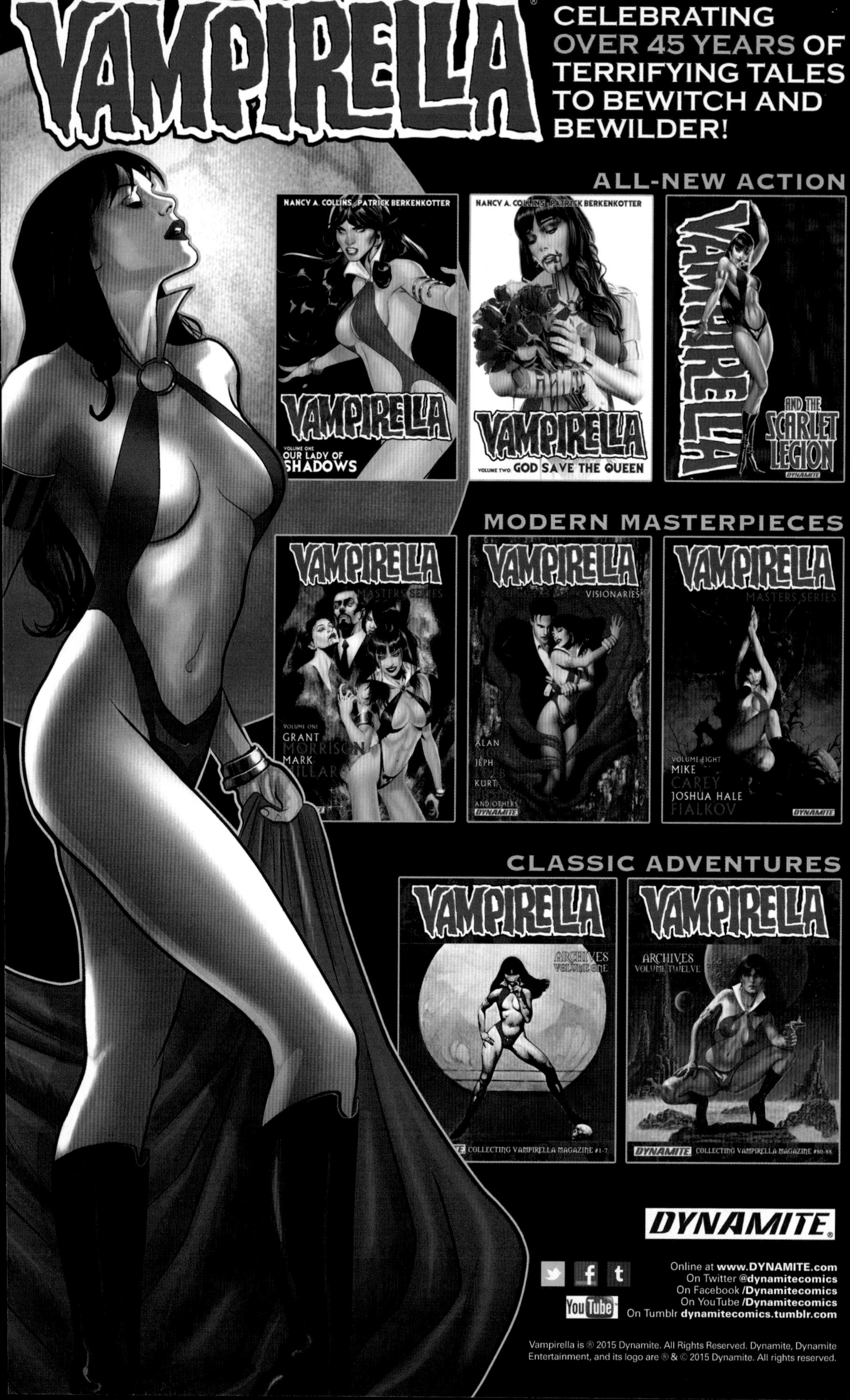
VAMPIRELLA
CELEBRATING OVER 45 YEARS OF TERRIFYING TALES TO BEWITCH AND BEWILDER!
ALL-NEW ACTION
NANCY A. COLLINS · PATRICK BERKENKOTTER
VAMPIRELLA
VOLUME ONE OUR LADY OF SHADOWS
NANCY A. COLLINS · PATRICK BERKENKOTTER
VAMPIRELLA
VOLUME TWO: GOD SAVE THE QUEEN
VAMPIRELLA AND THE SCARLET LEGION
DYNAMITE
MODERN MASTERPIECES
VAMPIRELLA
MASTERS SERIES
VOLUME ONE
GRANT MORRISON
MARK MILLAR
VAMPIRELLA
VISIONARIES
ALAN MOORE
JEPH LOEB
KURT BUSIEK
AND OTHERS
DYNAMITE
VAMPIRELLA
MASTERS SERIES
VOLUME EIGHT
MIKE CAREY
JOSHUA HALE FIALKOV
DYNAMITE
CLASSIC ADVENTURES
VAMPIRELLA
ARCHIVES VOLUME ONE
COLLECTING VAMPIRELLA MAGAZINE #1-7
VAMPIRELLA
ARCHIVES VOLUME TWELVE
DYNAMITE
COLLECTING VAMPIRELLA MAGAZINE #80-88
DYNAMITE
Online at www.DYNAMITE.com
On Twitter @dynamitecomics
On Facebook /Dynamitecomics
On YouTube /Dynamitecomics
On Tumblr dynamitecomics.tumblr.com
Vampirella is ® 2015 Dynamite. All Rights Reserved. Dynamite, Dynamite Entertainment, and its logo are ® & © 2015 Dynamite. All rights reserved.

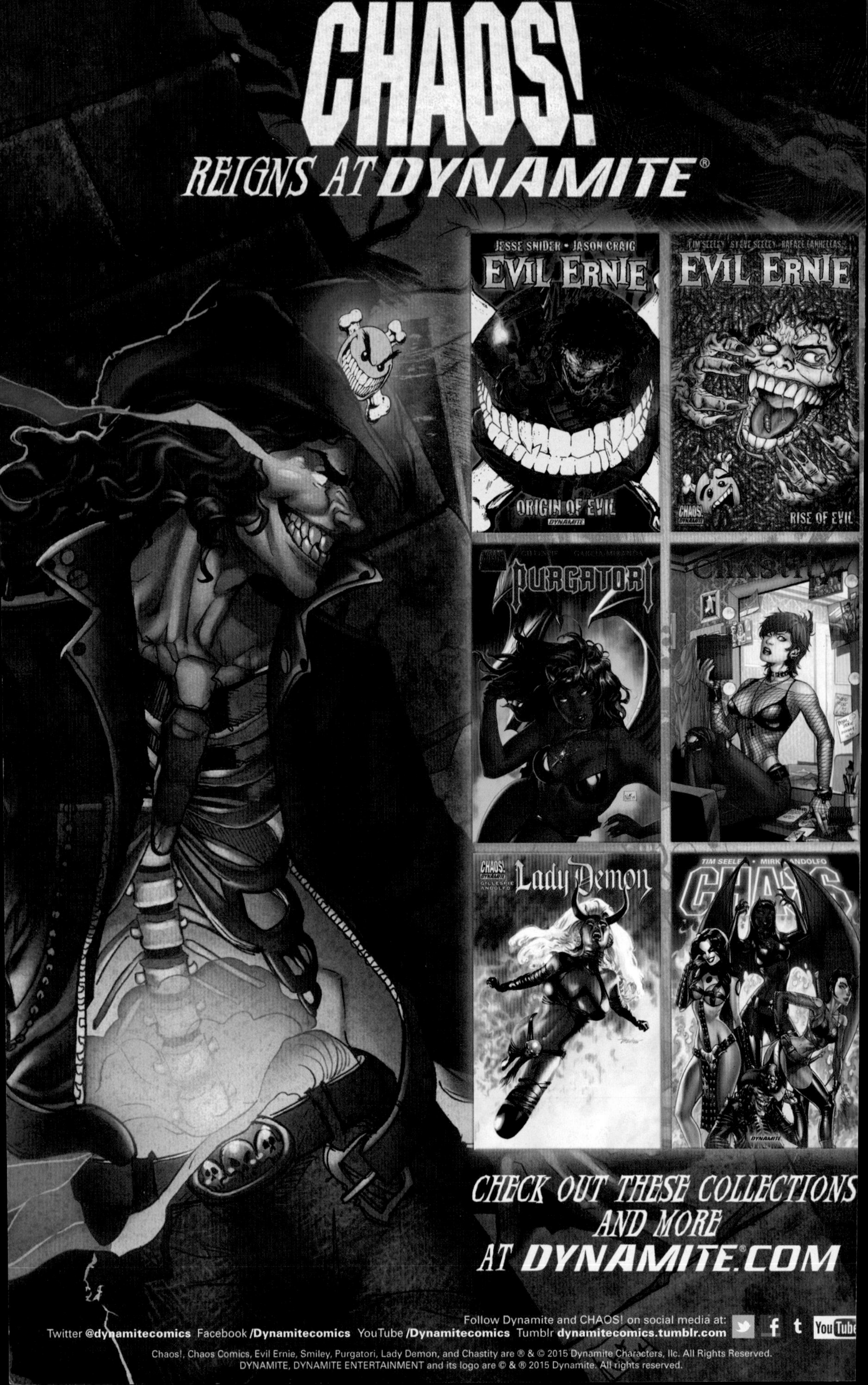

CHAOS!
REIGNS AT DYNAMITE®
JESSE SNIDER • JASON CRAIG
EVIL ERNIE
ORIGIN OF EVIL
DYNAMITE
EVIL ERNIE
RISE OF EVIL
PURGATORI
Lady Demon
GILLESPIE
ANDOLFO
CHECK OUT THESE COLLECTIONS
AND MORE
AT DYNAMITE®.COM
Follow Dynamite and CHAOS! on social media at:
Twitter @dynamitecomics Facebook /Dynamitecomics YouTube /Dynamitecomics Tumblr dynamitecomics.tumblr.com

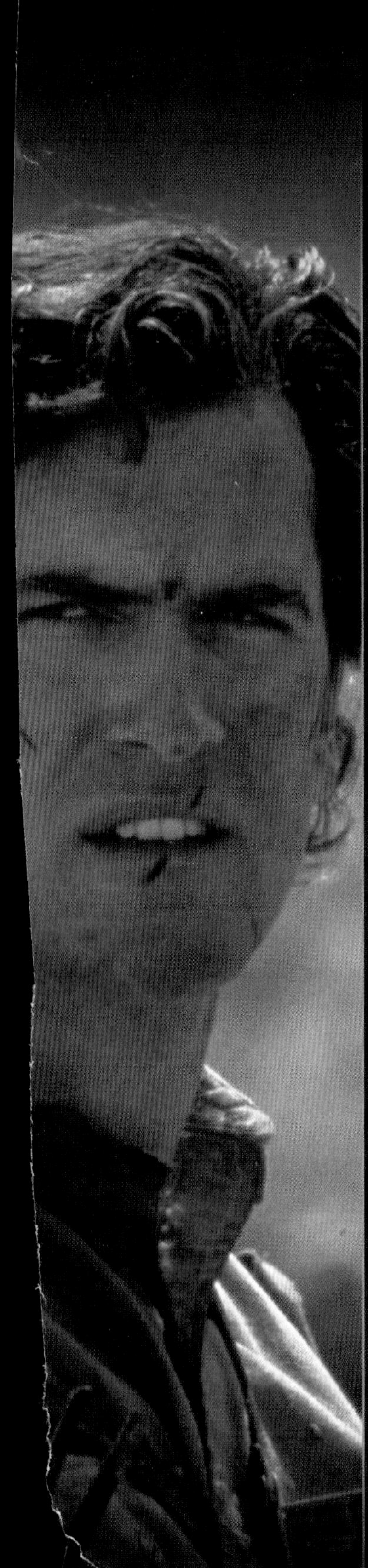

BEST OF ARMY OF DARKNESS™ COLLECTIONS

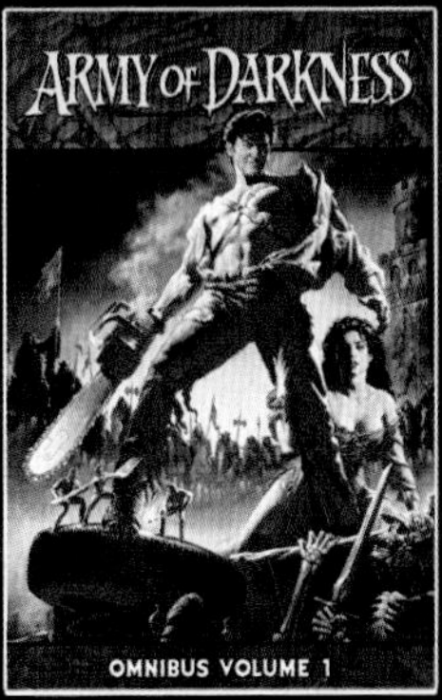
ARMY OF DARKNESS
OMNIBUS VOLUME 1

OMNIBUS VOL. 1

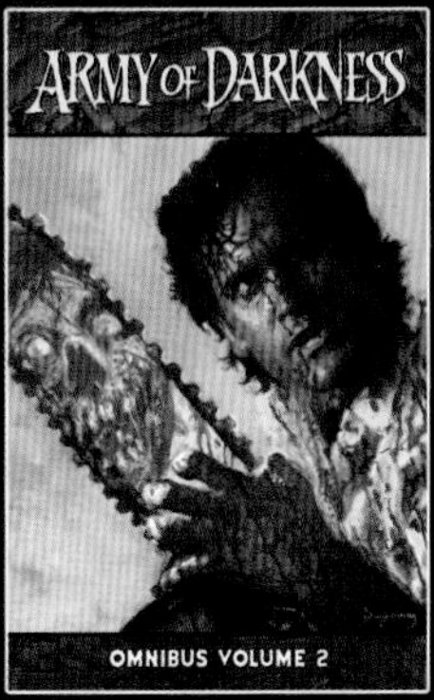
ARMY OF DARKNESS
OMNIBUS VOLUME 2

OMNIBUS VOL. 2

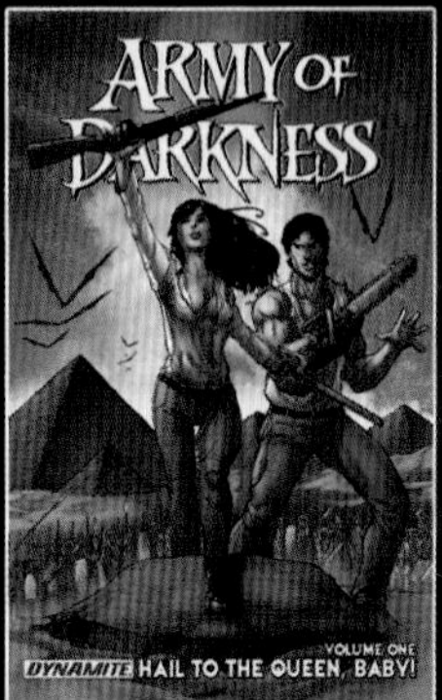
ARMY OF DARKNESS
VOLUME ONE
DYNAMITE HAIL TO THE QUEEN, BABY!

VOL. 1: HAIL TO THE QUEEN, BABY! TPB

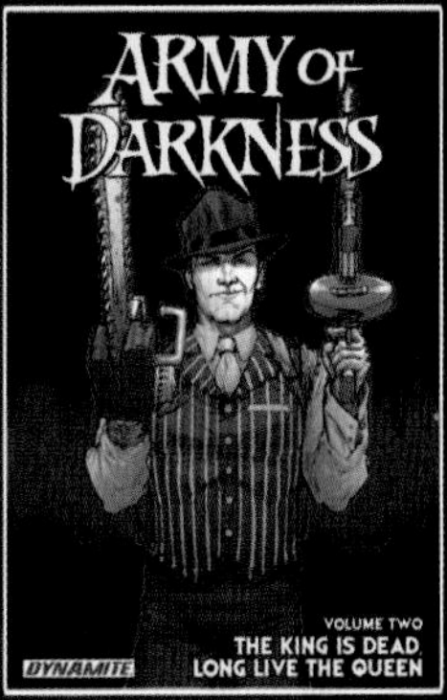
ARMY OF DARKNESS
VOLUME TWO
THE KING IS DEAD
LONG LIVE THE QUEEN
DYNAMITE

VOL. 2: THE KING IS DEAD, LONG LIVE THE QUEEN TPB

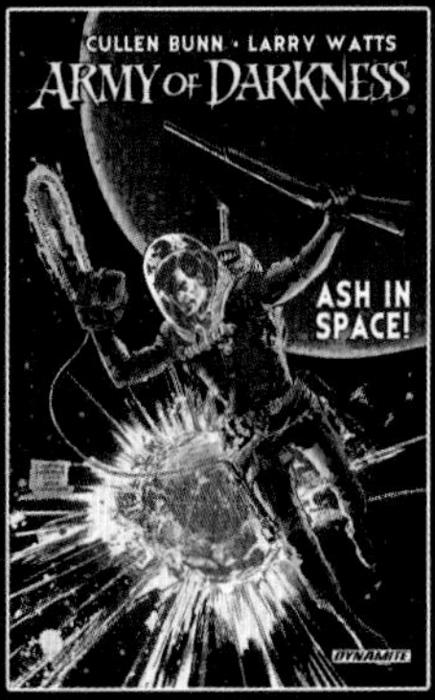
CULLEN BUNN · LARRY WATTS
ARMY OF DARKNESS
ASH IN SPACE!
DYNAMITE

ASH IN SPACE TPB

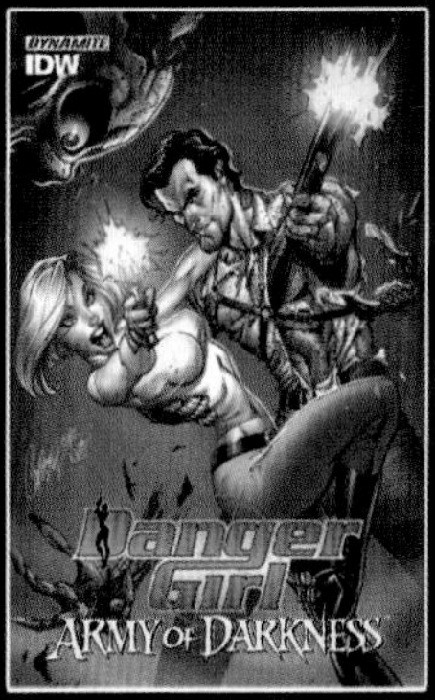
DYNAMITE
IDW
Danger Girl
ARMY OF DARKNESS

DANGER GIRL AND THE ARMY OF DARKNESS TPB

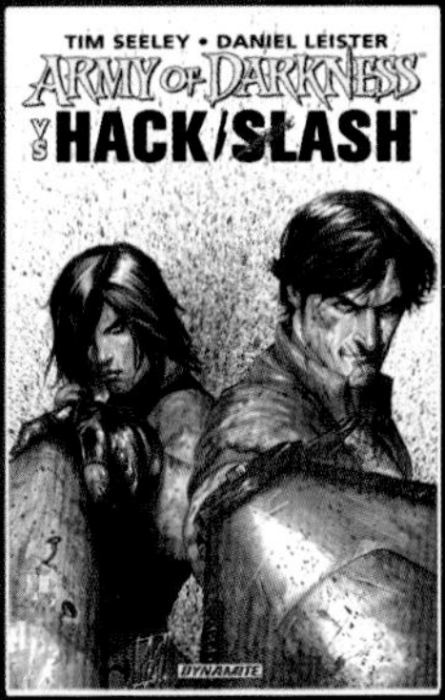
TIM SEELEY • DANIEL LEISTER
ARMY OF DARKNESS
VS
HACK/SLASH
DYNAMITE

ARMY OF DARKNESS VS HACK/SLASH

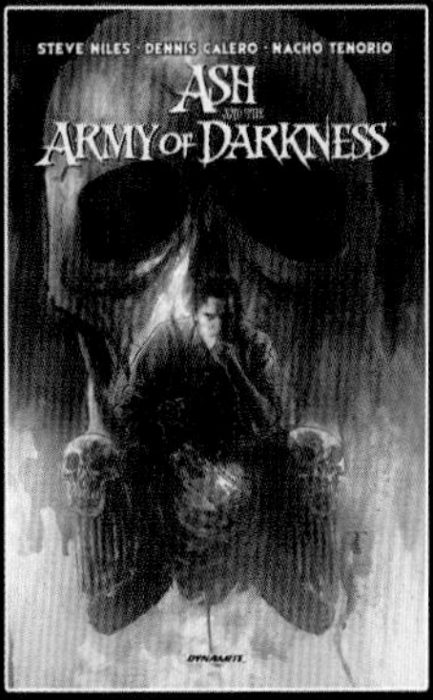
STEVE NILES · DENNIS CALERO · NACHO TENORIO
ASH AND THE ARMY OF DARKNESS
DYNAMITE

ASH AND THE ARMY OF DARKNESS TPB

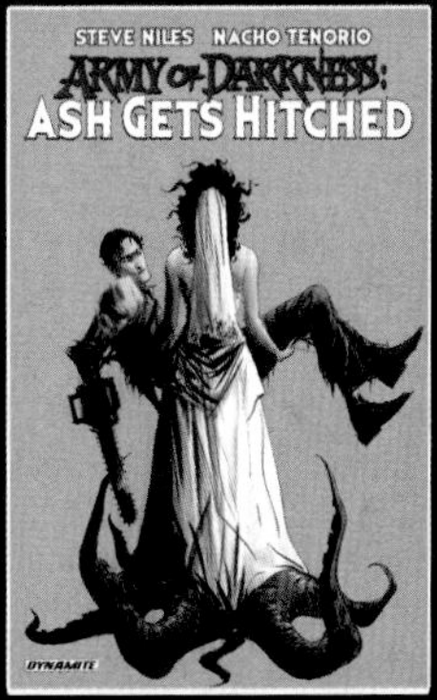
STEVE NILES · NACHO TENORIO
ARMY OF DARKNESS:
ASH GETS HITCHED
DYNAMITE

ASH GETS HITCHED TPB

DYNAMITE® WWW.DYNAMITE.COM @DYNAMITECOMICS /DYNAMITECOMICS

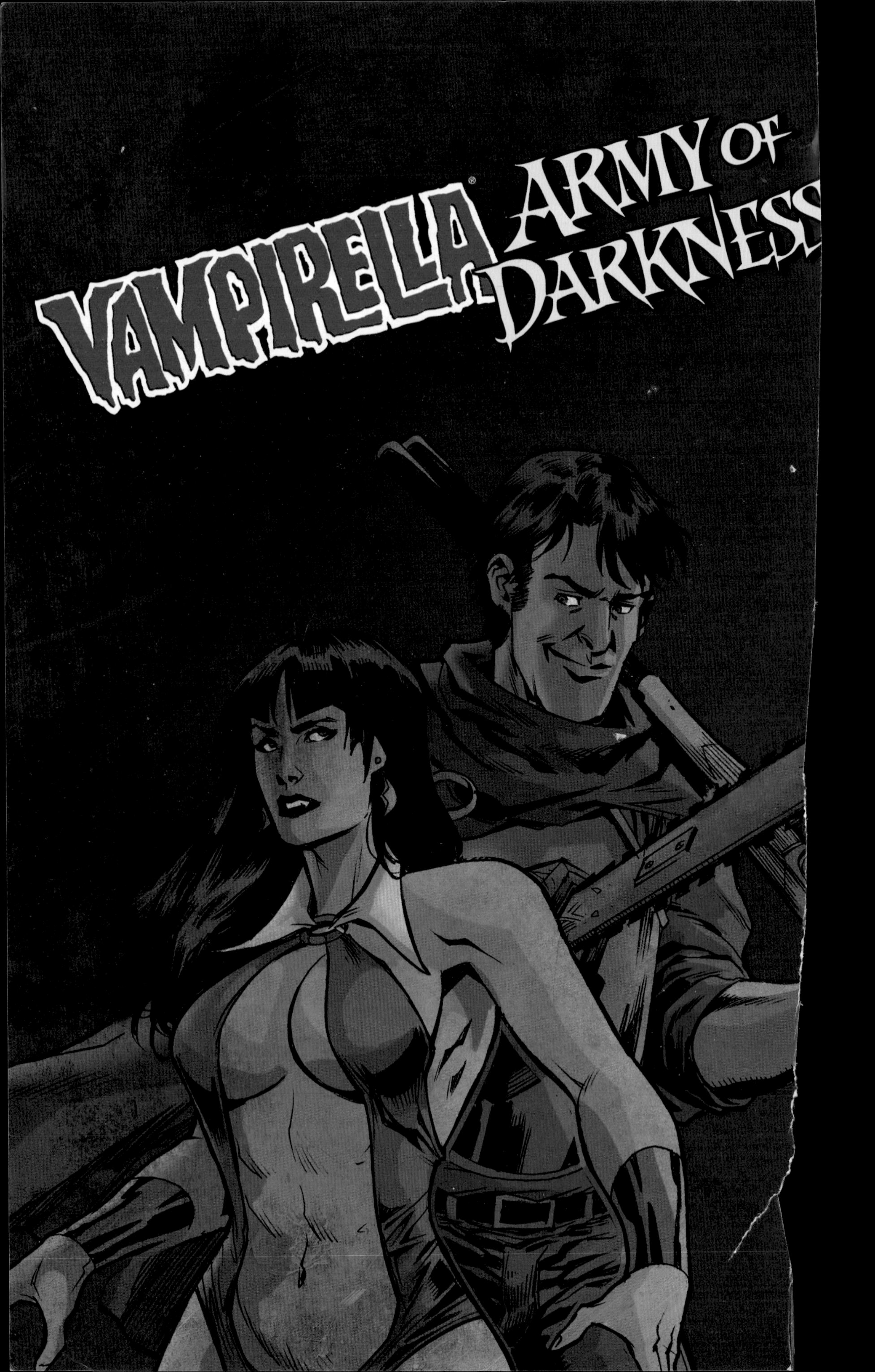
VAMPIRELLA®
ARMY OF DARKNESS